BUILDING TRUST AND RELATIONSHIP AT THE SPEED OF CHANGE

A WORLDVIEW INTELLIGENCE LEADERSHIP SERIES
BOOK 1

WORLDVIEW INTELLIGENCE
Change The Outcome

AUTHORS
KATHY JOURDAIN, MBA AND JERRY NAGEL, PHD

COVER DESIGN AND PAGE LAYOUT

They say, don't judge a book by its cover. But, books get judged by their covers all the time. We went to 99Designs and initiated a competition for cover design. There were many great possible designs submitted by a number of designers. As we provided feedback, U.T. Dezines showed excellent responsiveness and incorporated our requests in a way that was aligned with what we were asking. We were delighted with the professional business look of the cover he designed. So much so, we asked him to do the page layout for the interior of the book. He has worked diligently and collaboratively with us throughout the whole process and we are delighted to acknowledge him for his creative talents.

https://99designs.com/profiles/2860518

© 2019 Kathy Jourdain, MBA and Jerry Nagel, MA, PhD

All rights reserved. No part of this publication may be reproduced or transmitted in any form or by any means, electronic or mechanical, including photocopying, recording, or by any information storage and retrieval system, without permission in writing from Kathy Jourdain and Jerry Nagel. Reviewers may quote brief passages.

Library of Congress Control Number: 2019911994

      Kathy Jourdain and Jerry Nagel, co-authors

      ISBN 978-1-7332822-1-5

FOREWORD

The landscape of organizations and leadership is strewn with failed change efforts and broken strategic plans. Many of these have been well-designed, well-funded, and overseen by skillful leaders. A close inspection would reveal that many different factors contributed to each failure. But one factor emerges that is central to them all, and this central factor is the subject of *Building Trust and Relationship at the Speed of Change.*

Most simply put, the actions we take, and indeed the very ways we lead our lives, are a direct outcome of our most deeply held opinions and assessments about who we are and how the world works. These deeply held views are not readily transparent to us, but they dominate how we see and act on the world. They are made manifest and reinforced by the language that we use, both for internal self-talk and for external communications.

Inevitably, at some point, we seek change and need to take action, from the simplest to the grandest scale. Then, when things don't work as we hoped, when the world doesn't bend to our wishes, we routinely blame some set of external circumstances. That doesn't help because, in fact, the obstacle to success is how we envisioned the situation in the first place.

It's important to keep in mind that we all do this. Obstacles of this sort aren't generated solely by human failure. For evolutionary purposes, science tells us, our brain is geared to simplifying our understanding of the world by sorting and categorizing so we can deal with the massive input we receive. This is just how our brain works, and the obstacles generated by our limiting habits like cognitive bias can't be totally fixed by new management techniques, flatter hierarchies, or more data.

And, as if that weren't enough, all of this is exacerbated by growing organizational complexity, the proliferation of digital communications, mountains of data to sort through, and the rapidly accelerating pace of change in the world. For leaders seeking effective action, the "speed of change" is a polite term for the chaos they face daily.

Jourdain and Nagel take this obstacle head on and offer us a pathway through to effective action. They show us the importance of a greater awareness of how our own deeply held assumptions—our worldviews—shape our actions, and how we must start there to effect real change. They present us with Worldview Intelligence and the family of tools they have developed to implement it. Underlying all is a presentation of the most basic capability all successful leaders possess: building trust and relationship with those around them.

As many scientists and systems thinkers point out, the world can be explained as a network of inseparable patterns of relationships, where the key element is not the contents, but the connections between things. If you want to affect this world, to change things, then you must be connected to be part of these relationships. It follows, then, that more than charisma, more than brilliance, more than super social media skills, building trust and relationship are the key ingredients of successful leadership.

If leadership were an economy, then trust and relationship would be the coin of the realm.

Building them requires careful and relentless cultivation. Even in the most mundane campaigns, execution depends upon getting commitment from relevant stakeholders, and that depends on establishing common ground, language and culture. This is critical work in an age that emphasizes difference and solidified positions, and when digital algorithms are pulling us apart.

Building Trust and Relationship at the Speed of Change can help us with this important work. This wisdom arose from the authors' response to real situations in relationship with their clients and their clients' organizations. It provides engaged change-makers with a systematic, holistic, and employable methodology for understanding their own worldview and working with the worldviews of their clients. It doesn't just present skills and strategies, but ways of looking deeper, of sorting through surface noise and working with underlying causes.

The urgency of working more effectively with organizational change is that we've got some big hairy problems and we've got to get better at working together to solve them. We could be talking about nurturing more diversity and inclusion, diminishing the impact of a monolithic dominant culture, responding to an environmental crisis that's become an existential threat to us all, or...pick your poison.

Organizations are the biggest levers to effect change so that's a good place to start. But they are also the toughest things to change. Right now, and for a little while, the window is still open. If we can expand the way we see ourselves and work with the world, more creative options for effective action will emerge. Worldview intelligence tools can help us find them, and If you want to be an agent in this work, *Building Trust and Relationship at the Speed of Change* will take you by the hand and guide your way along the journey.

James Gimian
Author of The Rules of Victory

TABLE OF CONTENTS

Foreword by James Gimian.....................................i
Introduction.. 1

Section 1:
Change, Complexity, Trust, Relationship
and Worldviews 11

Chapter 1: When Time is the Enemy....................... 13
Chapter 2: Worldviews, How They are Formed
and Why it Matters 33
Chapter 3: The Scope of Worldview Intelligence
Applications 47
Chapter 4: What It Means to be Worldview Intelligent 55

Section 2:
The Worldview Intelligence Six Dimensions
Framework.. 69

Chapter 5: Introducing the Worldview Intelligence
Framework...71
Chapter 6: Reality.. 83
Chapter 7: History 93
Chapter 8: Future...107
Chapter 9: Values 117
Chapter 10: Practices 127
Chapter 11: Knowledge 137
Chapter 12: The Strategic Use of the Worldview
Intelligence Six Dimensions Framework.....................147

Section 3:
Worldview Intelligence, Brain and Behavioral Science. . . 159

Chapter 13: Brain Science and Worldviews: 161
Chapter 14: Understanding Worldview and Identity Reactions
Through Behavioral Science. 175

Section 4:
Building Trust and Relationship: Application One-on-One
and in Teams **193**

Chapter 15: Worldview Intelligence Theory
of Change Planning Model 195
Chapter 16: Building Trust and Relationship One-on-One 215
Chapter 17: Building Trust and Relationship in Your Team . . . 229
Chapter 18: When the Team is Dysfunctional–Is It Possible
to Build Trust and Relationship? 247

Conclusion 263
Acknowledgements. 266
About the Authors 272
Endnotes 277
A Request from the Authors, Jerry and Kathy 283

INTRODUCTION:
A WORLDVIEW INTELLIGENCE APPROACH TO BUILDING TRUST AND RELATIONSHIP AT THE SPEED OF CHANGE

Worldview. Have you heard this word or perhaps even used it? Have you thought about what it means? Over the last decade it is a word that has been increasing in use in popular vocabulary, social and print media. It is used by any number of people to sweepingly describe another person or an organization's entire ideology by declaring that a single statement or action describes how they see and experience the world around them – their worldview. Worldviews are commonly ascribed to celebrities, sports figures, or politicians by writers and reporters based on such statements or actions.

How many of us want to be wholly described by one statement? We are not uni-dimensional as human beings; we are multi-dimensional. One statement will never completely capture the essence of who we are. So, why do we do this? Why do we try to condense our understanding of another person, an organization, culture or community into a single statement?

In an increasingly complex world, we are looking for ways to simplify our understanding of other people. While simplifying can be helpful, it also gets us into trouble as it involves a myriad of assumptions we don't even know we are making. It is akin to stereotyping which is the unconscious application of a fixed and oversimplified set of beliefs and assumptions to an individual or group of people.

We are living in times that seem to be moving ever faster and complexity is increasing. The diversity of people and backgrounds in our communities, our countries and our organizations is growing. It is welcomed by some and feared by others. Whichever way it is perceived, it is a growing reality. How do we find our way in times that are asking more of us?

This is a question many of our clients are asking as they deal not just with increasing complexity but also with accelerating change in their organizations and the environments in which they are operating. We heard the question: how do you build trust and relationship when things are moving so fast? What is the leadership we need to bring to our teams and our organizations? That query resonated with us and our own evolving work with Worldview Intelligence. However, it is also important to be mindful of an assumption in the query which may be some version of: how do we do this fast? What is the silver bullet that will solve all the challenges that arise when Building Trust and Relationship at the Speed of Change?

This book is not a silver bullet solution since no such thing exists. However, it does provide insight into what is needed to lead change, build trust and relationship at the speed of change and over time. It addresses the depth of leadership needed to create and nurture high performance teams while keeping the focus on the "prize" of better outcomes. It does this through the lens of Worldview Intelligence.

Our awareness of worldviews came into being as Jerry began his PhD dissertation on the topic of worldviews. As he did his research, we started to experiment with the concepts he was examining in our programs and client consulting. We noticed a strong interest in exploring the idea that each of us, our families, cultures, communities and organizations all have worldviews. Worldviews are the lenses or sets of lenses through which we see and experience the world. They are different for each of us and they influence relationship, communication and conflict or tension without us being present to this because they operate largely in our unawareness.

We grew increasingly curious about the appetite for the ideas on worldviews we were exploring. There was particular interest in the language we were using which was opening doors for new explorations on topics that have been difficult to address, particularly around differences.

As we introduced our Worldview Intelligence approach to more and more of our clients, we continued to create new applications for what has become the Worldview Intelligence Six Dimensions

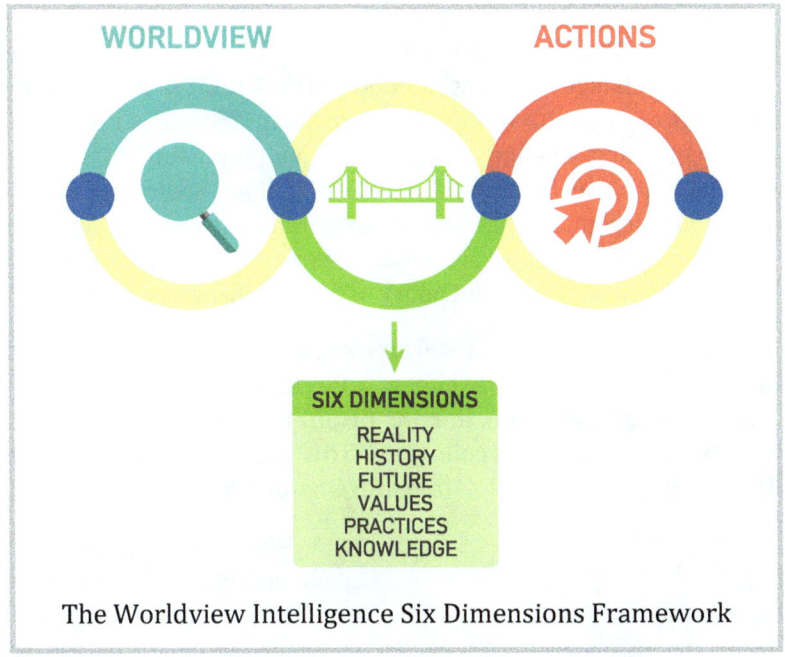

The Worldview Intelligence Six Dimensions Framework

Framework. This framework is based on the work of Belgium philosopher Leo Apostel and the Worldviews Group he founded. We developed exercises for people to explore the fullness of their worldviews using each of the dimensions which are covered in Chapters 6-11.

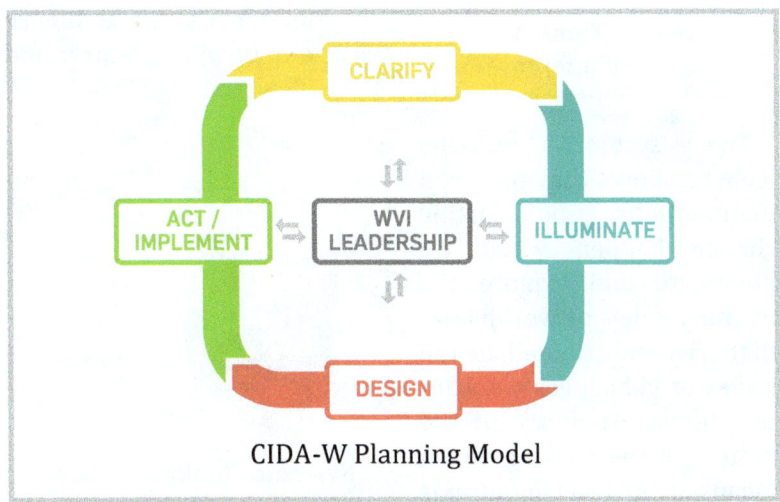

CIDA-W Planning Model

Then we articulated our planning, design and implementation processes and strategies in what is now the Worldview Intelligence Theory of Change Planning Model (CIDA-W). CIDA-W is a four-step approach to the design and implementation of strategy for future planning, change management, employee or community engagement. The four steps in the planning model are clarify, illuminate, design, and act. Worldview Intelligence leadership – the W – informs all four steps. The model is explained in detail in Chapter 15: Worldview Intelligence Theory of Change Planning Model.

We also created the SHEER Framework (stance, hopes, empathy, engage, results) and worksheet to address the question: how do I have THAT conversation, the one I want to avoid, with my family member, friend or work colleague? This is introduced in Chapter 16: Building Trust and Relationship One-on-One.

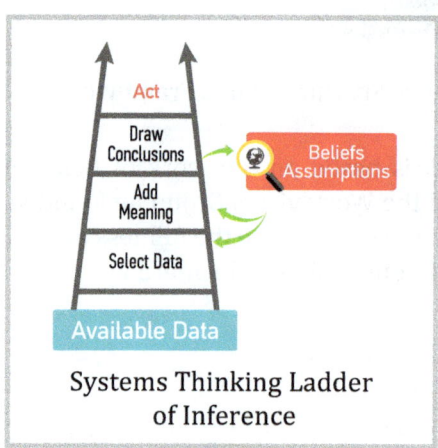

Systems Thinking Ladder of Inference

We found ourselves bringing systems thinking into our work, recognizing it as a valuable contribution to Worldview Intelligence. The Ladder of Inference demonstrates worldviews at work and how quickly assumptions and judgments can influence our opinions, beliefs and views.

The systems thinking Iceberg shows that powerful interventions and lasting change happen when we illuminate and explore the mental models or worldviews that have contributed to the issues or challenges we want to address. They are at the bottom of the iceberg, which means deep level inquiry is

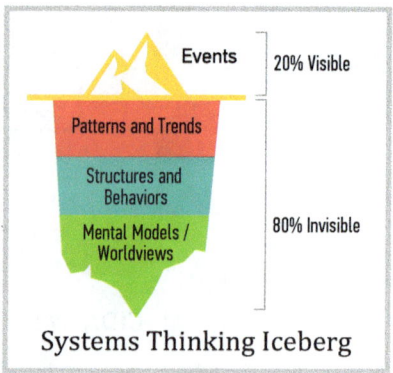

Systems Thinking Iceberg

needed to surface and illuminate the worldviews so they can be examined and shifted.

Because worldviews are closely linked to our sense of identity or who we are, we discovered that brain and behavioral science offers additional ways to understand how worldviews work and our reactions to worldview challenges. Understanding this influence also offers us ways to improve our communication and to build trust and relationship.

As our work became more robust, it led to more opportunities to offer Worldview Intelligence as well as requests for more complete explanations of how we approach our work. People started asking us for 'the book'. While we made a few attempts to convert Jerry's dissertation into non-academic language, we stalled a couple of times along the way. The book finally came together because the time was right. We have created a rigorous set of structures, frameworks, models and skills unique to Worldview Intelligence. We've now had years of experience speaking in front of groups that have honed the language we use, the stories we tell and the application of the frameworks and models. Finally, we received an inspired title for the book in conversation with a close friend and colleague reflecting on leadership, relationship, trust and change. This is a personal development and a leadership development book with a focus on high performance teams. They go hand-in-hand.

Our writing has drawn from experience and hands-on learning. Our hope is that it provides insight, clarity and practical examples that will inspire you. We begin each chapter with a story from our individual or collective experiences and we have woven stories and examples into the body of each chapter. Questions and frameworks you can work with for your own inquiry or with your team are also provided.

The book has four sections. Section 1: Change, Complexity, Trust, Relationship and Worldviews, provides context for the book and our work. Chapters 1-4 answer questions related to change, trust and relationship, what is a worldview, what does it mean to be Worldview Intelligent and what becomes possible when you focus on illuminating and understanding the influence and impact of worldviews.

Section 2: The Worldview Intelligence Six Dimensions Framework is, not surprisingly, focused on the Worldview Intelligence Six Dimensions and the Framework. The framework is coherent and straightforward yet unique. It enables you to discover your worldview, the worldviews of others or of your team, organization, culture, social system or community. It is adaptable to any application we choose to focus on. This is one reason why it is so effective. Chapter 5 introduces the framework. Chapters 6-11 each highlight one of the six dimensions. Chapter 12 shows how the framework is coherent and how the dimensions work together in ways that are strategic in illuminating blind spots in strategy, policy development or planning and implementation processes.

Section 3: Worldview Intelligence, Brain and Behavioral Science draws on these two knowledge areas as they relate to worldviews. As Worldview Intelligence unfolded, we had a growing awareness of how brain and behavioral science describes and explains our attachment to our worldviews, how our worldviews are reinforced without our awareness and how we can work with this knowledge to become more worldview aware and Worldview Intelligent. Chapter 13 focuses on brain science, brain development and particularly the amygdala and the fight-flight-freeze response that happens when the amygdala is hijacked. It offers a way to work with your response to change it over time through awareness and practice. Chapter 14: Understanding Worldview and Identity Reactions Through Behavioral Science, dives into a number of terms and concepts from behavioral science, what they mean, how they relate to our worldviews and how this awareness can improve success in communication and relationship.

Although each section provides examples, strategies and application stories, Section 4: Building Trust and Relationship: Application One-on-One and in Teams, is specifically dedicated to practice. In Chapter 15 we share the Worldview Intelligence CIDA-W Theory of Change Planning Model and how we use it. Chapter 16 explores how to build trust and relationship one-on-one. Chapter 17 looks at how to build trust and relationship in our teams, looking at the characteristics of high-performance teams and the structures, processes and practices that support high-performance teams. Because there are dysfunctional teams and toxic work environments, Chapter 18 examines what to do when the team is dysfunctional.

A STORY THREAD TO BRING AWARENESS TO YOUR WORLDVIEWS

Early readers of this book, prior to publication, offered great suggestions for edits and additions to the book. One suggestion was to include a storyline on a specific, easily illustrated topic throughout several chapters as a way to invite readers into thinking about their worldview. We discussed a number of options for such a narrative including current domestic politics, international issues like climate change, forms of discrimination and economic justice.

Two recent incidents led us to choose a storyline focused on disability and ableism. One occurred at an Art of Hosting Program where we were told the facility was accessible. This was important to us as a general principle and also because we had participants who required the space to be accessible. While strictly speaking the space was accessible, it required driving on a narrow dirt road and coming in through the backdoor. In other words, accessibility was an afterthought. The other incident involves a good friend who has had a reoccurrence of polio that has impacted her daily reality and practices and her sense of self.

Before embarking on her consulting career, Kathy was the Executive Director of an Atlantic Canada Health Charity. This charity provided financial support for research into the cause of an auto-immune disease that leads to disability and services to people whose physical mobility was impacted by the disease. This has given her perspective and experience addressing the challenges faced by people with disabilities. Both of us have first hand experience with parents who aged into physical challenges.

Additionally, we felt it would be good to deepen our

understanding of the personal experiences of people with disabilities and so we reached out to a colleague at the Minnesota Department of Human Rights. Several elements in this storyline throughout the book come from those conversations.

In some chapters there will be a dialogue box speaking to a specific matter regarding worldviews around disability – both visible and invisible. We offer a brief description of the worldview challenge and a few questions for your exploration. As you consider your views concerning disabilities, we invite you to also explore your worldviews on other matters of the human condition.

Worldviews we touch on include the medical model approach to disabilities, what is considered normal or not normal, attractive or not. We highlight the role of fear in our reactions to people with disabilities, the privilege of being able bodied and how societal views about disabilities gets internalized by people with disabilities.

This narrative is directed to able-bodied people. It is worldviews we hold regarding disabilities that we are inviting you to reflect on. We recognize that this has an exclusive element to it for readers with disabilities. We ask your understanding for this approach and invite you to reflect on the stories and questions from your own experiences and worldviews. We hope all of us gain greater understanding of what it means to be disabled or able bodied and how this impacts our worldviews.

SPRINT OR MARATHON?

Building relationship and trust is not a sprint; it is more like a marathon. But we don't always have time for the marathon as we point out in Chapter 1: When Time is the Enemy. We are often asked to build trust at the same pace as change in our organizations. These do not have to be mutually exclusive. It is our intent with this book to provide the knowledge and skills to begin building trust and relationship at the pace of a sprint and to sustain that trust and those relationships over the long-term, the marathon.

What do sprints and marathons have in common? They both have a common core activity – running. They both have specific techniques and they require practice. While different in purpose, a skilled runner can do both with varying degrees of success. Some of the elements can be transferred to other activities, like marathon rollerblading or Iron-Man events, which also require conditioning.

While building trust may be more of a marathon than a sprint, in our workplace environments the process often must start quickly and then can take time to support and strengthen the trust over the longer term. Whether building trust at the pace of a sprint or a marathon, trust is the common denominator. Building trust and relationship requires dedication and practice. Both approaches require specific techniques and those techniques can be used inter-changeably.

Worldview Intelligence skills to do both are similar, with some perhaps more important for one activity than the other. Being curious and non-judgmental is essential to both and early curiosity and non-judgment may be critical to the sprint. Creating safe space is essential to both and an ongoing practice, but during the first stages this is critical. Taking time to understand the worldview lenses through which we each see ourselves and the situation, whether it is the workplace, the community or social relations, will carry us through the sprint to the longer-term. The Worldview Intelligence Six Dimensions Framework, the SHEER conversation framework or the CIDA-W Planning model can be applied whether beginning the sprint or building long-term relationship and trust.

It is our hope that as you read this book you find ideas, concepts and practices that will help you grow personally and advance both your leadership skills and your ability to support your team in being a high-performance team. Perhaps you will be inspired to build trust and relationship in your organization or community with new skills, planning strategies and more informed ways of acting. In doing so, you, your team, organization or community will become more Worldview Intelligent, carving out new ways to be together in service of the purpose you aspire to personally or professionally.

SECTION 1
CHANGE, COMPLEXITY, TRUST, RELATIONSHIP AND WORLDVIEWS

CHAPTER 1:
WHEN TIME IS THE ENEMY

In the classical story of the Tortoise and the Hare, the tortoise challenges the hare to a race after the hare boasts about how fast he is. In his arrogance, the hare takes off with a burst of speed and then, because he can go so much faster than the tortoise, he decides to take a nap. While he is napping, the tortoise plods along, making slow and steady progress. By the time the hare wakes up, the tortoise has crossed the finish line.

Today's typical work environment wouldn't necessarily find the hare asleep. More likely, it would find the hare distracted by the challenges, demands and expectations alive in the workplace, all moving at a great pace. With change moving so fast, there is barely time to breathe or take stock. Yet it is those who slow down -- to take stock, to make sure that things are aligned and moving in the right direction -- who will win the race. We need to slow down to go fast.

THE RATE OF CHANGE IS SPEEDING UP

There is a feeling that time is speeding up. While that isn't actually happening, the pressure of time and expectations about how fast things can be accomplished is building. It is fair to say that the debate is about how fast change is accelerating and the impact this has on careers, workplaces, organizational growth and change, in communities, and even in families. Influenced by increasing globalization, 24-hour news cycles, competitive pressures, new cultural and social norms, rapidly changing technology, emergence of the new and accelerating obsolescence (planned or otherwise) of products and services, the world is moving faster than ever. It's like the merry-go-round spinning wheel on the playground, going faster and faster. You better hang on for dear life or you just might fly off.

When looking at the rate of change or the pressure of time, speed often means: how fast can change be executed in an organization or business enterprise? But, make no mistake, execution doesn't necessarily translate into success.

One of our Worldview Intelligence clients is growing exponentially through mergers and acquisitions. They have characterized the pace of change in their organization as "driving down the highway in a bus at 80 miles an hour, changing the tires as we go." We have shared this description with many of our other clients and it resonates with them. Expectations placed on people for how fast things need to be accomplished can be unachievable. This can set people, teams, departments and even whole organizations up for failure, not success. If this is the case, what is needed for successful achievement of outcomes and the evolution of our teams, organizations and communities?

The focus on fast results de-emphasizes the value of relationship. Time becomes the enemy of relationship and trust building. Yet, it is through relationship that work gets done. And the best work gets done in trustworthy relationships and well-performing teams. In toxic environments work still gets done, but at what cost? Quality and innovation are diminished in addition to the human physical and mental health toll and the impact of low morale on productivity. One increasingly likely cost for companies could be going out of business. There is growing competition and increasing demand for workers who will have more employment choices in the coming years. Where will people chose to work in the future? In organizations that support and encourage employees to thoughtfully and strategically engage in conversations or relationships to improve trust and change the outcomes. In organizations that clearly know what their worldview is and recognize that there can exist vastly different worldviews amongst employees, clients and partners. In other words, in Worldview Intelligent organizations with Worldview Intelligent leaders.

WE LIVE IN A TIME OF A MULTIPLICITY OF WORLDVIEWS

Of course, individuals and businesses don't exist in isolation. They are located in society, in large and small cities and in rural communities across countries. They exist in social and cultural systems and networks of partners, stakeholders, customers and suppliers. Walk down a street in any major city, and increasingly in small towns too, and it is clear the composition of our societies is changing. With increasing mobility across countries and cultures leading to a rise in immigration, this is an ever more present reality. We are living in a multicultural age where a defining characteristic of contemporary culture is the presence of a multitude of differing perspectives or worldviews. These community and social multicultural experiences exist in teams and organizations as well. If it isn't already showing up, this multicultural experience will likely be a necessity in the future for surviving, if not thriving.

It is much easier to trust people who look and act like us, who believe the same things we believe whether that is basic beliefs with respect to the nature of human beings or similar spiritual or religious belief systems. The more different people are or are perceived to be, the more conditional trust becomes. If trust has been jeopardized in any way, then relationship responses tend to range from more cautious to outright suspicious or hostile. These kinds of responses get in the way of producing results. When moving at the pace of change, trust and relationship are often disrupted because things are moving so fast it is easy to lose touch with the basic tenets and principles that allow trust to grow and relationships to thrive.

THE NATURE OF TRUST

The dictionary treats trust as both a noun and a verb. As a noun, it uses words like reliance, confidence, care, hope, and the person or thing in which confidence is placed. As a verb, it centers on the act of trusting, placing confidence or to hope. For us, trust is a far broader and more nuanced personal connection or act. It is more a matter of the heart than the mind. It has many characteristics depending upon context. The trust we might place in the person we love is different than the trust we might place in a co-worker or neighbor.

Many people hold a personality characteristic referred to as trust propensity. They start with offering trust when they first meet someone. This comes from life experiences with people and from an underlying belief about whether people can be trusted or not. The offering of trust to new people is part of our meta-beliefs discussed in Chapter 6: Reality. For many in the dominant culture this is relatively easy to do and for those who have had their trust abused it is much more difficult. Expecting trust is not something to be taken for granted.

Some people like to describe trust as something you have to earn. This means a starting point or worldview of no or little trust, building trust from ground zero. We think of trust as a gift given to someone. They can keep and nurture this gift or lose it. We start from a position of trust that can grow or expand or be lost. Once lost, it becomes difficult to get back.

In your personal interactions with new people you meet outside of a work or professional context, you can become aware of which stance you want to start from: little or no trust or a kindness towards others that has within it strong elements of trust. With awareness, you could then choose which stance you might want to take rather than default into one or the other.

THE CONTEXT FOR TRUST MATTERS

How far interactions with new people may go is context dependent. You may meet someone on an airplane and expect to never see them again, so nurturing trust is a moot point. You may meet a new neighbor or the parent of your children's classmate or someone in a recurring social activity and expect to see them again. You can choose to grow a friendship and nurture trust or to be casual in your contact and have limited need to attend to trust.

In the workplace, however, we are often put in a position where we have no or limited choice concerning our interactions with our co-workers, whether in ongoing relationships or new ones. With ongoing relationships, established patterns of relationship and trust will exist. This can work in our favor if the relationships are good and can be problematic if the relationships are challenged. If relationship is challenged, building even basic trust can seem impossible. It requires some of the kindness mentioned above. It demands that someone take the responsibility and initiative to break the patterns that contribute to and likely compound the lack of trust. That someone is likely you since you are the one reading this book. We offer strategies for how to do that throughout the book and Chapter 16 is dedicated to Building Trust and Relationship One-on-One. It may be a game changer for you in that relationship.

In the case of new co-workers, the circumstance of a new hire or interdepartmental transfer, you may have limited or no pre-conceived notions concerning that person. With awareness, you can choose your stance with them regarding a starting point of trust.

In other circumstances co-workers can be brought together in forced ways, such as a company merger or acquisition. Constant leadership change or continuous and sometimes contradictory change initiatives can also force circumstances of new team configurations. These situations bring with them many differing emotions, worldview clashes or pre-conceived distrust. You may oppose the merger or fear it will impact you or your job. You may have heard stories in the community referring to employee dissatisfaction within one of the companies. Your organizations may have very different worldviews. Examples include family versus shareholder owned, faith centered versus more secular in practice or deliberate decision-making versus rapid action. All could lead to worldview clashes.

In many of these situations the starting point is one of uncertainty, skepticism, worry or mistrust. Building trust requires care and dedicated attention. We have worked with a merger of a growth-oriented enterprise and a faith-based organization. The specific departments we worked with have taken the time to slow down and learn about each other's worldviews. The result has been a shift from concern about what might happen to employee practices in the faith-based organization to a recognition they can be a family of co-workers who trust each other and work together relationally. As noted earlier, it is as much or more a matter of the heart than the mind or an intellectual exercise.

The Worldview Intelligence approach to building trust invites you to explore your starting point when you are asked to begin a professional relationship with others. Are you approaching the person, team or organization from a stance of offering trust or are you starting from a different place? Why? What worldview does your employer have that impacts how you see other organizations? If you are being judgmental or defensive, how could you be more curious and open? What might the other person's starting point be? Are you taking that into consideration as you begin working together?

Jerry worked with a staff team that had concerns about timecard reporting which resulted in growing animosity toward a specific person. The team leader had told her to be precise in managing timecards and her worldview was to do her job correctly. To her this meant staff arrive at 8:00 and leave at 4:30 and, if not, it was noted on timecards. The team leader told other staff members they could be flexible with their time. This means if they work late, they can come in late the next morning. This allows staff who facilitate public meetings that often take place in the evenings to manage their time in a way they perceive as fair. These mixed messages led to a worldview clash that wasn't evident to everyone until a team conversation about how each member's worldview influenced how they did their work and reporting was held. The clash was eventually resolved as deeper understanding emerged and the conversation shifted from one focused on individuals to one focused on worldviews.

Using a Worldview Intelligence approach, we can begin a dialogue with new co-workers that helps each understand the individual and organizational perspectives regarding daily experiences, history, what the future holds, our values and practices and how we learn together. Having a better understanding of each other offers a path to nurture trust and build relationship.

As a leader you can begin to imagine what your role is in each of the circumstances described above. How do you help your team members build trust and relationship with each other? How do you set the tone for your expectations within your team? How do you role model your expectations?

THE NATURE OF RELATIONSHIP

Trust and relationship generally go together. Relationship is a type of kinship or connection where people see themselves as interrelated. Like with trust, good relationships can have many forms, including the loving relationship between life partners or between parents and children, the love siblings or close friends may share, or the warm and friendly relations between professional colleagues.

It is not possible to be in healthy relationship with someone when there is no trust. And like trust, relationships are more matters of the heart than the mind. People can be in shared context with each other – the workplace, family, social setting – without trust, but they are not in relationship as we think of it here. They are not in a relationship that is supportive and can maintain itself through interpersonal challenges that will inevitably show up.

Like trust, with awareness you can choose your starting point for building relationships. You can start from a stance of openness and curiosity toward another person and begin a journey together that builds trust and relationship. Or you can start from a stance of suspicion, judgment or mistrust based upon previous experiences or pre-conceived notions in which case you come to relationship reluctantly or not at all. If you hold open the willingness to be in professional or personal relationship with another and that person does not reciprocate or acts in a manner that negatively impacts the relationship, then it becomes hard to rejoin the journey of building relationship. Examples could be a spouse having an affair or a co-worker saying something harmful about you to other colleagues or a supervisor. Trust is lost, relationship is fractured, and both are difficult to rebuild.

While relationship is a noun, the action of building relationship is a verb, as in being relational. Being relational is a practice. It is an ongoing approach to how we interact with people. It is a continual action that has several components. Being relational invites us into the work of listening as well as speaking. Listening is a heart-felt participation in a relational process. We listen as a participatory process and for participatory knowing.[1] We listen deeply, openly and compassionately without judgment, to let go of fixed views and to be fully present to the other persons or people.[2]

In being relational we keep ourselves open to experiencing the full richness of the people around us. We are open to multiple forms of relationship with others by being in dialogue with them rather than a having a monologic view of other people. From this stance we open up the possibilities of new ways of being in relationship or new possible futures rather than focusing on how things are.[3] By being relational we open up possibilities for new ways of being together or new possible futures.

This relational perspective has been described as deeply ecological. It is a participatory way of relating that gives us the opportunity and the power to speak from the multiple of voices we hold or represent – parent, grandparent, host, employee, employer, teacher, preacher, Buddhist or any other voice we may have – and not just a single voice that does not represent the richness of who we each are.[4] This ecological or relational stance is one where each of us cares for each other and for our moral selves. When we approach relating in this way, we are less focused on knowledge and truth and more centered on the ethics of our work and the local, interconnected and extended pragmatics of our work.[5]

Bringing this Worldview Intelligence relational approach to a new professional or personal context, whether it is a new team member, a merger of departments or organizations, a new supervisor or other situation, establishes a starting point that lays the foundation for building trust and relationship.

WORLDVIEW CLASHES AND CONTRADICTIONS – VISIBLE AND INVISIBLE PATTERNS

For many people it is a revelation to discover that not everyone sees or interacts with the world in the same ways. This is especially true for people who are part of the dominant culture where they are located. This is partly because like attracts like and many of us are surrounded by people who share many of our views. When confronted with different worldviews, we may seek to move away from any discomfort we might be experiencing and back to that which is comfortable or familiar. We may also contradict another view, or simply ignore it as if it doesn't exist. In the process we talk at or past another human being without connecting. This can result in an imposition of worldviews. When this happens, it diminishes connection and trust.

Most people who are not part of a dominant culture, whether social, national, cultural, or racial, have developed the skill and facility of interacting with the worldviews of the dominant culture. We hear repeatedly, it is a survival skill. People who are not part of the dominant culture have fewer choices about how they interact with the prevalent worldview. It could literally mean life or death for them.

For people who are part of the dominant culture, it is easy for a multiplicity of worldviews to remain "invisible". When misunderstanding or conflict shows up, it catches people by surprise, often triggering defensive or dismissive responses instead of curiosity, compassion or humility. Later in the book, in Chapter 13: Brain Science and Worldviews: Rationale and Strategies for Working with Fight-Flight-Freeze Response, we explore why people get triggered and how this kind of response restricts explorations as people become more attached to their own worldview and less open to other views. Without interruption, these responses become individual and collective patterns of communication and relationship that are harder to disrupt the longer they go unchecked.

The impact of these patterns is not invisible. A multiplicity of worldviews contributes to and feeds into the fragmentation in our societies. This fragmentation is reflected in our professions, teams, organizations and communities, even in our families. Fragmentation seems to be increasing, as does the complexity of the situations we encounter. We are far more likely to experience a clash of worldviews that leads to the polarization of perspectives and entrenchment of attitudes rather than a generative exploration that leads to progress and changes outcomes. In anticipation of a clash, we are also far more likely to try to avoid the interaction or the conversation to begin with than we are to lean into and embrace it because we lack the tools, strategies, methods and confidence to do it well.

DEFYING A DOMINANT WORLDVIEW

Myrna Kay Olsen Peterson has a larger than life personality and presence in any room she enters. On June 21, 1995 she was involved in an accident that put her in a wheelchair for life. Over the years, she has had 25 surgeries in 24 years in her chair and has had some life-threatening incidents related to her health. Despite the health challenges, her worldview remains one of "live life to the fullest".

Part of what's made the journey difficult over the years are the barriers to navigating outside the home if you are in a wheelchair. Limited public transportation, a lack of accessibility getting into and through buildings, sidewalks without cutaways for curbs, and a lack of accessible trails and recreation paths make life in a wheelchair harder than it could be, even in supportive community like Grand Rapids, MN where Myrna lives.

In 2015, Mryna and her neighbor and friend, Les Isaacs who also uses a wheelchair from a separate accident coincidentally on the same day as Myrna's, decided to organize a gathering for the record books - for Guinness World Records. To bring awareness to the plight of the differently abled, they brought 351 people together in Grand Rapids, MN for the longest moving line of wheelchairs on record. It didn't just break the Guinness World Record, it expanded worldviews.

The event, called MyrnaLee Mania, had 100 manual wheelchairs on hand for able-bodied people who wanted to participate, but what struck Myrna was the sheer number of actual wheelchair users—251—who showed up. "The reason that was so impacting is that we don't see them out anywhere," she says. "Only 25 or 30 of them were from the Twin Cities, Duluth, or out west—the rest were pretty local, but we never see them."

The lack of visibility and the lack of accessibility it implies is why Myrna and others started a steering committee of wheelchair users, local politicians, city workers and engineers, and other prominent people in Itasca County. "A lot of people in chairs don't have a voice or even the opportunity to have a voice, so we're speaking for a lot of people," she says. "Our focus is that these improvements in accessibility will benefit our entire communities of all ages, abilities, and concerns, not just those of us in wheelchairs."

In 2019, Myrna was appointed to the Minnesota Governor's Council On Disabilities. In her words, "I'm so honored and pumped to be able to have closer contact and relationships with legislators who can help make a difference. Yesterday is gone and no one is promised tomorrow, so let's live life to the fullest today! My motto is still: 'Dream BIG, Give it to GOD, Make a SOLID PLAN & GIT 'ER DUN!' It always helps to add a little jazz to the mix!"

Myrna's story and her presence are inspiring. What do you think life would be like for you if your mobility was suddenly dependent on a wheelchair? When you are out walking do you notice accessibility of sidewalks and roadways? When you enter buildings do you scan for wheelchair ramps, accessible buttons or automatic doors?

When clashes happen, what are your touchstones, the things that help you stay grounded or centered? What is important to you? How do you know what is real or true? How do you build trust and relationship in the time pressured environments of your team, department, business or organization, especially when these environments are further complicated by a multiplicity of worldviews?

THE WORLDVIEW INTELLIGENCE LEADERSHIP APPROACH TO COMMUNICATION AND BUILDING TRUST AND RELATIONSHIP

Recognizing the growing complexity of work and the composition of work environments, compounded by the speed of change, demands new approaches to communication, to building relationship and trust; new approaches to dialogue, engagement, team development, business and workforce strategies. If relationship is important and trust is essential to healthy relationship – and it is – then how do you *Build Trust and Relationship at the Speed of Change?* It is relatively simple, but it doesn't get done for a variety of reasons. Time is perceived as the enemy. We are unsure how to sprint in a way that supports building trust and relationship for the marathon. Demands for impossibly quick results increases tension and conflict in teams. The work of building trust and relationship is viewed as time not well spent, misnamed "soft skills" when they are essential skills in any team, organization, community or family.

Someone must do this work and most of us would prefer it be someone else. However, as a leader of your team or in your organization or community, this is your responsibility. As far as family or friend relationships go, the person who recognizes or is willing to acknowledge the issue is also the one who must step into a leadership role, otherwise nothing will change.

Discovering new approaches to communication, relationship, connectivity and building trust is essential. Some approaches or ideas are not entirely new but rather a reorientation to tried and true actions and ways of being that stand the test of time. Some would say there is nothing new under the sun. We know proven leadership, communication and change management practices have existed for millennia. In most situations they are not well practiced, they are not coherent, or they are ravaged by the pressures of time. They are rejected because people look for the quick fix. In this book the "tried and true" are reoriented through the Worldview Intelligence approach. This approach offers new ways of thinking, new language, frameworks and models to support structured explorations.

In our work with clients, we know several ways to befriend the enemy of time and they are essential to building trust and relationship. We mention them here and they are woven in throughout this book. They are: question your assumptions, slow down, do your homework, be transparent, apologize when you are wrong and align worldviews.

QUESTION YOUR ASSUMPTIONS

Begin by questioning the assumption that there is not enough time. See where that leads you, especially if you have been struggling with things that slow you or your outcomes down. This might include resistance to change, misaligned worldviews, communication challenges, not knowing what someone (or a department) does or organizational silos. Time must be made available when things need to be done over if they haven't been done successfully in the first place or if they have been rushed. It takes more time if you have to stop to address dysfunctional team dynamics or relationships as we explore in Chapter 18: When the Team is Dysfunctional, Is It Possible to Build Trust and Relationship? It is not a question of not enough time; it is a question of how your use of time can become a strategic advantage for you, your team and organization.

SLOW DOWN

Slow down. Employ the strategies of the tortoise. What's that, you ask? Isn't that the exact opposite of dealing with the enemy of time? Take a breath – a deep breath – right now and notice what happens when you do this. There are so many health benefits to pausing for a deep breath, let alone the space it opens to pay attention. It can literally take a second. Someone needs your time and attention? Take a breath, turn away from your screen, put your phone down, turn your attention to the other person. Taking a moment to do this minimizes distractions, creates connection and is a step or factor in building trust and relationship.

Bring a breath to your team culture and see how individual and team trust, relationship and performance improve as a result. You can bring a breath by using strategies like check-in and check-out processes. A check-in is a way to invite everyone in the meeting to bring their minds and attention into the space, especially if they have been running from meeting to meeting or are distracted by some other issue or concern. A check-out is used at the end of the meeting to seal it, to wrap up loose ends or to discover how participants experienced the meeting. Both processes are guided by purpose or what you want to achieve with the check-in or check-out and the use of skillful questions.

You could bring a breath by offering a skillful question or a helpful observation. You could pass a talking piece from person to person. The person with the talking piece speaks, everyone else listens. Or you can simply invite people to pause, listen, collect their thoughts and speak with intention – thoughtfully, with care and with purpose. We often say, "You have to slow down to go fast". While it may seem counterintuitive, you can turn this into a solid results strategy.

DO YOUR HOMEWORK

Worldview Intelligence is a leadership skill. Becoming more aware of your own worldview, your way of seeing and experiencing the world and what makes you angry or joyful, unsettled or present will increase your own confidence and give you a strategic advantage in building trust and relationship. Awareness of your starting point for any conversation allows you to thoughtfully and strategically engage that conversation or relationship to improve trust and change the outcomes.

Individually or as a part of a team, at work or in other contexts, it becomes important to clearly know what your own worldviews are and to understand that even within your own local, organizational or community contexts there can exist vastly different worldviews; even within yourself. Yet worldviews largely operate under the surface, invisibly and unconsciously influencing communication, relationship and cultures, so how do you begin to understand their influence and impact? This is an aim, intention and result of Worldview Intelligence and an objective of this book.

BE TRANSPARENT

Tell the truth. As much of it and as often as you can. People know it or sense it anyway. If you are not truthful, it can pick away at or explode relationship and trust. If you can't disclose something, say so. Don't make promises you can't keep. Advocate with your senior leadership or CEO to be as transparent as possible. While less can be more, some organizations rely a little too heavily on the old maxim: "on a need to know basis – and you don't need to know". All too often this happens unintentionally, either because there are too many moving parts or there is no overarching strategy that holds it altogether.

Trust is compromised when people sense something is inconsistent or out of alignment. Our actions speak louder than our words. Not sharing what you know, or even not naming what you don't know, does not keep people focused on their tasks, as we prefer to believe. It distracts them and leads to higher stress environments, suspicion of intent, lower productivity and damaged relationship, the opposite of enabling people to respond appropriately and move at the speed of change.

APOLOGIZE

Apologize when you are wrong. Contrary to some beliefs it is not weakness, it is strength. Jealously guard your own integrity. In the end, it may be all you have. Brene Brown is a leading researcher, author and speaker on the topic of vulnerability and shame. She says, "Apologizing ranks right up there as one of the most courageous and vulnerable things we can do."[6] It is worth checking out her work on this topic. People trust when they believe you are reliable, good, honest, effective and worthy of confidence. There is a lot of power and social capital to be gained with a solid, appropriate apology.

CONNECT AND ALIGN WORLDVIEWS

In most workplaces and many communities, the many and varied worldviews are muted, discouraged or disallowed as the dominant worldview prevails. Not only do these multiple perspectives exist, it can be a competitive advantage to create the conditions and mechanisms for them to be expressed, acknowledged and valued. It is healthy for discussion, innovation and better solutions. When diverse worldviews truly are welcomed, trust and relationship are built. Within any organization or business unit there will be multiple worldviews – across departments, in different divisions, locations or subsidiaries, amongst different partners or stakeholders. The challenge is not to try to make everyone think the same, but to connect people to the larger story or inspiration that ignites and fuels the fire of why people engage. The more connected people feel to the shared story, the greater the engagement, trust and relationship.

Rather than seeing a diversity of views, experiences and opinions as something that needs to be eliminated or merged into one or two perspectives, find more ways to open opportunities for exploration, creativity, emergence, and innovation. There is substantial evidence that the greater the diversity of perspectives the higher the level of creativity, innovation, productivity and success in business. Do a Google search on this and any number of journal articles will appear including:

- How Diversity Makes Us Smarter; October 2014[7]
- Millennials Have a Different Definition of Diversity and Inclusion, May 2015[8]
- Kellogg Insight: Better Decisions Through Diversity, October 2010[9]
- Innovation Management: Why Diversity is the Mother of Creativity[10]; and,
- Harvard Business Review: How Diversity Can Drive Innovation, December 2013[11]

If it is true that increasing diversity creates better business results, it is also true that it causes some social discomfort, particularly when encountering people and views that are different, new and unfamiliar. As a leader in your team, business or community, developing the capabilities to work and live in these multi-varied and rich systems of many worldviews will elevate your skill and reputation and make you a leader in demand. The more skilled you are in strategies and dialogue practices that build trust and relationship, the more able you are personally and as a leader to find ways forward on issues that matter, on topics that may be fundamental to our survival, whether in our organizations, communities or families. To do so requires adept ability to hold differing and even opposing views, paradoxes or multiple truths at the same time.

A RELATIONAL APPROACH TO BUILDING TRUST

Worldview Intelligence is a relational approach to leading, building workplace cultures, creating trust, transforming differences into progress and changing outcomes. It is a relational approach to connecting, planning for challenging conversations, developing strategies, engaging stakeholders and systems change. This is also how we work with our clients. Trust often falters when exchanges are primarily transactional, when people are only focused on where, and from whom they have benefited lately and when it is only success or failure of the immediate tasks that matter.

A Relational Leadership Approach to Building Trust and Relationship	
From Transactional	**To Relational**
• What's In It For Me (WIIFM)? • What have you done for me lately? • One-off or episodic • Interested in the "sale" or individual transaction	• Build connections through genuine interest in others • Cultivate long term relationship • Collaborative/co-creative – drawing on the knowledge, expertise and experience of each contributor • Value added exchanges • Emergent, generative and responsive • Vested in each other's success

Central to a relational approach is developing an understanding of worldviews and to be able to work skillfully with them in building trust and relationship. Relational leadership recognizes that our experiences, like our worldviews, are socially constructed. A social construct is an idea that would be widely accepted as normal by a group, community or organization. It can be invisible to that group and it may or may not represent a reality shared by those outside the group, community or organization.

Relational leadership understands the fundamental role of language in creating experiences and in influencing relationship and communication. Worldview Intelligence offers new language that aids in entering difficult or challenging conversations or in diffusing challenged team dynamics and relationships. Understanding the role of language can be an asset in *Building Trust and Relationship at the Speed of Change* and it is a skill of Worldview Intelligent leaders.

James Sire, an author and lecturer who writes on the topic of worldviews, offers that the ability to consciously think in terms of worldviews is foundational to our ability to understand our own ways of thinking and that of others.[12] Perhaps most importantly, it is a way to understand and then genuinely communicate with others in a multiplicity of worldview experiences including in teams, business environments and communities. Worldview Intelligence offers a structured, organized method to be able to do this, beginning with the Worldview Intelligence Six Dimensions Framework and including the Worldview Intelligence Theory of Change Planning Model (CIDA-W) and the SHEER conversational planning worksheet shared in later chapters in this book.

In a diverse society, people believe many different things and tolerate each other's beliefs even when they don't match their own. Often, there can be an acceptance of a multiplicity of worldviews, but tolerance is not enough to get to acceptance or to transform differences into progress. For many of us, this is a challenge we do not always know we are facing, especially if we have muted out or shut down the very voices that could help improve performance or results. Our businesses, our teams, do not function in isolation. They are influenced by and influence the environments and communities in which they are located. As a leader, recognizing these external influences and worldviews as well as internal ones, gives you added capacity to build relationships to get the results you are being asked to deliver.

Marilyn Schlitz and her colleagues at the Institute of Noetic Sciences (IONS) go a step further than Sire in worldview thinking. They suggest that developing the capacity for greater cognitive flexibility, being comfortable in unfamiliar settings, appreciating many and diverse perspectives, being able to hold multiple views simultaneously and working at high levels of creative problem solving are essential skills for survival in the future.[13] We offer that these are essential skills for productive dialogue on issues that matter in the present and for the future. Having the capability to appreciate how worldviews shape our thoughts, conversations and actions is a foundational skill for working in the 21st century world and this is fundamental to *Building Trust and Relationship at the Speed of Change*.

REFLECTION QUESTIONS

1. What has been your experience of change in the last few years?

2. What have you been noticing about increasing diversity in your organization, community or country? How do you feel about this?

3. What is your default starting point when considering whether to trust another person or establish a relationship?

4. What are your thoughts or experiences in building trust in:
    a. New relationships
    b. Maintaining strong trust in existing relationships, or
    c. In re-building trust in a relationship that has been challenged

5. How do you think about time? Is it something to be precisely managed or are you open to approaching time based on the cultural or social context you are in?

CHAPTER 2:
WORLDVIEWS, HOW THEY ARE FORMED AND WHY IT MATTERS

I grew up in Lunenburg, Nova Scotia in the 1960s and 70s. It was, and still is, a homogenous small town of 2,500-3,000 people, almost exclusively white. Its economy centered around the fishing industry. Surrounding towns and the rural spaces in between were not much different. Although their economic bases differed somewhat, they were all dependent on natural resources. Skip ahead 25 years – past my attending university (several times), moving to the small city of Halifax, travel experiences, leading an Atlantic Canada based charitable organization and contributing to and participating in the National agenda of that organization, and so many other life experiences to 2005.

I was a member of a facilitation team designing and delivering curriculum for a nine-month community-based leadership program called Envision Halifax. For the first time in my life, I encountered difference in a way I had never experienced before. There were three women of color in the program that year – two were African Nova Scotian and one an immigrant. Early in the year, these women began raising concerns about racism including, among other things, the use of language. Examples might include negative connotations attributed to words like "dark" or "black" as in someone is in a black mood.

Although we each brought different worldview experiences, our facilitation team was poorly equipped to address the concerns being raised, and that was certainly true for me. At first, I was confused and then I was shocked. It never occurred to me that the experiences these women described happened to anyone, let alone women who were as professional as they were. They described walking into stores and being followed by store staff or security, even when professionally dressed. They shared their challenges in the workplace and with systemic racism, something that was not even a concept to me at the time.

Their experience was very different than mine as a middle-aged white woman. Age, education levels, career and professionalism were not necessarily the differing factors. Skin color, pure and simple, was. I was dumbfounded, then outraged. Especially when I discovered the even greater extent of this life experience for young black men living in my own city. One young man described being arrested as he was leaving his place of employment – a community library – locking the door behind him as he left. Not just once. Several times. By police waiting in the back parking lot. They knew he worked there. Another young man, a social worker, described being stopped by police as he was running an errand to pick up ice cream for his pregnant wife. He was walking down the street wearing a hoodie. The police pushed him up against the side of the squad car and would not let him speak. For more than an hour. Meanwhile, his wife was at home, wondering what had happened to him.

This began, for me, a journey that continues to this day, to understand other people's experiences, cultures and the impact of not being part of a dominant culture, learning to take care to not impose my worldview on others, but to be curious. When confronted or challenged with statements or perspectives offered in public forums and in the work we do, to pause, hear, acknowledge and incorporate it as new growth and worldview expansions whenever possible.

Kathy Jourdain

WORLDVIEWS AND HOW THEY ARE FORMED

What are worldviews, how are they formed and why does it matter? How does Worldview Intelligence provide strategies for Building Trust and Relationship at the Speed of Change?

Worldviews are the lenses through which we see, experience and interpret the world around us. They provide a symbolic system of representation in which we can place our own experiences. It is important to recognize that we don't have just one worldview but each of us can have many, usually interrelated, worldviews.

You have a personal worldview that influences how you act with family or friends. You may have a professional worldview that impacts how you think and act at work and in professional situations. You may be influenced by a cultural worldview that is prominent in your family or community. There is a societal worldview that influences how you act with, view or treat others in social settings, your community and your country. These worldviews operate principally in your unconscious or unawareness. They are invisible, like the air we breathe, and yet they have a vitality to them that infiltrates who we are and how we act. And because they are largely invisible, we think with them and through them but rarely about them.

How are worldviews formed? You were not born with a worldview, but you were born into a multitude of worldviews. Your parents, family, culture, community, faith institutions and schools all have worldviews.

Worldviews are socially and locally constructed. Socially constructed means constructed in relationship with and to other people. Our first interactions are with parents, family members or other caregivers. It is in relationship with them that our first worldviews take shape as we unconsciously assume the perspectives of those around us. Conversations and relationships throughout your whole life will have you continually constructing and reconstructing your worldview, even as you are unaware of the process.

Locally constructed means that place has a role in shaping worldviews. Where you were born, where you grew up, where you live now or have traveled to, all inform your worldview. The worldviews of place, people, organizations, culture and systems are communicated in many ways. Some of this is communicated in obvious and overt ways, but most of it is subtle, operating invisibly and impacting internally. Your worldviews become just what you know or how you act. Think of a place you've travelled to where you knew right away, "this place is different". It might have been another country, a different part of your own country, a different size city or town, more rural or more urban. How did you know it was different? Most people notice it "feels" different, but what generates that feeling? What are the components that contribute to the whole that generates that "feeling"? It could be the landscape, architecture, road design, the interactions and behaviors of local people or any of several other things.

The physical characteristics of where we grow up can also impact our worldview. Jerry grew up on the prairies of North Dakota with the wide expanse of space and far away horizons. He describes himself as a flatlander. While he enjoys visiting large metropolitan areas, he finds himself becoming uncomfortable in the canyons of tall buildings after a few days and longs to see the broad expanse of the sky. He also wonders how anyone could live in such places.

Kathy grew up next to the ocean and spent summers out on the water with her family. Her parents were able to identify far off specks on the horizon accurately as one boat or another. Her experience growing up with hills and trees of Nova Scotia makes the long prairie expanses seem boring.

Family members, neighboring communities, similar businesses, churches within the same faith, teachers in the same school can have similar or differing worldviews depending upon, among other things, local contexts and social and family experiences. Because they operate in your unawareness, these worldviews can be an invisible part of your conversations, relationships or any tension or conflict you may be experiencing. Values differences, impatience with different sources of knowledge or different relationships with the future may all be sources of conflict, as we explore in subsequent chapters.

Generally, the impact of worldviews is unknown prior to conscious exploration. It is quite common to be unaware of our own contribution to challenging dynamics in relationships, conversations or conflicts, which means you may be equally unaware of how much power you have to influence positively and strategically.

As you may have surmised by now, worldviews are not fixed. They continue to be socially constructed over the course of your lifetime. Individually, worldviews are influenced by the contexts in which you grew up, choices you've made and the life path that unfolded and continues to unfold, as a result of those choices. As you age, mature and/or grow, your worldviews often also grow or expand, as one of the ways in which you make sense of your experiences. Alternatively, some experiences may cause worldviews to contract, creating a desire to withdraw or isolate, possibly making you less open to other perspectives. We will say more on that in a minute.

WORLDVIEW AND IDENTITY

Psychological research tells us that because our worldviews are closely linked to our sense of identity, when our worldviews are challenged, we might respond as if our life is threatened.[14] Responses could look like lashing out, emphatically defending our own views or dismissing another person or their views. This explains why some people respond to seemingly small things out of proportion to the event they experienced. Perhaps it explains your own response to something where you feel you were overreacting but don't know how to pull back. We touch on why this is in this section and explore it more fully in Chapter 14: Understanding Worldview and Identity Reactions Through Behavioral Science. There we share how our worldviews and attachment to them are strengthened.

Finding yourself feeling like you need to defend your perspectives can cause you to come to an oppositional position with someone else. If someone offers a different or contrary perspective or view to your own, the most common reaction is to debate rather than reflect on what was said. The more you defend your views, the more attached you become to them and the harder it is to be curious about why someone has a different view or how they came to see the world the way they do. Of course, the same thing is true of the other person you are in a debate with – they become more attached to their worldviews and perspectives. This attachment to worldviews makes it hard to find points of connection or common ground. When worldviews are made explicit, yours and that of others, you create the opportunity to draw upon them for generative, creative, and innovative actions.

WORLDVIEWS IN ACTION – FASTER THAN THE BLINK OF AN EYE

We are constantly making decisions at lightning fast speeds, most of the time without knowing we are doing it. When was the last time you sat at a café or in an airport, watching people go by? Have you ever created a story about someone you saw? Of course you have. It is a natural, normal, typical human behavior. We all do it. The story appears in our minds fully formed, without words, carrying many assumptions about who that person is. Where did that story and those assumptions come from?

Much of the research on how fast our brains process information is funded by marketing companies and political parties. They are interested in ensuring their messages influence us, our thoughts, beliefs and actions in a particular direction. A study done at MIT on brain processing showed that from the time we see something, interpret it, make conclusions related to it, and determine a reaction, less than 13 milliseconds will have passed.[15] That is faster than you can blink your eyes. Less time than it takes you to read this sentence. And the only reason it is 13 milliseconds is because that is as fast as it can currently be measured.

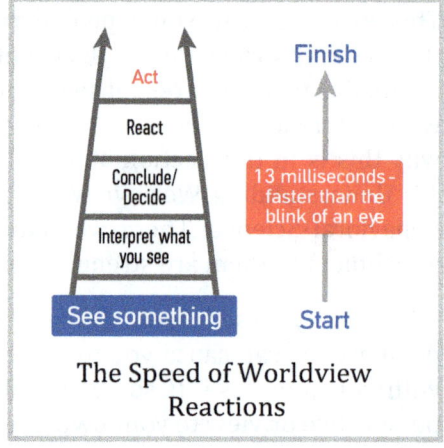

The Speed of Worldview Reactions

Your eyes are finding concepts and your brain is trying to understand them all day long. Even after the image has disappeared, the concepts may linger for processing in your brain, adding more interpretation, reinforcing belief systems about people, ideas and situations.

This rapid processing helps keep you safe, enables you to recognize complex patterns so you know instantly who familiar people, places and/or situations are and helps you develop habits to move through your days quicker. This can be valuable.

Having patterns for recognition and decision-making allows you to accomplish most routine actions quickly – like getting out of bed and getting ready for the day. However, it gets you in trouble when your interpretations, conclusions and reactions are wrong. It gets you into deeper trouble when you believe everyone thinks and processes information in the same way you do. They don't.

Your worldview, the way you have come to see and experience the world, influences even what you see or pay attention to. It shapes your interpretation of what you see and any meaning that you add, the conclusions you arrive at, reactions you have and any decisions or actions you take. If your experiences were different, you may reach a very different conclusion and act in a completely different way.

When considering the pace of change and the lightning fast speed with which this processing takes place, it is easy to see how misunderstandings, and in some instances conflict, occur.

Worldview Intelligence offers the opportunity to short-circuit unconscious messaging and to consider how to focus on healthy exchanges, relationships and communication. It does this by providing awareness, knowledge and skills to press the pause button, to be curious about your interpretations so you can act more mindfully, intentionally or strategically and to invite others to do so as well.

EVER CHANGING, EXPANDING AND CONTRACTING WORLDVIEWS

As noted already, worldviews are not fixed. Changes in worldviews can be quite small and hardly noticed. You might live in a similar pattern throughout periods of your lifetime and not notice how you have grown, shifted or changed. It could be that you have acquired a taste for a food you once did not like or an appetite for a new genre of fiction or non-fiction or you have taken on a new hobby. Sometimes new people in your life influence patterns around what food you cook, what movies you watch or how you use your time; and, again, it can be subtle or obvious.

Sometimes these changes or shifts add up to a transformative impact. Perhaps you discover a thirst for travel that you didn't have before or a desire to learn a new language. Occasionally, worldview shifts can be so transformative, due to life changing events like significant loss, a near death experience or a radically eye-opening experience, that a person can change spiritual beliefs, political philosophies, or even physical characteristics.[16] How a person looks, their physical stature or stance, how others perceive them, can be impacted by a shift in worldview.

While most people may not carry conscious awareness that their worldview has shifted or changed over time with minor events, for more significant shifts, there is often a more noticeable impact. However, few people take the time to truly reflect on the impact, what is different or how it has influenced their communication or relationships or their participation in society. When was the last time you paused to reflect on how your worldview has changed and what that means for how you live your life, what work you do, what kind of leadership you bring to your team, organization or community or how you show up in relationship? The value of doing this is not to be underestimated.

The work of Worldview Intelligence focuses on expansion, which means we usually think of a worldview shift in terms of broadening perspectives. As mentioned above, it also happens that some events cause people to reduce or contract their worldview. Travel is often cited as promoting worldview expansions and the threat of violence or terrorism in places people do not know or haven't been to is often cited as a reason for worldview contraction. This can manifest in a fear of traveling, fear of the unknown in an event, situation, place or groups of people. Fear is a strong motivator for contraction.

When we travelled to France in February of 2019 to teach at a University in Brittany, we had several people warn us of the violence in the country, attributed to the Yellow Vest movement, or mouvement des gilets jaunes. If we were not familiar with the country and the culture, we may have hesitated to go. But we knew that Paris and other places we would travel to were so much more than the representation in the media of one slice of the current reality. We did in fact see a Yellow Vest protest on the day we arrived in Paris, but it was more of an event to observe than a fear-inducing protest.

AVOIDING THE IMPOSITION OF WORLDVIEWS

As mentioned in Chapter 1: When Time is the Enemy, how people have come to see and experience the world is different for everyone. If you think of siblings or friends you grew up with, even with similar experiences in the same family or community, you already know that people hold different opinions, beliefs and views even when they have many of the same reference points. Someone who has grown up somewhere else, has a different faith, different culture, different skin color, different language or family values, had a different life experience. This means they see and experience the world differently than you – from a little bit differently to dramatically differently to anywhere in between.

When one person or group imposes their worldview on another person or group, whether on purpose or accidentally, this can be seen as an act of aggression between individuals and is an act violence between groups. This comes from the ancient text by Sun Tzu, called *The Art of War.* Sun Tzu was an ancient Chinese military general, strategist and philosopher.[17] His book is often sited as a treatise on how to win wars. In recent times, Mao used it in China and the Vietcong used it to defeat the USA in Viet Nam. Ironically, *The Art of War* can be interpreted as a text on why not to go to war because the minute you go to war, everyone loses. In war, the presumed victorious group imposes their worldview on the presumed losing group, wanted or not. *The Art of War* names this as an act of violence. You cannot do harm to another without also doing harm to yourself. According to the worldview expressed in that book, we are all interconnected. When imposing a worldview on another, it becomes an act of violence and harmful to all. Awareness of our interconnectedness and the impacts of worldview imposition can be part of a business strategy. This is outlined in careful detail in the *Rules of Victory: How to Transform Chaos and Conflict – Strategies from The Art of War* by James Gimian and

Barry Boyce.[18] As a leader, having an awareness of this might inform your approach to leading change and the care you take in tending to trust and relationship.

CHANGE – INVITATION OR IMPOSITION?

Simply having an awareness that different individuals and groups, teams or departments will meet change differently according to their own worldview experiences can offer different options and strategies to work with those impacted by change, planned or unplanned. People may be excited, daunted, resistant or somewhere else on the spectrum of the change curve. A range of responses is not unusual – it is normal and to be expected.

Too often, people leading change or other initiatives in the organization expect everyone to welcome change the way they do, or at least that everyone else will react in the same way. That is not what happens. Change managers often see acceptance of change as a matter of the mind, as an intellectual activity. They do not see it as also a matter of the heart, an emotional matter. If you are leading change, you are out ahead of the change curve and have already worked through your own reactions to the change. You are likely leading the change with excitement and enthusiasm. Creating the time and processes for people to catch up can be annoying and frustrating if you just want to get on with it. Pausing to allow people to catch up emotionally and intellectually goes a long way in building trust and relationship.

It is common to not take the time, or to believe you don't have the time, to slow down to allow the expression of the range of emotional reactions. By not slowing down, the reactions don't go away. They inevitably find a way to be expressed, which often then slows things down in unplanned, unhealthy and unhelpful ways. The patterns of reactions to change are predictable; some are visible, some are invisible. Building in time and opportunity for people to acclimatize to change not only maintains trust and relationship but it keeps things advancing. There are many ways this can be achieved including in informal sessions with the people affected by change, creating safe-enough space for what is on people's minds to be expressed. It could be an organization-wide change strategy with multiple forums for expression, including on-line forums.

Bear in mind that people's previous experience with change influences their worldview about change. If they have had a lot of positive experiences with change, they may be more change ready and trusting. If they have had bad experiences with change, they will be leerier. If your organization is one that seldom completes a change process before the next one comes around, employees may be change weary. Leeriness or weariness will both impact trust and relationship in change efforts. If parts of a person's life have stability (for example, at home), they have more capacity for change in other parts of their life (for example, at work) and the opposite is true as well. If their home life is not stable for whatever reason, handling change at work could be harder.

If you are dealing with a merger or acquisition situation, there will be many and varied reactions to the changes ahead. Attending to the emotional reactions will significantly increase the potential for success. Remembering that people in both the acquiring and acquired companies will be skeptical or even fearful of what will happen, what it will mean for their role, their career or their employment will influence your people strategy. A Worldview Intelligence approach will give you insight into potential reactions. A relational approach to leading can help you be aware of your team member's individual circumstances and their capacity for change and how you might support them during the change process.

This makes transparency and aligning worldviews referenced in Chapter 1 in the steps to Building Trust and Relationship at the Speed of Change, of paramount importance. Awareness of the various worldviews reduces the chances of accidental impositions and it affords you the opportunity to strategically address relationships and maintain trust throughout change processes you plan as well as when the organization gets hit with unanticipated changes due to other internal or external changing circumstances.

POINTS OF CONNECTION ESSENTIAL TO RELATIONSHIP AND TRUST

From a personal and leadership perspective, finding points of connection can change the nature of interactions and allow for more opportunities to build trust and relationship. Too often this is seen as superfluous to the tasks at hand and little relationship building gets done. The myth is to focus on tasks, attend to them and check the to-do items to accomplish change objectives. Rarely is anyone's work done in isolation, especially these days. Work projects and larger scale initiatives require sequential tasks, handed from one person, team or department to another and possibly back again. More likely, with the increasing complexity of many work environments, interdependent and cross functional teams work together, sometimes collaboratively and usually with competing demands or loyalties, on initiatives and especially larger ones.

Poor relationships and lack of trust get in the way of accomplishing tasks and effective job performance. This can lead to poor morale and, in too many cases, become a toxic work environment. None of these things are conducive to working well at the speed of change.

Building team coherence does not have to be spending days away together on a retreat, testing physical endurance, doing trust falls or role modeling bad and good patterns of interaction or dynamics – although it could be. One of the best ways to build team connection and coherence is by attending to the work at hand, focusing on issues relevant to the team and the organization. Opportunities for people to explore their own worldviews, that of the team or the organization can be built into this. We have worked with organizations on attending to issues and questions surrounding recent mergers or undergoing other kinds of change initiatives where we have incorporated into the meeting design both Worldview Intelligence exercises and the opportunity to strategize and plan for the issues most top of mind. This helps team members find points of connection between each other, between other work teams and also between employees and their organization.

Finding points of connection changes how people deal with the differences they experience. It points to more opportunity for information sharing, collaboration and generally strengthens the ability of the team to be in good, even if challenging, work together. They bring more curiosity to the tougher questions or conversations and the environment is often more conducive to exploration than otherwise.

WORLDVIEW INTELLIGENCE IS A LEADERSHIP PRACTICE

Your worldviews contain and influence your sense of what is real, your past, your future, the values you hold, the practices you live your life by and your sense of how you know what you know, how you evaluate the relative truth of what you think you know. They influence your communication, relationships and any tension or conflict you may be experiencing. As we have already noted, most of this happens without your conscious awareness. Worldviews operate in the places of habits, "taken-for granteds" and automatic reactions. They influence your assumptions, conclusions and actions, even before you think.

Worldview Intelligence is a leadership practice. The structure and approach it offers provides the opportunity for self-reflection to illuminate your ability to understand your perspective and your starting points in any conversation, team convening or strategic undertaking in your organization. You can use the personal and professional Worldview Intelligence explorations that you will find later in this book to choose to grow, learn and change with conscious awareness.

REFLECTION QUESTIONS

1. Recall a moment when you realized your worldview seemed to suddenly expand or contract. What was the circumstance, event or situation? What was the movement in your worldview – expansion, contraction, something else? How did that impact or influence you in the days, weeks, months or even years that followed? What else changed for you?

2. When you reflect on a team you are leading or are a part of, what would you consider the quality of relationship and trust in the team? Does this support or get in the way of results? What could improve? What might be the result of improving? As a leader of a team, how does your current understanding of worldviews (based on these first two chapters) inform your understanding of your team dynamics?

CHAPTER 3:
THE SCOPE OF WORLDVIEW INTELLIGENCE APPLICATIONS

Clients often look to Worldview Intelligence to support the innovative, transformational work they are in the midst of or preparing to embark on. One such client, a provincial Law Society, was changing the way it regulated the profession of law within the province. They were moving from a more unilateral, one size fits all, do as we tell you approach to what they call a 3P approach: proportionate, principled and proactive; more supportive and less punitive. The senior leadership in the Regulatory Body recognized they were asking staff, the Governing Council, members, stakeholders, partners and the public for a change in worldviews.

The scope of this work included asking staff to explore their own personal worldviews. It asked departments to illuminate departmental worldviews. The organization was charged with redefining some of the terms it was using, including what it meant by "risk management". Staff identified areas where they wanted to change outcomes, including increasing their ability to have animated, generative conversations and their ability to collaborate across what they identified as departmental silos – both of which were achieved.

The Governing Council explored a combination of their personal and professional worldviews. They examined how their worldviews had shifted from the time they agreed to serve on Council to this point, given their experiences and growth since joining the Council. Council members came to a determination that in order to support the regulatory shift and the changes in conversations with members, they needed to change some of the context and tone of their meetings and relationships for greater alignment and coherence.

Kathy Jourdain and Jerry Nagel

SCOPE OF WORLDVIEW INTELLIGENCE APPLICATIONS

The focus of this book is on personal worldview explorations, particularly as it relates to leadership practice and how to Build Trust and Relationship at the Speed of Change. While it is the ability to combine worldview explorations that makes the work so powerful, most programs begin with a personal exploration. Just like we each have a personal and perhaps professional worldview, our teams, organizations, communities, social systems and cultures have worldviews. These are also locally and socially constructed, and they are not usually visible or articulated. There are pervasive patterns of belief and behavior practiced as part of a shared experience, often implicit in the fabric of an organization, family system, a community, culture or social system.

The beauty of the Worldview Intelligence Six Dimensions Framework that we introduce in Chapter 5 and examine in more detail in Chapters 6 through 11 is that it is equally applicable to a variety of explorations. This includes personal, professional, teams and organizations, in community, across social systems or with partners and collaborators, and in looking at cultures.* You can also use it in your personal relationships with family and friends.

These explorations can build on and support each other, each offering new or different insights into the complexities of your organization, community, collaborations or partnerships and can help you imagine the leadership you could provide. Hidden dynamics that get in the way of achieving results can be illuminated and new ways forward can be discerned. We explore this more fully in Chapter 12: The Strategic Use of the Worldview Intelligence Six Dimensions Framework.

ORGANIZATION WORLDVIEWS ARE NOT IN VISION OR MISSION STATEMENTS

Organizations do not typically express their worldviews in their vision or mission statements. They are not generally explicit about their worldviews, largely because they are not articulated and haven't been thought through. During Worldview Intelligence explorations with one of our non-profit clients, they were struck with a realization. The mandate for their work in community was to eradicate poverty. Written into their codicil of incorporation is that the organization will exist in perpetuity. The insight: the worldview of the organization is that poverty will always exist. Unstated, it created a personal and unarticulated tension for staff that hovered under the surface as they worked in community. While neither the codicil nor the mandate will likely change, making it visible reduces the influence of this tension and allows the staff to work with the mandate more mindfully.

The worldviews of an organization impact how it operates, treats employees or customers or communicates with other organizations. These worldviews can significantly impact mergers, partnerships, collaborations or power structures. The same is true for communities. The patterns within a community and its social system impact its ability to interact with other

---

* These are all topics that will be more fully articulated in subsequent books.

communities, with new residents or with components of the community such as businesses, police, social services, education and more.

SOCIAL SYSTEMS AND WORLDVIEWS

Several years ago, Jerry lived in a rural community in Minnesota that had a reputation for not being particularly welcoming to newcomers. The saying was, "If you aren't four or five generations from here, you are not from here and never will be." This notion of not being from somewhere was also made visible to Jerry the first time he hosted in Maine. During the first circle check-in, people described themselves as from Maine or "from away". This is also a common expression in Atlantic Canada where the term CFA or "come from away" is often used. Now, interestingly, it is also the name of a Canadian produced Broadway production that shines the light on Newfoundland, Canada hospitality in the aftermath of the 9-11 tragedy[19].

A community is one version of a social system. In addition to a community, a social system could be one in which individuals, families, organizations or cultures operate. In a social system, there are overarching aspects of worldview, which draw the components of the social system together. However, under the umbrella of the social system there are likely to be different and sometimes competing worldviews at play. For instance, if you mapped out a social system related to health and health care as we have done, it would include hospitals, emergency rooms, clinics, the various health care professionals and their professional and regulatory bodies, pharmacies, community members and more. Within the system, the worldviews of community members might be different from that of the professionals who provide healthcare. There may also be some professions that are not mainstream healthcare like physiotherapy, chiropractic, massage therapy or naturopathy who also provide health related services but are not often recommended by physicians as part of holistic health care.

Worldview Intelligence is a powerful resource for revealing and understanding hidden dynamics and patterns that support or get in the way of trust or relationship, especially when there are fundamental differences in views that divide people. The rituals, stories, myths and metaphors that are a deep part of an organization, group, community, system, culture or family can indicate how the members see themselves, their group identities, what matters to them and how they make meaning of what is important.[20] When you bring an attitude of curiosity and non-judgment, then opportunities for connection and understanding of differences become clearer. This can lead to greater possibilities to find new ways forward on matters of shared interest or concern, to resolve conflicts, or step into spaces of emergence and to change outcomes.

LOCAL AND GLOBAL INFLUENCES

Just as individual worldviews can shift, expand or contract, so too can the worldviews of organizations, communities, social systems and cultures. Again, these shifts can be subtle, and some can also occur significantly. Local shifts can be sparked by global influences. This is evidenced by many of the changes in our organizations and in society as a whole in the past century resulting from scientific advances like flight, Internet, space travel, atomic energy or those in medicine; and historical events like wars, walking on the moon, acts of terrorism, epidemics; or social shifts like civil rights, same-sex marriage, food preferences and music. This means that, while worldviews are locally constructed, they are also influenced by changes in global constructs as well as individual and collective experiences. Since we know worldviews do shift, change, contract or expand, we can also become intentional in strategically shifting organizational or community worldviews. This can be particularly useful when working at the speed of change or needing to illuminate hidden dynamics. You can identify core elements to be nurtured and amplified and find ways to disrupt what no longer serves.

THE PERSONAL WORLDVIEW EXPLORATION IS FOUNDATIONAL – HERE'S WHY

The personal worldview exploration is foundational to the other explorations. We have discovered this repeatedly in working with clients and in offering open enrolment programs. It is reinforced by participant responses and feedback. As people begin to imagine how to create the space for multiple worldviews, stories and perspectives to co-exist, to fuel generative conversations of discovery or new, more comprehensive solutions to issues of mutual concern or interest it becomes obvious we need to know and understand our own worldviews before being able to understand or invite others.

To understand why you react the way you do when your worldview is challenged gives you the opportunity to respond differently to the challenge. This, in essence, means you can respond differently to the person who brings the challenge, which is an essential leadership skill. To be able to deconstruct your own worldview, what you naturally gravitate towards, to understand what you usually ignore and why, opens the opportunity to hold yourself in a position of not knowing, of curiosity, of willingness to hear something you disagree with without immediately dismissing it, debating it or trying to normalize it. Your response, your openness, changes the conversation and expands the possibilities. It does not mean you need to agree with another's worldview, but in making an effort to understand how they came to their worldview, how they came to see the world the way they do, you create an exploratory opportunity that can be held open for as long as needed, even for a lifetime if you wish.

This is why becoming Worldview Intelligent is a leadership practice. It is complete with a set of skills and capacity building strategies that enable you to grow as an individual and as someone who leads in your organization. The personal exploration is foundational to the other categories of exploration – professional, organizational, community, social systems, and more.

Fundamental to building or maintaining trust with those you lead is your own personal integrity, alignment and coherence. When your words and your actions are out of alignment, mixed messages are conveyed to others. Your actions speak so loudly people cannot hear what you say. Without the personal Worldview Intelligence exploration, this can be a dynamic that stays hidden to yourself.

In our Worldview Intelligence programs, we ask the questions, "What is your worldview? How do you know? What impact does it have on your relationships, communication or the challenges you experience? What is your starting point for any interaction or communication?" Most people have given little, if any, thought to these questions. The personal worldview exploration allows you to begin to understand your worldview, what has influenced how you have come to see and experience the world around you and specific issues, and it allows you to discern your starting point. You will have the opportunity to explore and discover the answers to these questions in subsequent chapters. The Worldview Intelligence Six Dimensions Framework introduced in Chapter 5 provides an elegant structure for this exploration. It will help you illuminate things that seem obvious once they are made visible but otherwise are running in the background, impacting you, your communications and relationships in unconscious ways.

Understanding your own worldview helps you understand where and how you might differ with someone else. The points of difference are often hidden or disguised. They look like something else, most commonly a disagreement on facts or a difference in opinion. It may be more fundamentally a values clash, how you see and experience the future or something in your history that is still alive in this moment. It happens often that we take offence without understanding what it is that has offended us or without understanding how to bring curiosity and compassion to another individual, their point of view or a situation.

In a recent Worldview Intelligence program, one of the participants was surprised at how they arrived at compassion for someone with whom they differ. They might not ever agree with that person but imagine how approaching that relationship with compassion changes the whole context for the conversation.

REFLECTION QUESTIONS

1. What is one relationship you are challenged by and why? What seems to be at the core of the challenge? What do you think the other person contributes to this challenge? What might you be contributing to this challenge?

2. In your leadership capacity, what one or two questions might you hold as you continue this worldview exploration in subsequent chapters?

CHAPTER 4:
WHAT IT MEANS TO BE WORLDVIEW INTELLIGENT

There was a tremble in our fourteen member Art of Hosting* team in March 2012 as we prepared to welcome over seventy Somalis, Native Americans, African Americans, Anglo Americans, Latinos, people from Liberia, Ethiopia, Malaysia, Mexico, Costa Rica and Columbia, together with two translators: one for Somali and one for Spanish. We were not sure how many would come, how many would stay, or how many would come back the next day.

This four-day community gathering was convened in the hopes that bridges could be formed across the multiplicity of cultures that had come to reside in the Phillips residential area of South Minneapolis. The original residents of this community were primarily African Americans, Native Americans and Anglo Americans. In the 1990s, immigrants and refugees began moving into the area in search of affordable housing. Over the years, the cultures clashed, tensions rose and violence across the cultures, particularly between youth in the Native American and Somali communities, erupted.

A local Somali woman who found herself at an Art of Hosting Conversations that Matter (AoH) training in March 2011, wanted to explore what might be possible if a training was hosted right in the middle of her community, in the community center, where the children congregate after school. Well, we found out!

The hosting team was comprised of AoH stewards and members of the community representative of those who were called to gather. The gathering was opened with a beautiful Lakota sage ceremony – to open the space, to cleanse ourselves, open our minds and, even more so, our hearts. It was an offering from one of the cultures present in the room, from a Lakota elder on the hosting team, inviting others to also offer something in a right moment or right opportunity.

---

* The Art of Hosting Conversations that Matter is a suite of patterns and practices for hosting or facilitating group conversations. It has been taught and practiced throughout the world. Kathy and Jerry are highly experienced AoH trainers and practitioners.

Each one of us was then invited to bring our voices into the standing circle by responding to: my name is..., I live..., I'm from..., my ancestors are from... and I speak .... languages. As we listened, we became aware, beyond the diversity of skin color already visible in the room, of the richness and multiplicity of cultures, languages and worldviews represented in the space, the richness that is contained sometimes in a single individual as well as in the collective. It took our breath away and opened our curiosity.

People were warmly invited into the space, in such a way they felt welcome, "safe enough" and ready and willing to offer their cultural rituals, ceremonies and stories into this collective space. In addition to the opening sage ceremony, we experienced a Somali coffee ceremony, an Aztek water ceremony, a Hmong friendship ritual and an African American dramatic story telling, Sojourner Truth, as well as Native American ceremony, song and round dance from the Lakota culture. We gifted each other with prayers and blessings.

Sometimes it was a bit uncomfortable with the varying perspectives and cultural norms around touch, song, dance and partaking in another culture's ceremony; but only just in that moment before understanding blossomed and more ease entered with the witnessing of things precious. Graciousness, curiosity and respect filled the space and the conversations. Deepening our individual and collective listening skills invited each of us to be even more fully present.

The realization that issues, concerns and passions arc across cultures and neighborhood history invited people into bridge building. Education, children, community housing, racism, racial profiling, relationship with police, healing, well-being were collective connection points. Learning to navigate the dominant culture and stand up, both for what is right and for rights of an individual no matter each person's roots or ancestral history. Awareness of commonality and connection in the diversity. We care about many of the same things even if our ways of approaching them or our cultural norms are different.

Jerry Nagel and Kathy Jourdain

A STRUCTURED APPROACH TO EXPLORATIONS

Worldview Intelligence offers a structured approach for exploring individual and collective assumptions, beliefs and value systems. It provides ways to strategize and then be in planning, conversations and relationship differently. It opens the potential for more comprehensive approaches and solutions to emerge on a range of issues and opportunities. And, it changes outcomes. In a world that is becoming increasingly fragmented and polarized, Worldview Intelligence gives voice and visibility to multiple worldviews. It creates openings for successfully leading different, more inclusive conversations on issues and challenges that routinely show up in teams, organizations, communities, social systems and families.

Worldview Intelligence offers two key things for leaders in organizations and communities, especially when working in fast changing and complex environments. The first is that it offers skills and strategies for surfacing the multiple worldviews or perspectives that exist in a team, organization or community in ways that build trust and relationship. In this way, it draws out the diversity needed for innovation and creative solutions to the challenges facing us in our organizations.

The second is that when seeking successful change, interventions or solutions to issues, especially in complex environments, it offers a way to sort through the obvious but sometimes misleading surface events to fully work with the complexity. It gets to the underlying dynamics and patterns that contribute to the issues under investigation. In the systems thinking iceberg model that we share a bit later in this chapter, worldviews are mental models. Understanding the nature of worldviews that are perpetuating stuck issues or questions, illuminates different leverage points for addressing the issues. This includes worldview shifts or expansions that may be necessary within individuals, teams, organizations or communities.

WORLDVIEW AWARENESS AS A FIRST STEP TO WORLDVIEW INTELLIGENCE

What is the difference between being worldview aware and being Worldview Intelligent? To be worldview aware is to feel, experience and notice that worldviews exist, individually, professionally, culturally, organizationally and societally. It is to know and understand more about what is happening in the world around you through this greater awareness, curiosity and openness. Worldview Intelligence is to bring skills, strategies and different ways of knowing into practice in situations where multiple worldviews exist, which is pretty much everywhere to greater and lesser degrees. It is to transform differences into progress, to succeed in *building trust and relationship at the speed of change* and to change outcomes that support what you are intending to achieve.

In our experience, developing new levels of worldview awareness changes how people come together in situations of varying complexity. Worldview Intelligence skills allow individuals and groups to build trust and relationship quickly, to access the collective wisdom and intelligence available in groups, teams, organizations or communities in powerful ways. It offers an easily understood framework with a structured way to engage in practices that invite dialogue, create places for people to speak from their hearts and spirits as well as their minds and intellect. Worldview Intelligence recognizes that we each have something to contribute to the well-being of each of us. This is essential in healthy relationships that enable progress to be made on important work. This is not just a feel-good exercise, which many people want to dismiss in the "practical" pursuit of concrete outcomes. Creating or finding connections is one of the conditions conducive to high performance teams and organizations. In Google's famous study on the conditions that create successful teams, the two most important characteristics they identified were that each person on the team has an equal amount of time to contribute to the team discussions and successful teams have higher levels of social sensitivity among individual team members, meaning they tended to the well-being of the team, individually and collectively [21].

Learning to effectively communicate in different or new cultural milieus, with people holding strongly different worldviews from your own, or in situations where there are many differing worldviews, is a deep-level process. It involves connecting at more than an intellectual level. As the Google study notes, to enter effective communication within these or other multi-varied circumstances you must open your heart to empathy that allows you to more deeply understand another's worldview. This does not mean you need to agree with or be sympathetic to another's worldview. It does mean you seek understanding by developing your capacity for vulnerability, to respect difference, to be curious rather than judgmental, to sit in the space of not knowing, the unknown or unknowing, and to be self-reflective regarding your own thoughts, reactions, and "carried in" thinking of another person, organization or culture. This is not just important in one-on-one conversations, at home or in your community. It is also fundamentally important to how you work in your teams, organizations and social systems, if you want to succeed when things are moving at the speed of change.

If worldviews are mainly locally and socially constructed within ourselves, our organizations and communities and our belief systems, then you could ask, what consequences do these locally constructed worldviews have for our ability to work together? One answer is that they can create barriers to understanding and finding common ground for working together. This is what happens when people are not worldview aware or worldview curious. With curiosity you could ask questions like: How can we come together in ways that build understanding and respect to work together on what matters in the moment? How can we come together in ways that allow each of us to hold on to that which is most important while advancing the conversation or relationship? How can we use the energy of collisions of worldviews constructively? What would happen if understanding our worldviews opens a new gateway to our most challenging conversations? What can we do about it? This possibility grows with increased worldview awareness and then increased skills and strategies and the illumination the Worldview Intelligence Six Dimensions Framework brings to any inquiry.

BUILDING TRUST TO SURFACE THE DIVERSITY OF WORLDVIEWS

For practitioners of dialogue (which is our background) the capability to build trust quickly is essential to our ability to create environments of safety or "safe enough" in many settings. This is particularly true for leaders when it comes to building trust and connection within their teams, organizations or communities.

In challenging and complex situations, there is a greater likelihood of silent views and a greater actual or perceived risk in voicing them. When voices are silent, groups, teams, organizations or communities lose some of the wisdom and intelligence that might otherwise be available to them. It is almost always challenging for anyone to speak a view that differs from the majority opinion, unless that view is intentionally invited in and welcomed – by a consultant, a leader or the group itself. This challenge is compounded when it is not just a differing opinion but also held or offered by a visible minority in the room. We have witnessed these dynamics in a variety of settings including open enrolment programs where visible minorities have been quieter in the conversations and in our client work when one or a few individuals are guarded in what they have to offer. Intentionally inviting this diversity of views is best done from a place of humility, exercising the qualities of curiosity, respect, vulnerability, not knowing and compassion.

If people on your team, in your group or organization are not contributing, consider the following questions and points: Is their contribution or voice truly being invited? What happens when they do speak up? Do you or others listen, question, roll your eyes (even in your mind)? Are their ideas acknowledged and sometimes acted upon? Are they a valued member of your team, valued as a human being? Have you expressed this in a way that they know it? These are important points to be aware of in the relationships you are building.

WHEN THE LEADER IS HESITANT

We have learned the hard way to push back when clients ask

to mute a voice or an issue in a group. We worked with a client interested in building more team coherence within a newly formalized team. The team members had previously worked together in more informal ways. The organization values diversity among its constituencies. This team was not representative of the diversity of the constituencies and this was an issue for a few people on the team. The team lead was concerned about the topic of racism overtaking the attempt to build team coherence. We were asked not to include the usual examples that demonstrate racism in our presentation. We acquiesced. No surprise, the issue of racism and diversity did not go away. It became the elephant in the room. The team leader recognized about three quarters of the way into the day that perhaps she had made an error in her request.

The members of the team particularly interested in racial and gender equity brought it up during small group discussions and in large group debriefs. While we welcomed those reflections into the room and addressed them as they arose, we knew we missed an opportunity to go deeper, faster with this team.

INVITING THE VISIBILITY OF MULTIPLE WORLDVIEWS

Worldview Intelligence offers a starting point from which you can create new, shared meanings or new narratives. We are not suggesting a singular story. We are offering that it is more powerful to have a variety of narratives woven together in the richness with which they are offered and lived, the intersectionality of worldviews.

If you think there is only, or should only be, one narrative, you may be strong in your own worldview perspective or you may be part of the dominant culture or population and not even be aware that there may be a multiple of worldviews. Holding strongly onto single worldviews often leads to societies becoming more fragmented into specific groups or worldviews. This diminishes our ability to communicate with each other and to work together on issues that matter to us. Jerry has a good friend whose political views are quite divergent from his. It would be easy for them to huddle within their respective reference groups. Yet, they have worked together on an issue that matters deeply to both for over 15 years, often traveling together internationally. In the course of this, they have built a close and lasting friendship despite their different political views. This has given them the ability to explore, in trusting conversations, how each has come to see the world the way they do.

To invite multiple perspectives means being willing to expand your own worldview just enough to allow other stories or perspectives to also have significance to potentially shift the dialogue. As you develop greater understanding of differing worldviews, together with your team, you can begin co-creating new stories or design new processes or even rituals to build a collective narrative regarding issues that matter. A ritual could be as simple as starting every meeting with some kind of check in process as described in the previous chapter, so every voice is heard early. This increases the likelihood of continued participation and contribution throughout the meeting. You can establish conditions for dialogue that can create a 'knowing together'. These conditions include inviting every voice and welcoming divergent points of view, increasing comfort levels in animated discussions, valuing and building on ideas and staying focused on the topic at hand.

When you start from difference, difference is amplified. When you find points of connection first, you can explore difference in new ways and from a more generative orientation. As a leader in your team or organization, it may not be helpful to look for that one new narrative that explains everything. Instead, look for the multiplicity of narratives that can co-exist together in a place of interconnectedness, where value is recognized in each of the perspectives and the people who offer those perspectives.

The Worldview Intelligence Six Dimensions Framework provides a mechanism for this exploration. Through this interpersonal exchange, in the exploration of worldviews or how different people have come to see, experience or interpret an issue or situation of importance to the work at hand, connectedness can and does emerge in ways that weren't possible before. As this builds relationship and trust, the team grows their capacity for lively, animated conversations focused on issues without offending or taking offence. Worldview Intelligence offers language that supports this capacity building as people begin identifying that they are speaking from their worldview or their perspective.

As the team develops facility in these conversations, solutions appear faster. There is greater capacity for risk-taking as "failure" becomes part of the process of learning and discovering innovations that will work. Fear of failure, or punishment of failure, will make teams risk averse, more bureaucratic and less responsive to changing circumstances and can irreparably harm relationship and trust. Or they take a long time to repair once damaged.

AVOIDING FIXES THAT FAIL – GETTING TO MENTAL MODELS

Leaders working in fast changing environments are no strangers to the phenomena of "fixes that fail" otherwise known as "backfire loops". This is when you, your team, organization or community implements a solution to a problem that doesn't solve the problem. In some cases, the problem stays pretty much the same. In other cases, the problem is either made worse or new problems are created, otherwise known as unintended consequences.

An example of an unintended consequence occurred with one of our health care clients. They had initiated a pilot project that had a select number of clinics working in new collaborative ways around patient care. One of the clinics in the pilot was in a city where there were two other clinics in which they had invested a few years building relationship and standardizing practices so that the patient experience in each of the clinics was similar. When one of the clinics entered the pilot project, they began to implement different patient practices. This put the relationship they had been building with the other two clinics, that were

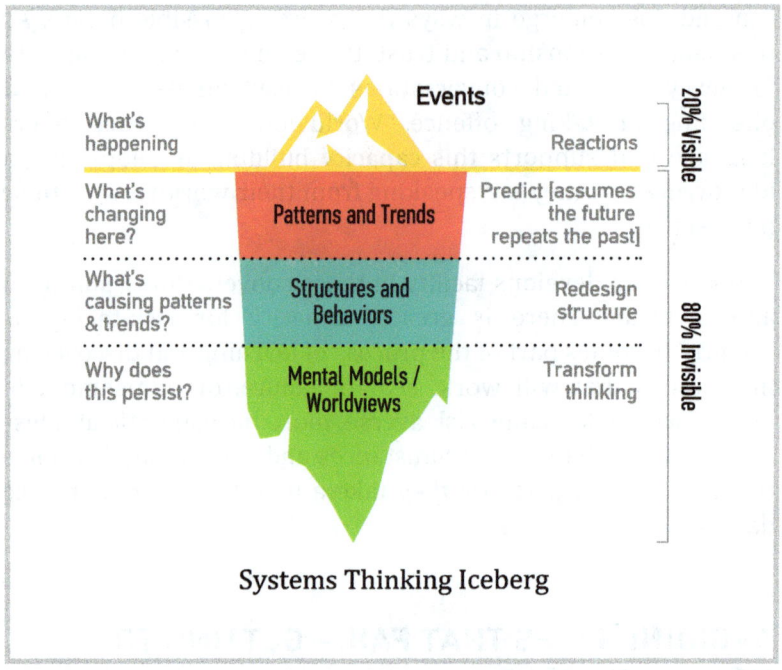

Systems Thinking Iceberg

not part of the pilot program, in jeopardy. It is easy to see it in retrospect, but it was an unintended consequence that could be attended to once it was illuminated.

To change the outcomes, the source of the issue needs to be discovered or uncovered. This can be done by reflecting on the patterns and trends that are creating the event being responded to. These patterns and trends are influenced by the structures in place and the behaviors of people in the organization or community. Ultimately, discerning the thinking or mental models that led to the creation of these structures and behaviors leads to the greatest opportunity for successful interventions. The deeper the exploration, the greater the likelihood of discovering strategies that change the nature of the problem.

An issue we have been bringing a Worldview Intelligence approach to is labor availability concerns in Itasca and Cass Counties in Minnesota. We have explored the iceberg with employers and community members to help everyone get a better grasp of the dynamics that are creating the challenges of workforce availability and workplace readiness, to understand why interventions need to be collaborative and comprehensive.

In this initiative the **"event"** is workforce shortage and competition for workers in a relatively small geographic area with a population of around 40,000 people. The typical actions taken by employers to address workforce shortage is to conduct career fairs, create committees and grumble about younger generations, believing that students need a reality check in their expectations of workplace conditions – but the reality check might be for employers.

The **patterns and trends** that are contributing to workforce shortage are demographic shifts, declining population rates and the ratcheting up of wages in other places. There are more people aging out of the workforce than aging in, expectations of work-life integration are different for younger generations and there will only be so much elasticity in wages. This region is not known to be a destination for immigrant or refugee populations and may not be perceived to be welcoming to people who come from other countries. Employee recruitment strategies are not creating long term gains but only have people potentially moving from one workplace to another, which does not address the larger issue of lack of available workers – only moves it around.

Looking at the patterns and trends it is obvious that the forecast or prediction for the next few years is that there will continue to be workforce shortages with no definitive strategies to address the issue.

Structures and behaviors that contribute to the patterns and trends include that youth are leaving the rural region to go to urban areas, newcomer populations do not feel fully supported and African American students attending the local community college don't permanently relocate to the region even though there are jobs available. Additionally, the workplace structures, processes and behavior expectations of most workplaces were created by Baby Boomers who generally have a different worldview of work and life than Millennials. It is hard for Baby Boomers who created the current structures to imagine different ways of structuring the workplace. They are expecting newer employees to conform to the existing structures, but more likely younger generations will break them. It is just a matter of time as Millennials begin to comprise the largest generation in the workforce, projected by several census reports to be 75% by 2025.

In considering how to redesign structures, employers, educators and the community are beginning to ask how are schools being engaged, what summer opportunities can be created and how can students be mentored, not just while they are in the education system, but to invite them to come back to the area when they are ready to settle down. They will be interested in working for Worldview Intelligent employers and organizations and living in Worldview Intelligent communities.

HOW THE WORLDVIEW INTELLIGENCE APPROACH CHANGES THE INQUIRY

A powerful question for exploration is, why is this issue of workforce availability and workplace readiness persisting? It would be simple to say it is a demographic trend and leave it at that, but that doesn't solve the issue or help the region thrive. A more comprehensive examination reveals that workforce availability is not just an employer issue, it is a community-wide issue. Is the region welcoming to youth and newcomers? Is it willing to create opportunities for Native American youth from the area? Are there supports in place for families to arrive? The question of daycare availability was frequently raised in the conversations around this issue.

Community members and employers are not completely aware of how they see themselves or what their worldviews are or of how they are seen by others. This is not unusual. They, like most of us, are not aware of their own blind spots. What became clear during our work there is that employers need to expand their thinking to be more open, innovative and welcoming, to think differently across the generations, become aware of their blind spots and biases in order to find transformational solutions for the region. But it is not solely an employer issue and will not be solved by employers alone. It requires a comprehensive, systems wide solution.

AGAIN, THE PERSONAL WORLDVIEW EXPLORATION IS FOUNDATIONAL

Worldview Intelligence offers a depth of invitation to step into working effectively with many differing worldviews. It can be easiest to support possibilities for the many differing worldviews of participants or clients to find ways forward on strategic, organizational and community issues of importance when working in a field that is collectively worldview aware and Worldview Intelligent. However, one person with such a practice can make a significant impact on their own, simply by bringing curiosity and understanding that many worldviews may be co-existing. This curiosity invites exploration through the use of thoughtful and thought-provoking questions, which is why the personal worldview exploration is so foundational.

We know that when working in situations with many differing worldviews, having clarity of your own worldview, being personally Worldview Intelligent, helps you to understand your responses to differing contexts or situations that can emerge. Understanding your individual, collective or contextual worldviews can be as simple as taking the time to reflect on them. Or, it can be a deeper exploration into the foundation of your worldview as was offered in the previous chapter. How were your worldviews formed? What is your daily reality? How do you see the future? What values guide you? What methods or practices do you live your life by? How did you come to know what you know?

In the next chapter, the Worldview Intelligence Six Dimensions Framework is presented with a description of its origins and a short introduction to each of the dimensions. Then there are dedicated chapters for each of the six dimensions and a wealth of questions for your reflections. This will be followed by a chapter that gives examples of the interdependence of the six dimensions and how the framework can be used to illuminate blind spots in change efforts or policy implementation.

REFLECTION QUESTIONS

1. Have you been in a meeting or involved in a longer-term initiative where you know that only one or two worldviews are being expressed? Might there have been other worldviews or perspectives in the room? What makes you think yes or no? Were more perspectives really wanted or was it "easier" to proceed with some voices not heard? Why do you think people stayed silent? What more could have been done to encourage more people to speak up or to bring different perspectives into the space?

2. Reflect on a situation in your organization or community that people have tried to address with limited or no success. What was tried and what happened? What patterns or trends might be influencing, impacting or informing the events you are responding to? What structures or behaviors are contributing to the patterns and trends or the event? What are the thinking or mental models that are operating in this situation? How could a different mental model or worldview lead to thinking differently to address this situation?

SECTION 2

THE WORLDVIEW INTELLIGENCE SIX DIMENSIONS FRAMEWORK

CHAPTER 5:
INTRODUCING THE WORLDVIEW INTELLIGENCE FRAMEWORK

I clearly remember the day I experienced the transformative question that started me on a journey that dramatically shifted my worldview, although I didn't know it at the time. It was July 3rd, 2003. I was part of a small group of people working on agriculture and rural policy issues in the United States. We had traveled to Europe to examine how environmental and social values were impacting European agriculture practices. Our group attended a meeting at the King Baudouin Foundation in Brussels, Belgium where we heard a presentation by Alain Wouters, a former Royal Dutch Shell Oil employee and member of their Group Planning Department. Wouters described a project he led to address a longstanding conflict concerning management of animal waste in the Belgium countryside. The design of the project included using scenarios as a way for stakeholders to consider the various possibilities that different actions could have on the future. Our entire group was fascinated by what we heard.

During dinner that evening a powerful question emerged within the group that influenced conversations for the rest of the trip. The question was: "Have we been asking the same questions [about rural development policies] over and over for so long that we don't even know what the right question is anymore?" This transformative moment started me on a journey of exploration, learning and self-reflexivity that led to a shift in my worldview, a change in my professional focus and a reconnecting with a curiosity around human behavior that I had explored in my early teens. It also reconnected me to a strongly held belief in human possibility that developed in my late teens and twenties and a deeper awareness of our relationship to something greater that I most sensed during my times in nature. Although I was not making a conscious choice at the time to change, that moment was a small spark of recognition that connected me to something I didn't yet fully recognize.

As I explored ideas, methods and programs to find the right questions for addressing current rural policy issues in my work,

I couldn't escape a similar question that was simmering within me: "What is my own personal 'right' question?" I spent my professional and intellectual life working as a research economist on rural development with a worldview that assumed that if we created investments in the material well-being of people and communities (jobs, buildings, roads, etc.) then rural communities would thrive. It came as a surprise to me that when I challenged my professional worldview, I was also challenging my own personal worldviews and related sense of self or identity as an economist. With each new idea on how to proceed with addressing current convention regarding rural development issues, I also discovered or rediscovered perspectives from my own experiences and views of what should be done. I found myself drawn more and more to actions that connected the work of rural development with one's own, or a community's, set of values and beliefs, which also connected with the work of my personal explorations. This led me, in 2006, to attend an Art of Hosting program in Colorado and eventually to become an AoH practitioner, trainer and Global Steward.

As I became more deeply involved in providing training in the Art of Hosting patterns and practices and using the practices in my own hosting and facilitation work, I started describing the Art of Hosting as having three main components. They are a specific worldview, a suite of patterns that set the conditions for good meetings, and a suite of methods or practices based on dialogic approaches to conversations. These practices include Circle, World Café, Open Space Technology and Appreciative Inquiry.

I began pursuing my dream of obtaining a PhD in March 2007. My original plan was to connect Theory U* with rural development approaches. However, as I wrote I was not able to find the core of what I was searching for. Then.....

Have you ever been working on an idea or challenge and the work just wasn't emerging with the level of clarity you wanted? Then, someone says something during a conversation, or you read a passage in a book, or hear someone on the radio speaking on

---

* Theory U (also called "U" methodology or U Process) is a change management method targeting leadership as a process of inner knowing and social innovation developed by Otto Scharmer.

a related topic, and suddenly the idea gels into a clear picture? That is what happened to me while I was attending a workshop in August 2010 at the Institute for Noetic Sciences campus in California on their Worldview Literacy Program. During one session I asked Dr. Marilyn Schlitz, then President of the Institute, a question regarding how the program fit into post-modern thought. Dr. Schlitz answered, "We are in the intersubjective space between narratives." Boom! Clarity emerged immediately for me regarding my explorations in researching for my dissertation. I knew then I wanted to center my research on worldviews.

My newly realized intention to deepen and expand my understanding of worldviews led to a change in focus for my dissertation. This became an exploration into ways to build bridges between social constructionist* and Art of Hosting worldviews and what this means for hosting and facilitation practices.

For my dissertation, I examined several frameworks for deconstructing and understanding worldviews and chose to use the Leo Apostel framework for four reasons. First, it offers a simple yet elegant way to examine what a worldview is, using six components or dimensions. Second, the framework was developed with input from a diverse field of contributors known as the Worldviews Group. Members were noted researchers, thinkers and authors from many disciplines, including theoretical physics, economics, theology, engineering, sociology, biology, and psychiatry. Third, Leo Apostel acknowledged that some deep-seated awareness of being related to a larger all-encompassing Whole is a requirement for a healthy and meaningful life. And fourth, the Worldviews Group worked to balance theory and practice, holding strongly that we are involved in the world not only by knowing, valuing or feeling but also by acting.

Jerry Nagel

---

* Social constructionism is a theory of knowledge in sociology and communication theory that examines the development of jointly constructed understandings of the world that form the basis for shared assumptions about reality. The theory centers on the notion that meanings are developed in coordination with others rather than separately within each individual. (Wikipedia)

OUR INITIAL WORLDVIEW INQUIRY

We were first alerted to the idea of worldviews through Jerry's research for his PhD dissertation. As he wrote, we began to bring the ideas that were percolating into our facilitation and consulting work and they were well received. We began using a simple diagram showing how our worldviews influence our actions and our actions inform our worldviews. Practices were identified as the bridge between worldview and action. This was inspired by James Gimian and Barry Boyce's interpretation of The Art of War in their book, The Rules of Victory[22]. In our work, we came to realize that the six dimensions of the Apostel framework provided a more robust description of the bridge and a clearer way of understanding worldviews so our diagram evolved to include all six dimensions.

The ideas we presented sparked new depths of conversation on challenging topics, including race, power and privilege. In one Art of Hosting (AoH) program we offered with our colleagues Bob-e Simpson Epps and Dave Ellis this really came alive for us. We had a late entry into the facility we were using and when we arrived in the rooms, we decided to reorganize them to be more

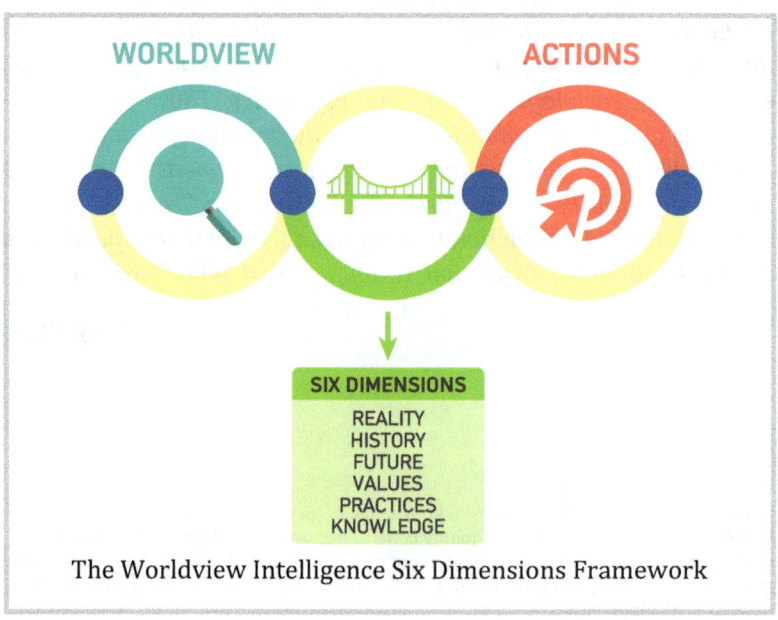

The Worldview Intelligence Six Dimensions Framework

conducive to the learning environment we wanted to create. This meant scrambling to move chairs between rooms, get registration started and make coffee and tea available for arriving participants. Each of us was involved in this. As participants arrived, they joined in re-setting the room. When we were ready, we took a collective breath, got started with an opening circle, offered some teaching on core AoH patterns, including a teach on worldviews. We ended our day with a World Café where we focused the questions on worldviews.

Dave is 60+ years old, African American and 6 feet+ tall with a football player's build. He often dresses casually and often wears a leather ball cap with the brim turned towards the back. During the final round of the World Café he sat next to a young white woman. She turned to him with tears in her eyes and shared her worldview shift experience. She said to him, "When I arrived here this morning and saw you moving furniture, I thought you were the janitor. Then, when you sat in our circle, I thought you were a participant. When you hosted the opening check-in, I realized you were part of the hosting team. I am embarrassed and ashamed. I thought I was over this. I had no idea this is how my brain was working. This has been an important moment for me, and I needed you to know." Dave was gracious in his acknowledgement of this heartfelt sharing and afterwards we, as the hosting team, were made even more aware of the importance of exploring worldviews.

Consistently in evaluations people noted the idea of worldviews as one of the most powerful and lasting impacts of their Art of Hosting experience with us. In the early days, we asked broad questions like, what is your worldview and how do you know? While it was almost too much for people to comprehend – we got the deer in the headlights look often – the conversations were still deep and revealing. We realized that the word "worldview" is being used with increasing frequency and few people stop to reflect on what it means. This took us on our inquiry on how to invite explorations more gently, which took us back to the Apostel Framework Jerry had used in his dissertation. Eventually, through application, experimentation and feedback, it developed into the full body of knowledge we are sharing in this book.

ORIGINS OF THE FRAMEWORK – LEO APOSTEL AND THE WORLDVIEWS GROUP

We are asked from time to time about the academic foundation underlying the Worldview Intelligence approach. This work is founded in extensive academic research. The initial primary source for development of the Worldview Intelligence Programs has been the Centre Leo Apostel for Interdisciplinary Studies (CLEA) in Brussels, Belgium. The references and resources section of this book lists a number of books and research papers written by academics, researchers and practitioners on worldviews that have influenced our thinking, offerings and writing.

In 1990, the Belgium philosopher Leo Apostel had a dream of developing an integrated worldview that could bridge the gap he perceived between the physical sciences and the humanities. To pursue this dream, he created a non-profit organization in Belgium called the Worldviews Group. He brought together people from many disciplines including Diederik Aerts (theoretical physics), Jan Van der Veken (philosophy and theology), Bart De Moor and Hubert Van Belle (engineering sciences), Staf Hellemans (sociology) and Edel Maex (psychiatry and psychotherapy). Of note, Hellemans served on Jerry's dissertation committee. Over time the group was joined by many other leading thinkers from various disciplines and from around the world.

Apostel and his colleagues proposed that our complex and rapidly evolving world was becoming extremely fragmented in the ideological, social, political, cultural and scientific arenas. There remained little or no trace of cultural unity. Additionally, in our everyday lives we often must deal with many cultures, subcultures and cultural fragments[23], and this seems even more true today in our rapidly changing world.

Apostel believed that this fragmentation was especially critical between the sciences and humanities. He also believed that this fragmentation, the rapid changes we were experiencing and the formation of the large-scale structures of the modern world were leading to increased alienation. The result is we often have the impression that what remains of the world is a collection of isolated fragments, without any structure or coherence. Our personal "everyday" world seems unable to harmonize itself with the global world of society, history and the cosmos.[24]

To address this concern, Apostel and his colleagues in the Worldviews Group embarked on a research initiative to construct integrated worldviews. The goal was to provide a framework in which the worldviews that were developing in various fields of culture and science could enter into dialogue with one another and overcome the situation of fragmentation.[25] They imagined this framework would be a basis for understanding society, the world, and our place in it, which could help us make critical decisions that would shape our future. In developing this picture of the whole it was thought we would be better able to understand and work with complexity and change.[26] A key driver for the Worldviews Group was society's inability to address some of the world's most macro- and micro-problems, which Apostel believed was related to this global fragmentation of worldviews.[27]

To be sure, the goal was not to develop one single imposed worldview, which is neither attainable nor desirable. It was simply to understand better what is going on and to do the best we can to consider the world as coherently as possible.[28] There was a clear recognition within the group that naively working to create one unique, single worldview could lead to totalitarianism. Instead, the objective was to discern which differing elements of the many worldviews lead to fragmentation that cannot be overcome and which are local constructs that have a global symmetry and connect us in our humanity.[29] The group was clear that the "task of our time is to search for worldviews in which different systems of interpretation and ideals can be incorporated and can converse with each other. This task is urgent, not only for the multi-cultural societies now found in all major cities of the world, but also for those countries in which a variety of cultural patterns, with quite different histories, are striving towards a certain symbiosis."[30] We would agree this is also true in our cities, communities and organizations.

The Worldviews Group noted, "We are experiencing the end of the big dreams and the 'great narratives'. It seems that there are no longer clear and generally accepted views on the nature of reality and about man's task in the world."[31] However, in reading through the work of Apostel and the Worldviews Group you can detect an optimism that new worldviews can be constructed. In effect, the acting subject of the Worldviews Group is the whole of humanity, the whole world and the entire universe. When we understand that our world is "not our land" and when we come to "live and think on a planetary scale, the urgency of a global worldview will become even more obvious."[32] One could say that there are many maps but only one world. The outcome is to be an integration of worldviews, which would help us to find our way in this ever-increasing complex reality and to act in a more coherent manner.

CREATING AN INTEGRATED WORLDVIEW

To pursue this work further, the Centre Leo Apostel for Interdisciplinary Studies (CLEA) at the Vrije Universiteir Brussel was founded in 1995. CLEA defines a worldview as "a system of co-ordinates or a frame of reference in which everything presented to us by our diverse experiences can be placed. It is a symbolic system of representation that allows us to integrate everything we know about the world and ourselves into a global picture, one that illuminates reality as it is presented to us within a certain culture."[33] Our worldviews are "connected to society, history, cosmos and to reality as a whole."[34] Essentially, our worldview(s) are assumptions, beliefs and images of the world that we use to guide us in our everyday lives. Our worldviews answer life's big questions.

Additionally, it is important to recognize that the CLEA works from a concept of the world in the broadest sense. It notes that what we think of as the world can differ depending upon our local context; for example, the modern world, the Western/Eastern world, the world of the Lakota or the world of Islam. It offers that "The World" should not be identified with "the earth," nor with "the cosmos," nor with "the observable universe," but with the totality in which we live and to which we can relate ourselves in a meaningful way.[35] This perspective opens the potential for exploration beyond words for ways to describe and reflect upon what is our world.

Apostel approached the task of constructing an integrated worldview as a philosophical enterprise.[36] He proposed a philosophical agenda to constructing and deconstructing worldviews, which would consist of core questions that could define the range of issues or problems addressed by a worldview. It is true that Apostel's own worldview originates in the Western world. Yet, as noted above he believed that societies throughout history and throughout the world have sought answers to questions regarding our being and becoming, what Francis Heylighen, current Director of CLEA, refers to as the "Eternal Philosophical Questions".[37]

THE SIX DIMENSIONS OF THE FRAMEWORK

As a philosopher, Apostel proposed that the concepts of 'philosophy' and 'worldview' are closely related. He believed that societies, as well as individuals, have always contemplated deep questions relating to their being and becoming, and to the being and becoming of the world.[38] He viewed talk about philosophy in the broadest sense, as talk about worldviews and constructing a worldview as the highest manifestation of philosophy.[39]

Apostel and the Worldviews Group identified six key components or questions that comprised their philosophical agenda. They believed that the answers to these questions constituted the components of a worldview. The questions are:

- What is?
- Where does it all come from?
- Where are we going?
- What is good and what is evil?
- How should we act?
- How do we know what is true and what is false?

In philosophical terms these dimensions hold questions of ontology, explanation, futurology or prediction, axiology, praxeology and epistemology. We have used more common terms for these components in the framework as the language is more accessible to us and the work we do. The translations we work with are reality, history, future, values, practices and knowledge.

The first three dimensions are "is-questions". They help us describe the world. How we ask these questions can change over time as our understanding of the world changes. These questions can often overlap with science. For example, questions on the nature of matter have changed significantly in the past 100 years. How we formulate and answer these questions can be influenced by other disciplines. They are sometimes referred to as mixed questions as they invite exploring philosophy with other disciplines.[40] The answers to these descriptive "is questions" can vary significantly between differing local contexts or realities. Something as simple or complex as the nature of life can vary between cultures. For example, one culture may see trees as having life but not sentience and another may see them as having something more than just life.

The fourth question is more normative and invites exploration of "ought-questions". This invites an exploration of what is good and evil. And we could ask two additional questions: How do I live a good life? And, how can we organize a good society? This question can also be seen as a "mixed question". On an individual level it mixes with the psychology of wellbeing and on a societal level it mixes with political philosophy and sociology.[41]

The fifth question takes us to the practical and addresses "act-questions". Once we've developed our model of the world or our understanding of reality and established a values system to guide us, then we could ask, "How can we act?" We are now in the domain of methodology or praxeology, which can be mixed with fields like operational research, problem-solving methods and management sciences.[42] It is here that we can think of our philosophy as a way of life. In the work we do, this would include the variety of practices we draw on to engage clients in the needed conversations and in building trust and relationship.

Finally, question six. If the first five questions invite direct exploration of what our world is and how we choose to interact with it, then question six invites an exploration of how we know the answers to all questions are correct. It is in this domain that the philosophical worlds of the study of human structures, experience and consciousness, individualism or agency, interpretation of wisdom and ancient philosophical texts, and the relationship between power and social behavior exist.

PRACTICALITY OF THE FRAMEWORK

While deeply philosophical in its orientation, the framework is also highly practical although Apostel did not live to see it applied in practice. Of the many approaches to looking at worldviews we researched, the Apostel framework was the most value neutral. It did not assume a religious, scientific or philosophical context as a starting point. With a little reframing and grounding, we found the framework's six dimensions illuminating, easy to understand and work with in our own explorations into worldviews and the applications we have developed for Worldview Intelligence. The six dimensions have been helpful in bringing structure and form to the journey of personal worldview awareness, to understanding another's worldview and in exploring professional, organizational, cultural, community and social system worldviews as we shared more fully in Chapter 3: The Scope of Worldview Intelligence Applications. We have also found this a helpful framework for exploring the components of complex situations and to getting to the core of issues quickly.

As the Apostel framework came to guide and inform our work in Worldview Intelligence we developed a more practical language for using it. We also explain that each of these worldview dimensions are interrelated and affect and influence each other as will be explored more in Chapter 12: The Strategic Use of the Worldview Intelligence Six Dimensions Framework. The dimensions as we explain and use them now are:

- Reality, which has two components: meta-reality and daily reality or experiences
- History, which is how we have come to see and experience the world the way we do, especially key influences
- Future, which is how we see and relate to the future

- Values, which are moral or core commitments
- Practices, which are the way we bring each aspect of our worldview to life
- Knowledge, which is our understanding of how we know what we know, the practice of how we acquire knowledge or information, and what sources of knowledge we trust; and how we know our answers to the six dimensions are true

We will explore each of these dimensions in some depth in the next six chapters, offering more definition and stories of how each are brought to life in the Worldview Intelligence explorations.

REFLECTION QUESTIONS

1. Have you ever been working on an idea or challenge and the work just wasn't emerging with the level of clarity that you wanted? What was the situation? Did something happen to bring clarity and, if so, what was it and what was the new awareness or knowledge you now had?
2. How has your worldview on your leadership changed over time? What were some of the key questions you held that catalyzed this shift?

CHAPTER 6:
REALITY

I am a middle-aged white woman with grey hair. I live in Bedford, Nova Scotia, Canada (near Halifax), twenty minutes from the airport, one hour from where my elderly father still lives in the town I grew up in. My adult children and one grandchild live within a 30-minute radius of me and my youngest son who is now in his late teens lives with me. I am in a long term, long distance, two-country relationship with a man who also happens to be my business partner.

I am an educated woman with an undergraduate honors degree in Sociology and a Masters in Business Administration, both from local universities.

I live in a mortgaged house, lease a car and drive pretty much everywhere in the city and region I live in. As a consultant and author who travels a lot, I have a home office and irregular patterns to my days. This means locally I can usually avoid driving anywhere during heavier traffic periods and there is no best time of the day for appointments.

My consulting practice means that in addition to local clients, I travel extensively for work to the US and also to other countries. When I'm working with clients, I am present to that work. When I'm not delivering services in this way, I might be writing proposals, reports, blog posts or books and surfing social media.

I basically believe in the goodness of people, that for the most part we create our own reality. I have an online yoga practice, which I do almost every day when not traveling and I have meditation and spiritual practices I can do anywhere. If you wanted to classify my belief systems or practices, you might call me an animist – someone who believes that objects, places, nature and creatures each possess a distinct spiritual essence. I also believe I have spirit guides, power animals, guardians and angels who I have a direct relationship with and who watch over me, aid and protect me.

My belief systems influence my day-to-day experiences and

patterns as much as my gender, age, relationships, where I live and what I do to live my purpose in life – or my reality.

Like each of us, I have many facets to my life and to who I am. I am, and we are, multi-beings.

Kathy Jourdain

REALITY

Reality is all that is real to us as individuals, families, communities, disciplines, teams, organizations and systems. It includes relationships, places, events, daily experiences, objects or things and structures - actual and conceptual. At a meta level it includes phenomena or belief systems, whether you can observe them or not.

In everyday life, there operate many local-cultural 'relational' realities. They include cultural or community norms, local slang, ways of dress or other behaviors that are acceptable within a social group. These local constructions or realities are closely tied to the values of social groups. The realities are communally agreed upon, whether implicitly or explicitly. What is meaningful for us comes to us primarily as a result of our relationships with others, whether it be within specific communities, professions, religions, or traditions. It is one way we know and understand ourselves.

Your personal reality can be considered from two perspectives: how you experience the world around you in your daily life, in essence your physical reality; and a philosophical or metaphysical perspective or your belief systems. Each of these two components of your reality can be explored through sets of questions that can help you further develop your personal worldview awareness. Since we are multi-dimensional human beings, you could also explore your professional or leadership realities. Not only can you begin to understand yourself better, you can use the same questions to understand someone else's experience or reality too.

At an experiential level, reality is your everyday experiences, whether in your family, at work, in your social life or everyday occurrences as you interact with your community, cultural group or another's community or cultural group. It is how physical characteristics influence the way you experience the world around you like skin color, age, the way you dress or whether you are able bodied or not. It is how your gender or sexual orientation impacts your experiences. It is how income and social status impact you as well as other things that influence how you see yourself and how others might see or interact with you. To try to understand someone else's experience you could use these elements mentioned in this paragraph to consider their reality.

During Worldview Intelligence programs we often tell the story of Alan Page[43] as an example of reality (as recounted by Mr. Page in an interview). Alan Page was a professional football player, is a member of the Football Hall of Fame, was a successful attorney and served with high distinction on the Minnesota Supreme Court until he retired. It would be difficult to be more accomplished than that. Yet, Mr. Page often had the experience of being followed by security guards when shopping because he is an African American male. This is part of his daily reality, his lived experience. Something most white males will never experience.

META-REALITY: BELIEF SYSTEMS

At the meta-level, your reality includes your perspectives on the nature of the universe. Do you believe there is a spiritual aspect to your experience? What beliefs do you hold about the nature of a deity or supreme being? Or, do you believe there is no deity? This could also include questions regarding the existence of consciousness within nonhuman "natural" phenomena like rocks, trees, the earth. Is nature conscious? You might ask yourself, what beliefs do you hold about the degree to which "the Truth" is valid across situations? Is there universal truth where "the Truth" is true always and everywhere, what we might call a "capital T Truth"? Or is truth relative and "the truth" varies in its accuracy and applicability by situation?

There are several beliefs or perspectives that you could hold in relation to the nature of creation, higher beings, human nature or the basic orientation or tendency of people. How you view people deeply impacts your reality. For instance, do you think people are basically good or evil? This will influence how you interact with other people, whether you are welcoming or fearful.

What beliefs do you hold about the human species relative to other species? Do the rights and privileges of human beings have priority over nonhuman species or do humans and nonhumans share equivalent rights? Your belief systems reflect what you imagine is the relationship between humanity and the natural world.

Do you believe people are at the mercy of nature or are people a part of nature and should work with it? Or is it humanity's prerogative to exploit or subdue nature? This is playing itself out right now in disputes over pipelines, fracking, access to natural sites deemed sacred or of national significance and dumping plastics and other garbage in the oceans. It is perhaps this belief that humanity has a right to subdue nature that has us in this current climate crisis, where 97% of scientists agree that climate change is caused by human behavior. But almost half the population does not want to believe this.

Social constructionism suggests that you have made choices that have come to represent your reality and your understanding of your reality. In making choices, you emphasize certain things and not others. This means what is described as reality is dependent upon your interpretations, the instruments of observation you use and the purpose you have in describing reality[44].

THE ROLE OF LANGUAGE AND VOCABULARY

Shared language or vocabulary is part of an unspoken agreement with those around you that is part of your own reality and part of a shared reality. The language and vocabulary you choose to use to describe your reality influences the description. This makes you an active participant in the construction of your reality whether you realize this or not.

Since language and vocabulary are part of a shared reality in your family, community, team or organization, you can become conscious of the language and vocabulary you and those around you use. Are there particular concepts that are part of your shared reality? How do you become aware of them? Most teams and organizations have a long list of acronyms that can function like a secret code. If you know it, you're in; if not, you're out – or an outsider.

Language matters. We move in the direction of the language we use. Our brains think in images more than in words, as we discovered in Chapter 2: Worldviews, How They are Formed and Why It Matters, when we looked at the Ladder of Inference. How things are described creates images in your mind and imagination. When details are left out, your imagination will fill them in. Sometimes we say we fill in the gaps with blinders on and those blinders are elements of our worldviews. Important to note is that the brain cannot create an image of a negative. If we say to you, don't think of a purple ostrich, the first thing that pops into your head is an image of a purple ostrich. Right? Or if you say to your children "Don't go play in the street," what is one of the first things they do when you aren't looking?

When you consider the team you lead, what are the words you use to describe your team as a whole or individual members of your team? These words and images influence how you approach your communication or relationship with them. Millennials are often described as entitled, lacking work ethic or loyalty. If you are part of an older generation and that may be how you think about the younger members of your team, how does that influence you before you are even in a conversation with them? On the other hand, if you believe Millennials are hardworking and focused and value their time off because of the desire and preference for work-life integration, that may influence your relationship and communication in a different way. If you are a Millennial, what assumptions do you carry about Baby Boomers you might be on a team with or report to? How does that influence your communication and relationship?

One more note on language. When we use language like "illegal immigrant" or "alien" to describe people who are new to a country, it already influences how they may be received in a workplace or a community. The more words are used to dehumanize another individual, the easier it is to think of them as less than human, as 'the other', which then influences how they are treated. Using language in this manner can also create stereotypes or "essentialize" a whole group. Examples include describing women as the weaker sex, or someone receiving public assistance as a 'welfare queen', or certain cultures as smarter or more athletic or more moral. The more we use language in these ways, the more likely these perspectives are to become part of our worldview.

Each of us, consciously and unconsciously, makes a reality commitment. We each hold a perspective on reality – or a worldview. While philosophically your reality may provide answers to some of life's biggest questions, another person may do so in a different way, if their reality, belief systems or experiences are different.

SHARED REALITIES

As noted in the exploration of language and vocabulary, reality is not just an individual phenomenon. Realities are also common concepts shared by a family, team, organization, community or cultural group. These communities and groups can be societal, religious, geographic, organizational or professional. They can vary by discipline, topic or focus. They can be quite local such as a marketing or engineering department in a company, or quite broad such as Western civilization. They can be groups of people who have who convene online about something that is important to them, whether they have ever met in person or not. These shared realities become, in effect, shared worldviews, most of which operate in the collective unawareness.

Because of this, perspectives on reality are not always held or manifested in the same ways within a specific social, cultural or organizational group. For example, the marketing department in your organization could have a different reality than the finance department. Each group's reality can be self-contained and adequate in the sense that it provides for them a coherent worldview as they perceive and experience it. The marketing department's daily experience might generally be more frenzied if they stage public events or have significant customer interaction. The finance department's daily reality could be more subdued, with limited interaction with clients or the general public. A group's sense of what is real to its members is deeply embedded in their history, practices, purpose, social groups and place in a larger culture or organization.

This shared vision of reality is usually not articulated, operating as it does in the unconscious. This shared sense of reality can be so deeply internalized that nobody questions where it came from. Realities or worldviews become so embedded within a group, organization, institution or society that it isn't necessary to even speak of them. Everybody already knows them and accepts them without question and acts or behaves based on them. They become part of the shared experiences of the group and contribute to the ongoing formation of the group. They are shaped by and shape organizational and community cultures, which are self-perpetuating and generally function below the surface. We can view an organization, institution, cultural group or society as the sum of its shared experiences, values, beliefs, history, and practices.

COLLISIONS OF WORLDVIEWS

Collisions of worldviews can be experienced when different groups come into contact with each other and they make assumptions about the collective or shared experience across groups that turn out to be inaccurate. They might project their own experience on another group as a way of assuming the same or similar experiences. This is often revealed when assumptions are challenged or it becomes apparent there are different interpretations of the same experience or situation being addressed. For example, a white professional will have different experiences in business or social settings than a professional person of color, yet often the white professional will assume that everyone has the same experience they have.

COLLISION OF ABLY-DIFFERENT WORLDVIEWS

Reality contains both our daily experiences and our meta-views regarding spirituality, beauty, good or bad, or truth. If you are an able-bodied reader, pause and think about your daily experiences regarding access to buildings, parks or transportation. Do you ever feel concern about what choices for access you will have? Have you ever considered that a person with a disability will always have fewer choices than you? Have you ever reflected on the fact that as an able-bodied person you have that privilege and what that means to how you live your life?

Think about your worldview regarding what is normal, beautiful, worthy or attractive. As you walk down the street or ride the bus and see someone in a wheelchair, on a scooter or walking with crutches or a cane, what assumptions do you make? Do you consider the person in the wheelchair not normal? What is normal or not normal?

Each of us, when we meet a person for the first time, initially responds to what we see on the outside of the person – physical stature, dress, and other elements of appearance – and we put people into worldview categories related to our personal perspectives regarding beauty, attractiveness and even worth. When you see a person with a physical disability do you see beauty? Worthiness? Attractiveness? Something to be fixed?

When worldview collisions become evident, the typical response is often to discount the other person's experience or to try to impose worldviews on each other. However, if we are paying attention, this provides an excellent opportunity to open a shared exploration of the realities of all involved and possibly incorporate other dimension explorations as well. Curiosity toward the circumstances of each group can reveal hidden dynamics that may be influencing communication and relationship. Once revealed, there is an opportunity to align realities enabling the differences to contribute to progress on shared issues of concern.

As we think about building relationship within rapidly changing environments, a constructionist approach shifts us away from the perspective that we each hold independent, fixed worldviews to one that recognizes that our worldviews are situated within our particular relations with others.[45] With that being the case, we are free to create new, shared realities and related ways of working together.

As a leader in your team, organization or community, it becomes important to recognize that you, consciously and unconsciously, have made a reality commitment. You hold a perspective on reality. While your reality may provide answers to some of life's biggest questions or to more immediate questions, another person or even another society may have different perspectives or worldviews on the same questions. Your challenge, when Building Trust and Relationship at the Speed of Change, is to be aware of the role that language plays, especially the language you use in constructing realities. Become self-aware and leadership aware in ways that support the various realities that are naturally part of any team or organization or community through both individual and shared experiences. Create ways to support constructive or generative dialogue that enables individuals and teams to use their collective experiences to achieve the outcomes expected of them. There are many examples throughout the book of how to do this and particularly in Section 4 where the focus of the chapters is on practical application.

REFLECTION QUESTIONS

1. What is your personal, professional or leadership reality? What are your day-to-day experiences? What beliefs do you hold about human beings, nature or higher powers? How do your beliefs influence your day-to-day experiences?

2. Reflect on some of the people you lead. What might their realities be? How might this create a different experience for them in contrast to your own? How might this be influencing your communication and relationship with them?

3. Notice the language you use. For yourself, how do you categorize, name or describe things, actions, outcomes or people? In your team or organization, what is the nature of the language and vocabulary you use? How does this create or contribute to the shared reality of your team or organization?

CHAPTER 7:
HISTORY

When I was growing up, I wanted to become an architect. I was especially attracted to the prairie style of architecture developed by Frank Lloyd Wright and dreamed of attending one of his student programs. In Jr. High and High School, I took classes in mechanical and architectural drawing. In High School I designed and built a model of a round house. I was certain this was my future. But things changed. The summer of 1967 before my junior year of high school I traveled to Denver, Colorado as part of a church group to do volunteer work in a low-income neighborhood. There I saw poverty in ways I hadn't seen or experienced before. I was quite impacted by it.

This was also the Summer of Love and the group visited Larimer Square, which at the time, was Denver's version of Haight-Asbury in San Francisco. I had recently discovered the beat poets and had just finished reading On the Road by Jack Kerouac. The book spoke to an emerging wanderlust in me. All of this came together to spark something in me that started a shift in my worldview.

During my junior year, opposition to the Viet Nam war was growing, Martin Luther King was assassinated and in the following summer Bobby Kennedy was assassinated. I met a political science professor at the local community college, and I met the new assistant pastor who arrived at our church. I engaged in deep conversations with both of them during the summer of 1968 and throughout my senior year of high school.

I started my freshman year of college still intending to be an architect, but something was bubbling inside. I enrolled in an honors political science course taught by the college professor I had met. By the end of that first semester I changed my major to political science and embarked on a new life journey with shifted and shifting worldviews. Eventually I achieved a Master's Degree in economics and a PhD in Social and Behavioral Science. A long way from that kid who read every book on Frank Lloyd Wright I could and dreamed of designing unique, modern structures.

Jerry Nagel

HOW YOUR HISTORY SHAPES YOUR WORLDVIEW

If reality reflects what is real for you in your daily, lived experiences in the present moment, history provides you with an explanation of how you got to your reality. Your personal history helps explain how you have come to see and experience the world, events or situations the way you do. It offers an explanation for who you are, who you are becoming and why.

Where reality focuses on the now, history, of course, is past focused. Obviously, history is inextricably linked to the present because your path, your experiences, your choices have brought you to this point in time. Exploring your history offers an opportunity for you to move beyond just experiencing or knowing your reality to trying to understand or explain how you arrived at this particular reality and not some other experience. This exploration seeks to answer many of life's big questions. Why is your world the way it is and not different? Why are you the way you are and not different? What is the origin of the reality in which you find yourself? How did your history contribute to this?

History provides a model of the past. You have your own model of your past and your own model of "the" past. You and your history do not exist in isolation. Minimally, your history situates your experiences within a network of relations that you have interacted with over time – family, personal, professional and social networks. Given this, there are multiple ways that your current situation could have been constructed. How your current reality is explained is dependent upon the local-cultural, local-historical characterizations of history and reality. This includes written and verbal narratives, paintings, music, metaphors and combinations thereof. History is part of the social construction of worldviews.

HISTORY IS MORE THAN EVENTS

Personal history, social history, world events history. They all have a strong influence on your worldview, how you have come to see and experience the world. When taught, history is mostly presented as a series of major events like wars, elections, disasters; or as singular events like Bloody Sunday, the march from Selma to Montgomery, Wounded Knee, Stonewall uprising, Trail of Tears in the United States, or the FLQ October 1970 Crisis in Canada. History is not usually presented as conditions of society or states of our public consciousness.

When history is offered as events, it becomes easy to remove or add events to history books that changes what we learn, like is being done now in Texas, other states and other areas where references to certain events like slavery or specific people like Hillary Clinton are being removed. When history is taught as events, we don't feel that history viscerally, in our bodies. However, when we read history that is not sanitized or, in our experience, is written by people who directly experienced the events or are living with the impacts, we often gain more profound and different perspectives and emotions concerning historical events.

One outcome of presenting history as a series of events is that, as readers or watchers of national news, we see racism, genocide, discrimination and, in the United States currently, police shootings of unarmed black men through the lens of events and not through the lenses of national consciousness or the worldviews that underlie what is happening within our society or our country. To understand these events, it becomes important to welcome the connective tissue that threads everything together and to have an awareness of lasting and lingering impacts of historical consciousness on different populations. When the various impacts of history and even historical trauma are not understood or even not acknowledged, finding ways forward becomes challenging as the alignment of reality, history and future courses of action cannot emerge.

SHARED OR COLLECTIVE INFLUENCES ON HISTORY

While we each have our own uniqueness in our experiences, individually and locally, we are also impacted by collective patterns, trends, and events that have influence regionally, nationally and globally and that touch our individual and collective consciousness. These events could include technological advancements, social movements, wars, economic trends, the influence of social media and more.

These shared experiences explain how we have come to see and experience the world, events or situations in a collective sense. Individuals can relate to the same experiences, share stories of events and assign their own meaning in relation to the collective sense. These shared experiences remind us that at any given present moment there can be a multiple of realities in play. Each of these realities has their own historical constructs and ways of explaining how that moment was arrived at. The model of a collective or shared history can and does vary by culture, region, sub-region, community, city, social system and country. This variability exists within our interactions.

UNDERSTANDING HISTORY AND EXPERIENCE THROUGH STORY

What takes precedence in our own history and our understanding of any collective history we are part of and why? It depends on the stories that capture our attention and our imagination, and it depends on the stories we tell.

Story is how we make sense of our experiences. We are constantly telling stories about what happened to us, whether we realize it or not. The way we tell our stories helps shape our understanding of our experiences. There are things that happen you might take no notice of. Think of a relative or friend who shares a story of a past incident that you have no recollection of even though you were there.

There are other events you remember but how you recall them and how someone else recalls them can sometimes be radically different. Why is that? It has a lot to do with your worldviews, what gains prominence in your experience and what doesn't. How many animated discussions are because of a different recall of past events? How many of these are friendly and how many are heated? What determines the nature and tone of these

HEART STOPPING MOMENT RECALLED

The Health Charity Kathy worked for had volunteer Chapters across the Atlantic Provinces and part of her role was to work with the chapters and the chapter executives. This involved attending Chapter meetings from time to time as a guest. She vividly recalls going to her first Chapter meeting in Halifax, shortly after she started her job. As she walked through the door and uneasily surveyed the meeting room, her heart rose up into her throat as she saw a sea of wheelchairs, walkers and canes. For a brief moment, she thought, "I don't think I'm the right person for this job."

Then, the chapter president rolled over to her and introduced himself in his warm, graceful manner. She saw the person in the wheelchair, the people in the room and her fears melted away. She worked for the organization for almost a decade.

Have you had an experience of encountering a group of people differently abled than you that stands out in your memory? What feelings or reactions did it evoke in you? Did you experience a shift in your perception and, if so, what was it, and what was it that enabled a shift?

discussions? We, Kathy and Jerry, can find ourselves offering different descriptions of a shared experience. When explored with curiosity and not defensiveness or the need to be right, this leads us to a deeper and broader understanding of the experience. With awareness and practice we have examined when our explorations have been generative and when they have been challenging to understand where the conversations sometimes go off the rails. This has resulted in fewer challenging, angry or defensive exchanges and more open, frank and collaborative ones. We also can each recognize our own role in exchanges that haven't gone as well as we like and focus on where we each have our own individual responsibility.

There are other things that happen that stick in your consciousness that you speak of repeatedly. Soon after something happens you may revisit it frequently and that may or may not wane over time. It is common to forget something that happened until something or someone reminds you of it. Then it may come flooding back. Some stories stay with you, running in the background even when you are not aware of them. You don't always "hear" your own thoughts or what we sometimes refer to as the "itty-bitty-shitty committee" sitting on your shoulder giving you bad advice and negative reinforcement.

How we relate to an experience right after it happens is often different than how we relate to it a week later, a month later, or years later. Your relationship to your story might expand or contract your worldview, might help a relationship flourish or might impede it, might nurture trust or not. Your experience of communicating on a particular issue or with a particular person might influence how well or poorly you are able to do so. Your experiences with trust or your propensity to trust may well shape how trusting you are and how you respond when trust is compromised.

We often don't take the time to reflect on how the experiences in our past have influenced how we have come to see and experience the world now or how they have influenced our worldviews. We are not often aware of the nature of the stories we are telling ourselves and others, or themes and patterns we carry or disrupt across time. It is powerful when people stop to remember who has influenced them, what events have had an impact, what books, movies or life events have caused new openings and worldview expansions for them.

DISCOVERING POINTS OF CONNECTION

The shortest distance between two people is a story. Sharing stories humanizes people and offers an opportunity to build trust and relationship. When people consider who or what has influenced their worldview and in what ways and then share those reflections with other people, it creates points of connection. When those points of connection appear, they offer the opportunity to explore difference supported by new insights and awareness. When we start with difference, difference is amplified, and it can be more challenging to find the connecting points.

Over and over in the Worldview Intelligence programs we offer, people marvel at how often similar worldview influences have appeared in the history exploration – whether it is parents, travel or particular life or world events. Then the discovery is that, even with similar influences like parents, the specific relationship and dynamics with them influenced each person in the discussion in unique directions. In one of our programs working with international graduate business students at a University in France, one young woman was in a conversation with a young man. Her view was that she would not want to date, let alone marry, a man whose parents were divorced as she imagined it would make it that much easier for him to consider divorce. In his experience, coming from a family where his parents were divorced, he knew the impact on him and he felt he would be more committed to a marriage because he knew how hard that situation is for the family members involved. Her worldview expanded in that moment – as possibly did her dating options.

THE STORY YOU TELL ABOUT ANOTHER GROUP OR CULTURE

What does the story you tell of some other group or culture look like and what does it look like when they tell it? We run into some of our most significant challenges and worldview clashes when we make assumptions about the experience and history of another group of people or another culture based on little information and little or no direct contact with them. Until you are in a conversation or relationship with someone from a different culture, have done some research or have lived in that culture, you are subject to how your own worldviews or those of the people around you have filled in the gaps or created the story. It is easy to be judgmental or fearful concerning someone or something you don't know.

BUILDING BRIDGES, TRUST AND RELATIONSHIP

If you want to build bridges, you have to reach out. Trust does not come by happenstance. You must be proactive in creating or co-creating it. The first step is to be curious about the assumptions you are making, where they come from and whether there are things you might not be aware of concerning another person, group or culture.

There are a number of conservative, alt-right or nativist groups that use language to ignite fear about immigrants, refugees, other religions or cultures. They brand whole cultural groups as being violent, terrorists or criminals with no basis in factual evidence. Or they brand others as lazy, wanting to come to their country to take advantage of the good will and resources available at the expense of the people born in that country. Or, paradoxically, they claim these newcomers will take all the opportunities and jobs from people born in their country. And of course, there are similar examples on the far left, from naming conservatives as ignorant or uninformed to describing those who support market-based economies as capitalist money grabbers to people that destroy property in the name of a cause.

These kinds of broad, general, "include everybody" statements should be questioned for their validity and used as an opportunity to understand the history of another people, even if it is recent history.

Recent history may help you understand current trends – why people are on the move for instance. A look at the longer historical context may well provide you with a stronger understanding of and compassion for the humanity of another group of people through their culture, the nature of relationships and their shared values.

VISIT PLACES OF HISTORICAL SIGNIFICANCE TO SHIFT CONSCIOUSNESS

One powerful way to shift your consciousness regarding history is to visit the actual places where historical events happened and sense into the stories of the people who were there. In 2018, Jerry went to Montgomery and Selma, Alabama to visit important sites and memorials to the civil rights and voting rights movements. He had the opportunity to hear directly from people who experienced the segregation that existed there within his lifetime and that, in many ways, is still subtly and not so subtly alive today. He wanted to learn more of the history of slavery and racism in his country. It was a profound and transformative experience.

This was not the first time he had gone on such a pilgrimage. He has also visited WWI and WWII cemeteries in Europe with friends who had family members that fought in WWII where he saw firsthand the thousands of lives lost there and heard the stories of local people who experienced the war. He has been to Wounded Knee to try to sense into what happened in 1890 and 1973. Each of these experiences touched an emotional rawness in him that stories in history books written by white authors have not.

Another way to shift consciousness is to take time to reflect on and to write out or journal the influences in your life that have shaped how you see and experience the world around you. When working with clients we often ask program participants to do an exercise that invites them to identify influences in their life and then select 2-3 to explore more fully before joining together in small group conversations to share what they may have discovered. This exercise, this experience, is quite impactful for participants.

A CASE FOR EMPATHY RATHER THAN SYMPATHY

It is important to be aware that understanding history is not necessarily to justify behavior or actions. This is an important distinction because, when actions are harmful, understanding them is different than sympathizing or agreeing with them.

Sympathy means that you are sorry for someone and express support for their point of view or position. It is largely used to convey commiseration, pity, or feelings of sorrow for someone who is experiencing misfortune. Empathy refers to the capacity or ability to imagine yourself in the situation of another person, experiencing the emotions, ideas, or opinions of that person. Both words have roots in the Greek term páthos meaning "suffering, feeling". The prefix sym comes from the Greek sýn meaning "with, together with" and the prefix em derives from the Greek en- meaning "within, in".

You can gain an understanding of how someone has come to see and experience the world without having to agree with or sympathize with their issue or their worldview. A Worldview Intelligent leader is skilled in the ability to empathize with another person, group or culture. In doing so, you can open the opportunity for exploration of difficult or challenging issues, discussions that might not be possible otherwise. Empathy is a skill that contributes to building trust and relationship. If you only want to condemn another person, people or culture for their views, behaviors or actions that you consider wrong, there is no opportunity for anyone's worldview to possibly expand – including your own.

There are perspectives or worldviews you might not be able to agree with or support. We certainly don't advocate that you need to. There are many groups or individuals you can choose not to be in communication with. Maybe you will never encounter the Taliban or ISIS. But ask yourself, if you have opinions on them or other potentially controversial groups, how did you arrive at those opinions? Refugees might be a better example. Do you know why they are leaving their homes? Do you know what their hopes and dreams are? If you are condemning them, do you know the basis of your condemnation? A little exploration of their historical context could go a long way to generate empathy for their experience and perhaps gratitude that you are not in their shoes.

HIDDEN DYNAMICS AND PATTERNS IN TEAMS, ORGANIZATIONS AND COMMUNITIES, ROOTED IN HISTORY

Current realities contain the history of an individual, family, team, organization or culture. This history can hold hidden dynamics or patterns that influence the relationships and interactions among people. They are often constructed and co-constructed by generation after generation, work group after work group, leader after leader, CEO after CEO. Elements of the past get carried forward into the present and new contributions are added to or replace parts of previous worldviews. Without understanding this, or deconstructing history to illuminate the patterns, these hidden dynamics can continue to be disruptive and be maintained as barriers to building the trust and relationship that is essential to discovering a shared or aligned future. The same applies to understanding patterns of trust and relationship within teams and organizations, how readily or not trust is or can be built and relationships developed.

Applying Worldview Intelligence strategies and explorations can reveal these hidden dynamics or patterns. They often show up in curious or strange actions and behaviors and they are often persistent. It can be hard to understand what is generating these dynamics until you look at history. The senior leadership of a medium sized not-for-profit association in Nova Scotia had a history of challenging interpersonal relationships. They had gotten to the point where disrespect was high, communication was almost non-existent, and five of the six team members often looked to and blamed the sixth member of the team for the issues. The situation was persistent, no matter the topic at hand. People felt the sixth member of the team was uncooperative on most issues, secretive, oppositional and arrogant. They asked Kathy to support moving the team to healthier relationships.

What nobody considered was that the department led by the sixth team member was actually established as a separate entity with its own charter, bylaws and Board of Directors. It had a unique structure or reality in comparison with the other departments. This person's greater loyalty or worldview focus was to this separate structure. The more the rest of the team tried to get this person to align to the goals the other five members had for the team, the more resistant this person became and the more the problem persisted. Once the impact of the organizational structure on goal alignment and relationships was made obvious, the structure was eventually changed. It took some time and a lot of work to overcome the historical structures and the reason why it was historically structured in that way and for the whole team to strategize ways to address related confidentiality concerns and financial implications.

YOUR INFLUENCE ON EXPOSING AND SHIFTING PATTERNS

Examining your history can help you understand why some relationships are solid and some are questionable. It may even point to ways for you to shift these patterns.

In your teams or organizations, there are patterns of behavior that sustain themselves even as people change, departments or organizations reorganize or restructure or as growth occurs. It can feel mysterious, stubborn and frustrating, especially if you believe the issues have been addressed but they keep reoccurring, like those "backfire loops" or "fixes that fail" we described in Chapter 4: What It Means to Be Worldview Intelligent.

In organizations and teams, these dynamics emerge for a few reasons. Here again, stories and how they are told are an important element. The stories told in organizations and teams shape the culture. If the stories are of failures, then whether they are told as warnings or as learnings can have a big impact.

Sometimes there are stories that are not told. They might be things considered immoral or unethical. They might contain some sense of failure or even shame. During a Worldview Intelligence program for the staff of another organization we worked with, they began to speak of the impact of a previous CEO for the first time in eight years since the CEO had departed the organization. His legacy of disrespectful and abusive behavior, internally and externally, still hung in the realm of unspeakables. Making this visible allowed discussion, acknowledgement and the opportunity to heal as an organization. This visibly improved trust and relationship internally and externally.

If, as a leader, you are trying to encourage or support certain actions, behaviors or outcomes but are not able to achieve the results, look at the messages you are trying to send and then look at the historic responses. Are people chastised for failure? Rewarded for caution? Is there healing from past events or leadership actions that is needed? Are you stuck in a pattern of "we tried that before"? Have you been consistent enough in your leadership and messaging that your team sees that you say what you mean and mean what you say?

WORLDVIEW EXPLORATIONS WITH YOUR TEAM AND IN YOUR ORGANIZATION

Don't underestimate the power of worldview explorations with your team to make connections and reveal patterns. Once they are visible, they seem obvious. Once obvious, different, more effective strategies can be used to address them. Be prepared to take the flack for proposing a "soft", "fluffy" or "touchy feely" approach, identify the importance of a relational approach and remain confident that this gets you to the hard outcomes and success you are seeking, confidence that will grow with each success.

Understanding the impact and influence of history on our individual and collective worldviews, seeing and understanding the patterns that lead to social change, acknowledging our wounds, finding our points of connection, helps us heal, if healing is what is needed.

As a leader, when *Building Trust and Relationship at the Speed of Change*, hosting a dialogue that seeks to build understanding between you and your team members or amongst your team can open opportunities for greater understanding and connection.

REFLECTION QUESTIONS

1. Over the course of your lifetime, who or what has influenced you and the way you have come to see and experience the world? In what ways do you think they have influenced your worldview? What was one subtle ongoing influence? What was one dramatic event or influence? Did they shape your experience in similar or different ways and how? Which

shared or collective "world" events have had an influence on your worldview?

2. When you think of specific members of your team, what kinds of things do you think may have influenced their worldviews? Reflect on someone you get along with well. What do you think the points of connection are? Consider someone you have a challenging relationship with. Might there be something in their history or your history that contributes to this challenge? How might that influence the pattern of relationship and communication you have with each other?

3. What is the shared history of your team or organization that might still be influencing current patterns of relationship or trust? What are some ways you might introduce that conversation to your team?

CHAPTER 8:
FUTURE

How the future is viewed by a group of people, a culture, a community can vary along with the relationship they want to have with the future. Nova Scotia is a prime example of how views of the future can be a source of tension and worldview collisions.

The province has one main economic center: the capital city of Halifax. Halifax has been in significant growth mode over the last few years, evidenced by the number of cranes visible across the city and including new innovative structures like the Halifax Library and the new convention center. I personally have my own moments of conflict around this as I love my city and its character, and I am also an advocate of growth. I worry that Halifax may lose its small city character in the midst of the growth.

There are smaller economic hubs across the province but, for as long as I can remember, smaller communities have been shrinking. For a province that has been dependent on natural resources, this was probably accelerated by the decline of the fishery and the collapse of the mining industry.

There are issues to be addressed in Nova Scotia and especially in more rural communities where industry is low, traditional sources of employment have dramatically decreased and where youth out-migration is a significant issue. There have been and are several attempts at addressing these issues, including the work of One Nova Scotia, which published the Ivany Report in 2014, and the ongoing work of Engage Nova Scotia.

One Nova Scotia was a coalition of 15 citizens from various sectors in the province, co-led by the Premier and the Leader of the Opposition Party. The Ivany Report it produced set out a 10-year future plan, which has had various degrees of success in implementation of the recommendations.

I had the pleasure several years ago of speaking with one of the members of One Nova Scotia – Dan Christmas. Dan is First Nations Mi'kmaw from Membertou, a successful community in Cape Breton, NS. He is now a Canadian Senator and he is a successful businessman. He shared a story that reflects the dynamic tension alive in so many of the rural communities in Nova Scotia as we consider the future.

In visiting one rural community in the province, differing worldview perspectives were brought home to him. This is a community that has become a shell of its former self because the young people have left, there are no new businesses, farms are disappearing and schools are closing. The One Nova Scotia team was testing out the idea of immigration as one means to revitalize communities. A resident of this particular community stood up and said, "Immigration will never work here. We are not that kind of people."

Dan was stunned as it dawned on him that some people would rather the community die than welcome newcomers to be part of a possible renewal. It was also a surprise to have this comment made in front of him as his culture and background as a Mi'kmaw would have made him an "outsider" in this community, but his presence as such seemed to go unnoticed.

One shift in Dan's own worldview was the comprehension that the barriers in Nova Scotia were not necessarily business related but attitude related. He remarked, "We looked into the well and saw the enemy; and it was us."

The dynamic tension across the province is between wanting the future to be an extension of the past and wanting the future to be vastly different. We have to find success in a global economy. Can our institutions work globally? Can our government? If Nova Scotia wants to be more successful, it needs to be more inclusive, diverse and welcoming. Can the horizons for Nova Scotia be opened enough to embark on a future informed by our history but different than our past?

Kathy Jourdain

YOUR RELATIONSHIP WITH THE FUTURE

This may seem like an odd question, but when was the last time you considered your relationship with the future? On the one hand, it seems simple. The future will always arrive, is always arriving; whether we are ready for it or not, planning for it or not. Relationships with the future vary from person to person, team to team, organization to organization, community to community and worldview to worldview.

Do you anticipate the future with excitement, anxiousness or a mixture of these two things? Given the times we live in, the relationships and change we must navigate, it could certainly be many reactions at the same time. If you pause for a moment and sense into the questions, what reaction seems most true for you? It might be something other than what is mentioned here.

As someone who is leading people and change in your organization, how are the members of your team reacting to the future – with enthusiasm, resistance or some other response? If things are changing quickly in your environment, how do you ensure the individual and collective worldviews are aligned around the vision you have and the future you are headed for? How change is guided and presented in your organization impacts trust and relationship. If change is viewed simply as a technical process with a series of steps to get from here to there, the people component is likely to get lost in the mix. When that happens, resistance will show up in force and trust and relationship will be challenged.

INVITATION TO EXPLORE WHERE YOU ARE GOING

Future is an invitation to explore where you are going. Your worldview provides you with a way of considering the future. This could be considered a model or prediction of what kind of future is ahead of you. Because the future is uncertain with more than one possible outcome, this dimension offers many possible futures, which then offers you choices to make[46], whether you are aware of choice or not.

At a personal level, it helps answer questions of: Where are you going? What future is open to you in this world? What kind of future is ahead of you? Can you see a future that is radically different than now?

WHAT DOES THE FUTURE HOLD IN STORE?

When you think about your future, are there things on your bucket-list that depend on your able-ness? Are you hopeful and looking forward to a long and busy life? What do you dream about? And, what do you fear? When you think about your future, what might change your hopes and dreams?

When you see someone with disabilities, do you pause and wonder how your hopes and dreams might change if you become disabled? Do you unconsciously hold a fear about becoming disabled? Or about dying or other health issues? Are these falsely placed fears? Or have you never given it a thought?

Have you ever thought that holding an unconscious fear might impact how you interact with people with disabilities? Might you have some reluctance to engage with someone if they touch into these hidden fears? Do you avoid or judge people with disabilities?

When you think towards the future, do you value tradition? If you value tradition, do you want the future to be an extension of the past or do you want to ensure that tradition is honored as you move forward?

From the perspective of leading your team, you could ask the same questions in relation to the individual members of your team and you could explore these questions collectively.

SOURCE OF TENSION OR CONFLICT

Future is a worldview dimension that offers a surprising source of possible conflict or tension. This can be particularly important knowledge for you as a leader of your team and in your organization, especially as you are confronted by the speed of change. How do you and your team members relate to the future? Are there some on your team who want to passively await the arrival of the future? Are there others charging ahead to find ways to shape it? As a leader, you are likely in the forefront of championing change in your organization. Knowing there are a wide range of typical or normal responses is critical to developing and implementing a change strategy that brings as many people along as possible.

Some people are futuristic thinkers, barely living in the present, although they may or may not have any idea of how to plan for the futures they imagine. Others are planners, imagining and creating the pathways to the future, sometimes in leaps and bounds, sometimes more methodically. Some people are concrete thinkers and need to know all the steps, in the right order, to get there. They want the detailed road map. And there are some who just want to keep doing what they've always done. Some people idealize memories of the past that may or may not reflect what it was like. They want the future to be a version of that past.

If you have a sense of the worldviews of your team members and their relationship with the future, you can strategize adaptable and responsive ways forward. It is important to make time for everyone, especially those more reluctant to imagine the future. Dismissing their perspectives as irrelevant or trying to drag them along will not serve either relationship or trust in the long run and will impede progress on change.

CRUSADERS OR TRADITIONALISTS

In his book, *Polarity Management*[47], Barry Johnson uses the terms Crusaders and Traditionalists to describe two "poles" of change. That language is useful in considering relationships to the future. People who are excited to engage the future are often crusaders for change. They may not be able to see the challenges inherent in any change process. They may not even be aware there is or could be a process that can alleviate some of the uncertainty and stress in a sustainable change process. People who value tradition, or the way things have been done, are tradition bearers. They may not see the positive aspects of change or may not be able to see themselves in it.

An important Worldview Intelligence skill is recognizing that there are practices and processes that can be used to open possibilities or new possible futures as well as practices that can make the journey to this future more accessible to a wider variety of people and responses. This happens when we make space for multiple voices or perspectives to be heard equally, thus creating the possibilities of discovering the future that the multiple perspectives invite.

Being aware of the different possible relationships to the future will allow you to tend to the relationships in your team. What is the balance between change and stability that will work for you and your team? What do you give your team that they can trust – in you as a leader and in the processes that bring stability even in times of fast-paced change? In what ways can you allay their fears concerning the future? How will you invite new team members into the ongoing work? When things change fast and roles or responsibilities change quickly there is a constant readjustment of working relationships that needs to happen – within the team and also between the team and its members and other parts of the organization they interact with. These moving targets can create a feeling of job insecurity for some, which can result in reduced loyalty as well as increased stress leave and lower productivity. With reduced loyalty comes challenged relationships and decreased trust.

Since change can and often does bring chaos – in structures, processes, transitions and relationships – what is the energy you might bring to your team to support them? In what ways can you help your team members stay connected to each other as you move toward the future you are anticipating, planning for and implementing?

BIG QUESTIONS APOSTEL AND THE WORLDVIEWS GROUP WRESTLED WITH

While operating at the speed of change, you and your team members may be holding some of the same questions concerning the future of humanity that Leo Apostel and the Worldviews Group wrestled with, although maybe you haven't thought of them quite so explicitly. An important component of their work was to clarify the place of humanity in the world and to provide insight into the most significant relations humans have with this world, both theoretically and practically.[48] They inquired into big questions like, what will be the fate of humanity in the universe, along with their concern about how to overcome the growing fragmentation of society.

The big questions generate many more questions regarding the future: How will cultures interact with each other in the future? Will Western culture become dominant over the whole world? What will be the role of science and economics in the future order? Who will make the decisions that will influence humanity as a whole? In the long term, and hence more speculatively, you can ponder the role of humanity in the universe. Does humanity have a future that reaches beyond the planet earth? Will we ever be able to bring human life to other planets? Does our species have a cosmic function and destiny?[49]

CRITERIA FOR CHOICES CONCERNING THE FUTURE

Thinking of the future provides you with the criteria that allow you to make choices about your future. The future contains more than one possible outcome. Your worldview gives you possible futures, which then offers you choices to make.[50] The same is true in your team, organization or community.

As a leader you may find yourself working in spaces of emergence or of an emergent future, which could also be thought of as working in a place of "not knowing" or openness to new ideas, opportunities and ways of working to be entertained. When the new emerges, you and the team can decide how to work with it and whether it will require you changing course or working differently. There is an assumption that what emerges is exciting and worth working with. It might also require the acknowledgement that we don't have all the answers, but we trust they will emerge. When you can hold yourself well in this space of not knowing, and hold the space for others, it will offer the opportunity to create or co-create the future that wants to emerge. In this way, you could find new ways forward that neither you nor your team imagined as you work at the speed of change.

How can you support your team in working in a place of emergent futures and not a fixed future? How can you support them in being responsive to changing circumstances to grab hold of the opportunities that appear? One way is to recognize that being in a place of not knowing or perceived chaos is uncomfortable for many people. Helping your team sit in this discomfort to create the conditions for clarity to emerge is an important leadership skill, as is managing any discomfort that you might be feeling personally. You do this by inviting a pause, reflection or more ideas. You could ask a skillful question or provide an observation of the quality of the energy or interactions in that moment that helps normalize the responses to not-knowing.

Another skill is recognizing and acknowledging that team members may have different worldviews concerning change or an uncertain future. Your task as a team leader may be to help people let go of the past and the present they know (or much of it anyway) for a promise of a better future they don't yet know. This can happen when you continually reinforce the future that is emerging and help people find ways to see themselves in this future.

CO-CREATING THE FUTURE

There is value in bringing people affected by change together for exploratory conversations that lead to strategic action. A component of this is to invite explorations of personal or professional worldviews, which we often do through one dimension, setting the stage for explorations of team and organization worldviews. This exploration of a single dimension makes pathways forward visible by illuminating connections, possible clashes and potential alignments that allow for thinking strategically on how to collectively move into a future that seems more approachable together. It allows those involved to draw on the diversity of views to develop a new shared story related to the future.

The context we are working within will influence the dimension we choose to explore as a starting point. We often invite people to consider significant personal historical influences on their worldview as we highlighted in the previous chapter. Then we might suggest a reflection on how those experiences influence thinking about the path to the future. We might look at whether their values will help guide them to the future they want. We might ask if their practices are keeping them stuck in the past or present instead of opening them to future possibilities. Or, we might look at how they get their knowledge or information. Is it from sources that affirm how they have operated in the past or do they look for disconfirming data that challenges their perspectives on the past, present and future?

How does your organization view its relationship to the future? Is your organization risk averse or risk taking? How sure does your team or organization need to be to move into the future proactively? Is the organization trying to attain certainty on everything or is your organization jumping in, willing to take risks and learn from them as it continues moving forward? Which views are rewarded and which are punished? What happens when these views clash?

As a leader who will likely encounter this in a fast-changing environment, what is your strategy for aligning the views while honoring the future vision set out by the organization? In Chapter 10 we provide more information concerning the practices needed to bring this alignment and support the future into being.

REFLECTION QUESTIONS

1. What is your relationship to the future? What does that tell you about how you function in reality? How does it inform your own planning process?
2. Given the various perspectives and possible relationships with the future, what is the balance between change and stability you can bring to your team?

CHAPTER 9:
VALUES

Each of us holds values that we consider core to who we are. For me, one of these values is around the taking of human life. That is why I am opposed to the death penalty and think that going to war should be an absolute last resort. The taking of a life is a personal matter for me and my family. Believing that murder is wrong touches us deeply. A decade ago, my sister's daughter, my niece, was murdered. She was sixteen. Our family feels the repercussions of it to this day, each in our way, according to our individual relationships with her, our connections to each other and the stories we use to understand and interpret this tragedy.

And yet, things are not always so clear-cut. When I was 17, my 79-year-old grandfather became ill with cancer and quickly deteriorated. My strong, healthy, independent, nature-loving grandfather became completely bedridden within a few months, unable to physically take care of himself in any way. Yet his mind remained strong.

I was close to all of my grandparents and especially this one. One day, near the end, as we were visiting, my grandfather looked at me and said, "Jerry, when we were on the farm and an animal was in this condition, we could put the animal down. Why can't we do that with humans?"

I have pondered this question much of my life. What are my values regarding death and dying? What is death with dignity? What is murder? What is freedom of choice about life? What is forgiveness? These are powerful questions that can have uneasy answers and I realize through my experience that deeply held core values have grey areas. I have made my peace with how I think about choices I might make regarding the ending of a life and the choices others might make.

Now, when my values are challenged, I try to think back to my grandfather's 'simple' question and the complexity of the answer. I try my best to remain open to listening to conversations on values from a place of not knowing so that I might learn and understand and open possibilities rather than shut them down.

Jerry Nagel

WHAT ARE YOUR VALUES

Each and every one of us has values but not all of us can easily name what our values are in thoughtful and accurate ways. For each of us, some values are more important than others. Although mostly interdependent, values do operate in a hierarchy. When challenged, some will have more importance than others. However, the interdependency can make it hard to isolate distinct values. Or, if we can, it is often a cursory list of things we think we should value, like family, success, respect, love, honesty. The question is, are these truly the values that settle deep in the heart or soul, that guide action and your way of being in the world? Are they core commitments you consistently live by?

In our experience, people who do values explorations to illuminate their own values are often surprised by what their values are compared to what they think they are or think they should be. They are sometimes surprised at the lack of alignment between these values and the choices they are making in life, work or relationships. While you could name a dozen things that are important to you, there are often only four to six that come into play at any given time, which is why they function in a hierarchy. Also, those four to six values can encompass or act as an umbrella for several other interrelated values.

Sometimes a crisis will illuminate your values. The crisis could be an existential identity crisis, the loss of a loved one, the collapse of a life style, marital discord or divorce, a promotion at work, a new job or job loss, perhaps a personal or professional development program or career coaching; basically any life event that sparks reflection or an examination of your life path or journey.

VALUES GUIDE YOUR CHOICES, ALTHOUGH THEY HAVE WIGGLE ROOM

Our values guide our choices, consciously or not. Value is the root of evaluate. This means we use our values to evaluate life choices, those we've made in the past, those in front of us right now and possible choices in the future. Our values help us know what is important to us now and where to focus our attention. Our values are a measure of what is important to us at a deeply personal level. Most of us feel good when our choices are aligned with our values and often discover, when things have gone awry, it is because we have strayed from what is important to us.

While many people think they hold true to their most important values all of the time, there are a times, and more than you might think, when this is likely not true. What happens when your values come into conflict with each other? Say honesty is an important value for you. And say kindness is also an important value. What happens when a friend asks your opinion of their new haircut and you think it is not flattering to them? Do you choose honesty or kindness? If the friend is a casual friend, you may choose to be kind. If the friend is a dear friend, you may choose honesty. However, this is also a false binary; you could choose to be honest with kindness. It may well depend on the consequences of choosing one over the other, like valuing the relationship enough to be honest or kind or both. You probably get the picture.

Another time our values do not hold true is when we act in a way that is in contradiction to a value that we say we hold. We each have what we call wiggle room in our values. It is the space where we can find a way to justify or rationalize a particular action or behavior. "I don't steal, that is wrong. But the waiter added the bill wrong so that's on them." "I always like to be on time, but this coffee date isn't business, so it doesn't matter if I'm late." "I know I said I'd go to that birthday party, but there will be so many people there they won't miss me, so I just won't go. I'll call my friend later (maybe)." These are minor examples reminding us to bear in mind that we judge other people on their actions and we often judge ourselves on our intentions.

Values is one of the places where we can carry a lot of judgment about other people. We judge others either based on what we think their values are or we judge them according to our own values, and how they aren't living up to an expectation we may have placed on them. You can ask yourself, what do you gain by judging another person? Is it possible to bring compassion and empathy instead of judgment?

Since 'value' is the root of 'evaluate' or 'evaluation' and the six dimensions are interrelated, as you experience your reality, locally or globally, how do you evaluate this reality? How do you choose your reality or your future? Is there another lens with which to understand or evaluate your history? The world we live in is not neutral. People love and hate; admire and despise; suffer and enjoy. We each determine what is good or evil to us; what is beautiful or not. We operate with individual and societal value systems and it can be hard to differentiate between the two.

VALUES AS A PHILOSOPHY OF LIFE

In philosophy, the subject of values can be looked at from a moral, ethical or aesthetic perspective. In the context of worldviews, values are individual and societal. We are each influenced by societal or cultural beliefs about what is good or evil, what is beautiful or ugly, what is right or wrong. We can think of values as a reflection of the importance we put on something. Every aspect of our worldview, from reality to knowledge is influenced by what we value and how we evaluate things.

Values are a central component of worldviews. They influence every aspect of life. They are a filter through which we choose how we will act in and interact with the world. They set the standards for our behavior. They provide moral guidelines. Our values help us understand which behaviors are acceptable and which are not, and when and where we can push the boundaries of our behavior. If our worldview reflects the basic values we hold, then it is plausible to consider our worldview as our philosophy of life, our ideology or faith or formula for life.[51]

As you explore your own values in order to develop a deeper understanding of your worldview you can ask yourself, what do you consider to be the source of moral guidelines or what society sanctions as right or acceptable? Is society the source of moral guidelines or is there a source of moral guidelines that transcends human society, such as a divine being or force? Reflecting back on the beliefs held within your meta-reality, you can ask yourself here how you think about values and especially your values in relation to the relativity of moral guidelines. Do you believe in

DISABILITY? PART OF THE HUMAN CONDITION OR SOMETHING TO BE FIXED?

The American Disabilities Act was passed 29 years ago, yet people with disabilities still experience discrimination in the workplace, in public spaces and buildings, in education and private facilities.

The ADA established policies to address discrimination against people with disabilities and provide remedies for acts of discrimination. Yet, as we know, policies do not change worldviews. As long as we hold a medical model worldview that we need to fix people who have disabilities, we will continue to focus on fixing the person rather than directing our energy, as individuals and as society, towards a narrative of worldview values of inclusion, openness, acceptance and seeing disability as part of the human condition. To be sure, it is important to continue with medical science to find cures for diseases and injuries that can cause disabilities. The focus on the source of the disability, not on fixing the person.

When meeting people with differing circumstances than you, how do you respond? Do you seek to expand your worldview through learning and understanding? Do you consider your situation mostly as normal and people with disabilities or differences from you as not normal? How often do you check in with your worldviews regarding difference?

absolute morality, that moral guidelines (values) are absolute? Or do you believe in relative morality, that moral guidelines are relative to time, culture, or situations?

Our values influence how we think about people who are different from us in some important way. Examples include skin color, religion or country of origin. Ask yourself, am I tolerant of difference or am I intolerant, which implies that another person or the different 'other' must be punished, changed or removed because of their values or worldviews? How do I know this? Am I more tolerant of some than others and on what basis do I make this decision? Is tolerance enough? What is beyond tolerance?

LEADERSHIP AND VALUES

As a leader of your team or in your organization, do your personal values align with your organization's values? To what degree? Does this help or hinder or have no impact on your ability to work in your organization? Has your organization taken the time to consider the relationship between personal and organizational values? Are there clashes in your team that could be attributed to differences in values?

One of our clients was an energy company in a small country. They were interested in creating new corporate values and wanted to create them in alignment with the values of the people who worked there. Jerry and local colleagues worked with a group of 40 employees who represented the various aspects of the company. Prior to coming together, group members explored their personal values through anonymous online surveys. The results were shared with the group and provided a picture of what personal values were most important across the group. From this foundation the group narrowed the range of values down to ten that they shared and then explored their thinking on these values in small group conversations as a way for the values to settle into the group. Next, they worked together in the large group and in small groups to identify a set of values for the company, eventually settling on five. They wrote five values statements and tested them with each other, knowing that the statements would need to be presented to and generally accepted by the company's employees. What is key here is that the company values aligned with employee personal values. By developing the values as a team, the employees 'owned' them and could live them within the company.

ARE VALUES AT THE SOURCE OF ARGUMENTS ABOUT FACTS?

Sometimes when people get locked into arguments or positions on certain topics, they resort to facts to explain their point of view. There are at least two problems with this. The person or people you are in conflict with have just as much ability to source their own information or facts that support their point of view. This is explored more in Chapter 14: Understanding Worldview and Identity Reactions Through Behavioral Science. The other problem is that facts are subject to interpretation, as much as we like to think of facts as that which is observably true. As Jerry would say, "Ask any three economists to offer a perspective on the same set of facts and you are likely to get three different answers or interpretations." There are few things that truly qualify as facts. The existence of gravity is an example of one fact. We are quick to fill in missing details in any conversation, story or observance and we do so through our worldviews. This is why eyewitness accounts can be so varied. The same facts can be interpreted to support very different points of view.

While stuck in an argument focused on facts, it could be that the true source of contention is values based. If you can shift the focus of the conversation to values, it could change the nature of the discussion. Then you can look for shared values to understand what's important. There you might find points of connection that allow you to focus on alignment rather than conflict.

We have labor union clients in the United States. Unions, and labor generally, are currently operating in a hostile environment in the US, with many organizations and court rulings working to dilute the power of the collective voice. It would be easy to end up in a debate of whether the fees members pay are better off spent in support of the union or left in the pocket of the member coping with increasing costs of living. Many anti-union political groups are actively trying to make the case for the latter.

Anti-union legislation is called "Right to Work", using language in interesting, possibly deceptive ways. What it means is the right to not belong to a union. When the conversation is focused on the amount of union dues, it is easy to get tugged back and forth in a debate. When the conversation shifts to the greater purpose and role of unions in society, to their role in making quality education accessible to all, to being a contributor to democracy and the better, safer, higher paying working conditions that support a strong middle-class, it changes the nature of the conversations that unions are having with their members. It also moves the conversation from individualistic values – everyone in it for themselves – to the collective value of stronger together.

WORLDVIEW INTELLIGENCE HAS A CORE SET OF VALUES

It is fair to ask, after suggesting that we as individuals and organizations have values, if Worldview Intelligence as a company has articulated its values. The answer is yes. The company holds to a set of simple values. These are things that are of importance to us. We believe in the powerful recognition that we live in a world of **fundamental relatedness**. We value **open-mindedness**, **compassion** and **curiosity over judgment**. We work to build **relationships** that create opportunities for followers to turn into leaders. We strive to bring forward and support an **appreciative stance to conversations**. We invite Worldview Intelligence practitioners to let go of fixed views and look for opportunities to learn and grow in new ways. And finally, Worldview Intelligence supports an approach to **power** that brings forth 'power to' and/or 'power with' rather than 'power over'. The former opens possibilities and the latter closes them down. Worldview Intelligence is an approach that supports "power to and with" values by working through multiple dialogues rather than top-down leadership edicts and the avoidance of dialogue.

REFLECTION QUESTIONS

1. What are your values? Allow yourself to reflect on this question and see what comes up for you. Then work with the process outlined here:

    - Brainstorm a list of values you think are important to you. Write down as many ideas as come to you. When you think you have exhausted ideas for your list, take a look at what you've written down and look for themes and patterns.

- It is helpful to take small post-it notes and write the individual values down on these post-its so you can move them around, cluster and theme them. Are there clusters of ideas that represent similar thoughts or values?
- If there were specific words that seem to capture or represent the clusters, what would they be? Write them down.
- Once you've identified these key values, do they feel true to you? Close your eyes and sense into the answers.
- Reflect on how each value is important to you and how they individually and together guide your decision-making and the way you live your life.
- Are there adjustments you need to make to be in better alignment with your values? What are they?
- Are there specific steps you want or need to take related to your values? When will you do this and how will you be supported in these actions?

2. For teams you are leading, are individual and team values in alignment? What informs your thinking on this? Does it matter? Does it influence individual or team performance in any way? What are some things you could do to make your team's values explicit? To bring your team's values alive, you and your team can find ways to hold yourselves accountable to and for these values. Accountability builds trust within the team.

CHAPTER 10:
PRACTICES

When I was in my late twenties, I was hired as the Executive Director of a health charity for Atlantic Canada. I had no formal leadership training although several patterns even from my childhood highlighted my leadership potential, like organizing my neighborhood friends for games of cards, tag, kick-the-can, hide and seek or baseball. If my friends were busy with chores, as often happened in the family with eight children – several of whom were my friends – I would pitch in and help so we could all get outside faster.

Flying by the seat of my pants, I had no idea what it took to skillfully lead a team, or an organization or a cadre of volunteers. I discovered it took consistency, focus and authenticity and I didn't have those things aligned or in practice all the time. I had good mentors and I had opportunities for education in addition to "on-the-job" training, which is how so many people are expected to learn how to lead.

A couple of years into this job, after having my first child, morale in the office nose-dived. Staff gossiped incessantly. They talked about each other behind each other's backs and they lacked confidence in my leadership. This was partly energized by the gossip and by the perception among staff that I was no longer as dedicated to my job because I had become a mother.

I became despondent and seriously considered quitting my job. Yet, when I considered the volunteer board and the initiatives we were undertaking at the time, I was energized. I realized I had a choice to make – not about whether to stay or go but on how I was going to act as a leader of the team and in this organization.

Some of these may seem like little things or little practices, but they were leverage points that shifted a number of things. I decided I would smile every morning when I walked into the office, that I would greet each person cheerfully, every single day, no matter how I was feeling. And I did. Every day. After a time, I realized I was feeling better and the morning smiles and greetings were *genuinely expressed. It brought back my joy and it brought back points of connection with and within the team.*

I also decided to directly address the issues of gossip and other patterns of behavior that did not serve the team or our work. One way I did this was in a staff meeting. I said to the employees, "There is a problem in this office. You know what it is and I don't." After an awkward silence and a repeat of the question, someone finally said, "You are never here when important decisions need to be made." Progress. Yet, when I asked for specific examples, no one had any to offer. Illuminating perceptions and misperceptions enabled us, as a team, to move past them.

When I encountered people clearly gossiping, I again tackled it directly. The result was that the nature of the conversations changed and, when we did a team building session, a member of the team commented on my morning greetings, helping me see the impact of my own choices.

These were simple behaviors learned the hard way on aligning my actions with my worldview through a deliberate, consistent choice of practices.

Kathy Jourdain

WORLDVIEW-PRACTICE-ACTION

As noted earlier, in the early days of our Worldview Intelligence explorations, we drew inspiration from *The Rules of Victory*, by James Gimian and Barry Boyce, based on the *The Art of War*. The *Art of War* is a book about how to conduct war and an explanation of why not go to war. It is based on the premise that once we go to war, everyone loses because you cannot do harm to another without also doing harm to yourself. This text assumes we are all connected or interrelated – to everybody and everything. We recognize that this is a worldview. In Chapter 9: Values, we identify this is also a Worldview Intelligence value.

When Europeans came to North America, took over the land and decimated the Indigenous populations, often referred to by our Native American colleagues as the Genocide, the Indigenous populations were socially, physically and morally harmed and the impacts continue to this day. The Europeans who did this gave up much of their own humanity by being a part of this genocide. Their descendants continue to experience the harm of the loss of this humanity. The same is true of the slave trade. Harm was done to Africans brought to North America and elsewhere on slave ships as human cargo. The choice of language here is intentional and an example of how language impacts how we see things. It was not 'slaves' who were brought from Africa but human beings forced into slavery. The nature of these traumas live on today in the history and patterns of all the populations. This includes the shame and guilt for many descendants of the European populations that, for the most part, have yet to be addressed in a way that is meaningful and offers healing.

In The Art of War, a framework is described that contains three components – view, practice or method and action.[52] Central to this perspective is the idea that our worldviews directly impact the actions we take in the world and that the methods we use to manifest or extend our worldviews into the practical realities of the world must be congruent with these worldviews. The Practices dimension provides a theory or practice of action. It answers the question: How are you to act and to create in this world?

ALIGNMENT OF WORLDVIEWS AND PRACTICES

When how you act is out of sync with what you say you believe or value, observers know it. When your actions do not align with your worldview, people will say you are inauthentic or out of integrity – bringing to life the adage of "do what I say, not what I do". Your actions speak so loudly, people cannot hear what you say. As an individual, if you aspire to personal integrity, this is fundamentally important. As a leader of a team or in an organization, it is even more so, especially as it relates to Building Trust and Relationship at the Speed of Change. If you and your team cannot rely on the environment to be stable, then you and your team have only your own personal integrity and alignment to count on.

> ## WHERE TO PARK?
> A while ago Kathy was helping her 86-year-old father with transportation for medical appointments. She had his accessible parking placard in her car window. During those few days she needed to pick Jerry up at the airport. As she drove up to where Jerry was waiting, a few meters away there was an accessible parking spot. The traffic attendant suggested she pull up to that spot because she had the placard. She explained she didn't need to and he suggested she do it anyway. She did not. In aligning practices with her worldview that space was reserved for people with accessibility needs and taking it, if only for a minute, would be inconsistent with her worldview.
>
> What would you have done? What is your worldview about accessible parking? Have you ever been frustrated when arriving at a store on a windy, chilly day and having to park far from the front door while accessible spaces are empty? Do you see accessible parking as inclusive for people with disabilities or do you see it as excluding you?

The practices you use to live your values directly impact the actions you take in the world. Your practices define and shape how you live your reality. They provide you with options and choices for how you act in various contexts – at work, in community, with family or friends, in school, or in social situations. They also provide you with a means to manifest or extend your worldview into the realities of the world in which you live, work and socialize. If your practices are not congruent with your stated worldview, it will be evident to those around you. When you practice something different from what you espouse, it calls into question the validity of your stated worldview, your authenticity and your integrity.

Knowing what your hopes and dreams are and desiring to get there does not necessarily mean you know how. As humans, we generally strive to act in meaningful ways and take actions to transform the world in ways that connect to our purpose. Your worldview not only includes your history and values system, but it also offers you thoughts and reflections on how to organize your actions to influence your life and perhaps the lives of others you interact with in the grand scheme of things, as a human in the world[53]. The practices you build, intentionally or habitually, bring life to your worldview and all that is important to you. In this chapter, we discuss various practices that demonstrate this idea.

DAILY AND INTENTIONAL PRACTICES

Practices generally fall into two categories that are not mutually exclusive: every day, how-you-live-your-life practices and intentional practices.

Every day practices are the realm of routines, habits and patterns. This is an important category of practices because so much of how we operate in the world is habitual. And even though the work of Worldview Intelligence is meant to draw attention to the habits or patterns we don't question that get us into trouble, if we had to think everything through all the time, we would not get out of the house in the morning. We create routines that offer us efficiency. This is a good thing – most of the time.

If you value the environment, you may have regular practices of recycling or composting or other environmentally friendly actions that allow you to demonstrate this. If you value food security, you may have a practice of buying locally or frequenting farm-to-table eating establishments. These are regular or daily practices that are intentional. Other intentional practices are ones you generally need to create room for or even schedule into your day or week or they won't happen. These kinds of intentional practices may include meditation, reflective practices or exercise; practices that if you are intentional about them they may eventually also become habitual. This could include how often and when you connect with family or friends.

Several years ago, Jerry moved to a new home in the countryside. The land had been a pasture and during home construction it was deeply disturbed. Jerry chose to plant the two acres around the house in natural prairie grass instead of a typical lawn. For the prairie grass to take, it required several years of active management, including occasional burning, pulling weeds by hand and hand cutting of invasive species like buckthorn. The result was better for the environment, created habitat for bees and butterflies and shelter for birds and small animals. This was a personal life practice choice, partly as a balance to the impacts of work-related travel.

HOW DO YOU TREAT OTHER PEOPLE?

How you treat people is a practice. Do you treat some people differently than other people? The answer is undoubtedly yes. The question is, what is the basis upon which you treat people differently? Do you treat family members better or worse than strangers? Do you treat your team members all the same and do you treat them better or worse than customers, suppliers or others in the organization? If you say you value diversity of people, perspective, opinions or expressions of differing experiences, is that evident in your practices and priorities and in how you interact with people who are different than you?

Practices that show you value diversity of all kinds could include listening practices, the cultivation of being present to the situation or other person and removing distractions from the interaction. As referenced in earlier chapters, in your team meetings you could use check-in and check-out practices or a talking piece to bring every voice into the room. Intentionally inviting worldview explorations and pausing to ensure that all views have been expressed can bring tremendous value to your team discussions and demonstrate that the various views are not only welcome but contribute to team creativity and innovation, leading to better outcomes.

It is important to note here that actions that may be valid in one context may not necessarily be so in another. For example, converting a rural landscape to prairie grass did not impact nearby neighbors, but doing so in an urban neighborhood may be met with resistance from neighbors or the local city government. A friend who has turned his front yard into the family garden has received many unkind comments as well as support from neighbors.

LEADERSHIP PRACTICES

The world is continuously evolving and your worldview with it, whether you are conscious of this or not. This is why the worldview explorations offer a key strategic advantage. It helps you make your own worldview explicit to you. It is also why it is a leadership practice.

As a leader, you can learn to adapt your leadership practices to the contexts you are working in and to the people you are working with. You may hold a general theory of action, such as conversations are important in building trust and relationship, however, what constitutes a conversation that builds trust and relationship could vary by local realities or contexts. To take effective action you need clarity of your own goals and values and those of your team and team members. Good individual and collective practices for acting on them will also be helpful. As you implement your practices you can seek self and collective reflections on the courses of action or practices you used in order to adjust as you go.[54]

BELIEFS AND PRACTICES ABOUT AUTHORITY AND PRIORITY RELATIONS

Your personal and leadership practices tell you a lot about your worldview, as they do other people like your team members or colleagues. One of the things your practices reflect is your beliefs about forms of authority relations and what you think are best or natural. Do you believe in a linear structure with a clearly defined leader and relatively fixed hierarchy where authority is top down? Do you believe in an egalitarian group with rotating or fluid leadership? Or some combination thereof?

One of the things subject to change in fast growing or changing environments is structure. What is your leadership style or what are your leadership practices in adapting at the speed of change? If there is work to be done, it is people who will do the work, so ensuring quality of relationship through sound leadership practices is a strategic advantage.

Your practices also reflect your beliefs about the natural priority of your personal, your team's or your organization's agenda. Does your individual agenda have priority over the team's need or does the team's agenda have priority over everyone's personal plans and goals? What is the balance that can work for most people most of the time?

On a societal level this could refer to your beliefs about the natural priority of the agenda of your reference or social group compared to another's reference or social group. This is at issue in many countries right now as opposition to immigration becomes more visible. Some people are concerned that people immigrating from other cultures or with different religions will impose their agenda on the country they immigrate to and these people want to be sure the country's agenda or culture is the priority. This may be more a perceived issue than an actual threat but some people are acting in accordance with a threat.

Individuals often have a combination of beliefs that are not clear-cut in relation to practices or have blind spots that enable them to rationalize or justify specific behaviors or actions that are not in alignment with their worldview, as we illustrated in the last chapter on values. The challenge is that conflicting belief systems and the resultant behaviors communicate confusion to others about what you mean or what you truly stand for.

Your beliefs on the natural priority of rights, privileges and prerogatives of your ethnic, religious or cultural group of reference relative to the rights of other groups also appear in your practices. Do you think that the rights and prerogatives of your group have priority over those of other human groups or are the rights and prerogatives of your group essentially equivalent to those of other groups? Or possibly, does your own group deserve less in the way of rights and prerogatives compared to other groups? How does this show up in your actions or practices?

PRACTICES FOR WORLDVIEW CLASHES

If your team has a diversity of cultural and ethnic backgrounds, does any of this create conflicts within the team or among members of the team? If so, what are your individual and collective practices in addressing these issues? In building trust and relationship, it is not enough to simply say, "You are all adults. You don't have to like each other; you just have to work together." We know that the best work gets done when people have better quality relationships, enjoy each other and take pride in accomplishing goals and objectives together. Remember the Google study discussed in Chapter 4: What It Means to Be Worldview Intelligent? One characteristic of high performing teams is that they have higher levels of social sensitivity, meaning they tend to the wellbeing of the team, individually and collectively.

Using Worldview Intelligent language and questions along with the practice of curiosity will give you and your team a strategic advantage. To be able to preface your own comments with something like, "From my worldview...." or "I imagine the worldview of our senior leadership on this issue is..." or to be able to ask questions like, "How did you come to see or experience this issue in this way?" creates exploratory rather than oppositional conversational spaces. To offer something like, "I value your perspective and it makes me think of...." keeps the exploration moving.

Worldview Intelligent practices offer ways to spark generative dialogue where all voices and perspectives matter, each contribution is valued in and of itself and for where it leads. Not only will these practices build trust and relationship, they will enable you, your team and your organization to benefit from the resulting creativity and innovative ideas and solutions that arise.

REFLECTION QUESTIONS

1. What practices do you have that support and reflect your worldview on your leadership – to yourself and to others? What additional practice(s) would offer even greater consistency and alignment?

2. What are the individual and collective practices in your team that continually build trust, relationship and exploratory dialogue? Are there practices that interfere with this? What

more could you or your team do to grow this skill and capacity in your team and in your organization?

3. What practices in your team or organization support the integration of work and life, health and well-being? What are your organization's practices around risk and failure? Around diversity, equity and inclusion? What do the practices tell you about the worldview of your organization or team? Are there practices that need to be introduced to bring greater alignment between worldviews and actions?

CHAPTER 11:
KNOWLEDGE

Have you ever had a moment when you have questioned everything you think you know? When you have questioned everything you have thought of as the facts of your life? This happened to me in my mid-forties when I discovered I had been adopted when I was just a few months old. I had had no idea.

Many of the things I had considered to be the "facts" of my life were stories I created to fill in the gaps that were not contradicted by anyone in my family. This included where I was born, why I was the shortest person in my family, why my hair went gray at an early age and why my middle son had curly hair. The physical characteristics in my experience I attributed to members of my adoptive family. For instance, my maternal grandmother was short and went gray at an early age so I assumed that was why I was short and started going gray in my teens. When I realized how many of the "facts" of my life were not really facts, it caused me to question absolutely everything.

In the end, what I knew to be true was that my family (the one I grew up in) loved me. While in some ways, everything had changed, nothing had changed. I was still the same person I had always been but now I had more information to expand on and inform my sense of who I am.

One interesting thing. My eyes continue to deceive me. When I look at pictures of myself with my family, I "see" my resemblance to them, even though "observers" would not. When I look at pictures of my birth family, except for my full sister, I do not see the resemblance. My brain still makes up a story that my logic now knows is not true.

Kathy Jourdain

HOW DO YOU KNOW WHAT YOU KNOW?

The dimension of knowledge asks you to consider the question of how you know what you know. Where did and does your knowledge come from? How do you know that what you know is accurate and correct? What sources of knowledge or information do you trust? There was a time when the Encyclopedia Britannica was the most comprehensive and trusted source of knowledge available to young students and their parents. Now those out-of-date books sit on the bookshelves of our parents and grandparents, hardly ever to be opened again thanks to the vastness of information available through the internet. However, just because information is readily available does not mean it is actual data or knowledge.

If you are getting your information from only one or a few sources and those sources are similar in perspectives, you are likely not getting a comprehensive picture. We are attracted to information that confirms our beliefs or what we already know or think we know. This reduces the possibility of our worldview being challenged. In Chapter 13: Brain Science and Worldviews: Rationale and Strategies for Working with Fight-Flight-Freeze Response and Chapter 14: Understanding Worldview and Identity Reactions Through Behavioral Science, we explore more fully some of the concepts offered in the research that help us understand why, as human beings, we become so attached to our views and why it is so hard to change.

If you get your information or knowledge from a particular set of sources and someone else gets theirs from a different and even opposite set of sources, you are ripe for worldview clashes. In these cases, it can seem like the other person has no idea what they are talking about. And they may think that of you. This is why it is important to have a variety of perspectives and sources of information to consult on a regular basis.

If you do check out another source of information, different from what you would usually look at, check your reactions and motivations for doing so. Is it to be curious regarding how someone else's views are being informed or is it to prove to yourself how wrong you already think they are and how ridiculous they are for carrying those views? Is it for a sense of superiority? If you are approaching your exploration with curiosity, there is room for expansion. If it is the former, you may only be locking yourself more firmly into your already established views.

Your worldview offers you an understanding of how it is that you know what you know, how you acquire knowledge or how it is you think you know something is true or false. This is especially important because what you believe about knowing or knowledge affects what you accept as valid evidence or facts. It also affects your interpretation of the evidence and thus what you believe or accept with respect to the particulars of the world [55] or the particulars of individuals or groups of people.

THE ROLE OF ASSUMPTIONS AND BELIEFS IN KNOWLEDGE

Like so much of your worldview, you make assumptions about how you know what you know, on the 'knowing' process itself. If you are like most people, you rarely question your assumptions. How do you experience reality? How did you come to believe what you believe? What is a belief? What is an opinion? What is your history? How did you develop your set of values? How does knowledge come into being?

What beliefs do you hold regarding reliable sources of knowledge? Do you value authority figures, opinions or traditional views on matters? Do you rely on your senses? Do you prefer logic models and rationality? Do you believe or trust in science or do you also believe in intuition, divination, or revelation? How much confidence do you place in each of these possible sources of knowledge? Perhaps you think that there are no reliable sources of knowledge.

The answers to these and many other worldview questions influence your daily actions. If you are to grow your leadership and communication skills and if you are to enter into dialogues that create opportunities to build trust and relationship, then you must periodically ask yourself how you came to know what you know.

You could also ask how does your team or the individual members of your team know what they know? The more a team holds the same or similar worldviews, the more confidence they will have in their knowledge, whether it is right or reliable, and the more they may be inclined to discount contradictory information if it is available. With your team, you may want to be asking the question of how the team knows what it knows, how reliable the sources of knowledge are and whether there is more relevant information or data or disconfirming information that should be considered. The more we are surrounded by people who think like us, the more convinced we are that our views are correct.

Diversity of views can provide for more comprehensive analysis and opportunities for new knowledge. The ongoing process of constructing knowledge is not just combining two or more 'knowns' into one new or different reality, but also the possibility that something not known before might emerge during the ongoing processes of knowledge creation.

Something else to take some care around is that different functions or departments in an organization that have different roles may well value different sources of knowledge. The engineering department may put more value on scientific studies and on the technology or processes that help them build things. The marketing department may put more value on communication, focus groups and relationship processes. The finance department may put more value on the spreadsheets and the numbers. Thus, what is real to a different department or team is constructed or co-constructed within their historical processes and contexts. Additionally, these processes may have their own forms, rules and sources of knowledge.

"COMMUNITY" KNOWLEDGE

From a constructionist perspective, our personal and professional communities are key sources of knowledge. Knowledge is not just what individuals believe, but what social groups or communities believe. Knowledge comes from what a community of people, the marketing or engineering departments or top management, for example, agrees to be true. This means knowledge or knowing or what professional or social groups hold to be real or true is fundamentally a social process. It can be seen as the common or shared property and experience of a group or culture.

So, it is important to pay attention to how you, your team or department responds to the valued knowledge of another team or department. Do you value your own team's perspective and knowledge more? Do you belittle another team because their focus or valued sources of information are different? Do you value a different way of thinking, recognizing it contributes to more comprehensive information and knowledge?

When building trust and relationship within your team, how you interact individually and collectively with other individuals, teams, departments or the organization influences trust and relationship within your team. This is the question of whether your practices are aligned with your worldviews and whether those practices allow for honoring different sources of knowledge and information. There is no long-term benefit or strategic advantage to building or promoting your team and its intelligence gathering at the expense of other teams, or other locations if your organization is geographically spread out.

MODELS OF ACQUIRING KNOWLEDGE

Francis Heylighen, the Director of the Center Leo Apostel, offers that there are six differing theories or models of how we acquire knowledge: empiricism, rationalism, pragmatic epistemology, constructivism*, evolutionary epistemology and memetics These are each explained a bit more below. What these six theories of knowledge invite you to consider is that there is no absolute true model of reality or way of acquiring knowledge or knowing what is absolutely true or false. Instead you are invited to recognize that construction of knowledge, of your worldview, must take into consideration which approach or approaches to knowledge acquisition you favor.

Knowledge acquisition, like worldviews, is locally situated or constructed. This means what we know can be influenced by the needs and characteristics of where we are located in an organization or geographically. It also means what we know is

---

* Empiricism, rationalism and constructivism are the predominant Western world theories of how we acquire knowledge.

influenced by our own needs and characteristics. We take the way we construct reality to be reality. We take the way we build our knowledge to be knowledge. Our teams develop a belief that what they know IS knowledge – or, all they need to know. In this way knowledge also comes from what a community of people agrees to be true. Our individual and collective practices for acquiring knowledge are a personal matter and they can be quite a passionate matter,[56] especially as knowledge becomes part of individual or collective identity.

SIX THEORIES OF KNOWLEDGE ACQUISITION

1. *Empiricism* emphasizes the role of experience in acquiring knowledge. Knowledge comes from sensory (as in the five senses) perceptions or observations. Empiricism emphasizes evidence-based approaches to knowledge, especially as discovered in experiments. It is a fundamental part of the scientific method that all hypotheses and theories must be tested against observations of the natural world rather than resting solely on a priori reasoning or knowledge that comes from theoretical deduction rather than from observation or experience, intuition, or revelation.

2. *Rationalism* views knowledge acquisition as a process of rational reflection. Knowledge is acquired by a process of reasoning and deduction rather than from experience or a priori reasoning.

3. *Pragmatic epistemology* asserts that knowledge consists of models that offer ways of representing the environment that make it easier to problem solve.[57] For an organization or team, there may be specific models for decision-making, risk taking, resource allocation, and communication. And these may vary across the organization.

4. *Constructivism** is the perspective that all knowledge is constructed. It assumes that knowledge is a product of social

---

* Constructivism, constructionism, social constructivism, and social constructionism are often used interchangeably. Heylighen uses constructivism as the word to mean the social construction of knowledge.

processes of communication. Social constructionism invites us to not be bound by the chains of either history or tradition. It invites us to consider that what may be true for me may not be true for someone else. It invites us to consider that there are many differing worldviews within humanity. First Nations or Native American groups will refer to the rock nation or tree nation or bison nation. For the empiricist, this perspective is fundamentally untestable and yet it is true knowledge for First Nations or Native Americans.[58]

5. *Evolutionary epistemology* gives a broader perspective on the acquisition of knowledge. In evolutionary epistemology, knowledge is constructed by individuals or groups in order to adapt to their local environment. This can be by observation, experience, intuition or revelation. This process of construction is ongoing.[59]

6. *Memetics* is the sixth model. In memetics, knowledge is transmitted from one person to another and thus is not dependent on any single individual. A piece of knowledge is a 'meme'. As long as the meme moves between individuals more quickly than the death of any individual holding the knowledge, the knowledge or meme will continue and possibly proliferate.[60] Societal and cultural norms are often conveyed invisibly through such memes. In a new city, one way to discover hierarchies between cars, pedestrians and other forms of transportation is to watch what the locals do.

In some cities, like Paris, pedestrians take precedence and they rarely obey traffic signals. Car drivers will stop. In Cologne, pedestrians could fear for their lives if they step off the curb and doing so is not synchronized to the traffic signals. In Geneva, with a mix of cultures, it's a mix of crossing patterns, not so easy to discern. And, in Amsterdam, the top of the hierarchy is bicyclists. They will run you down if you don't get out of the way fast enough.

Like constructivism, memetics attends to the role of communication and social processes in the development of knowledge. An important distinguishing difference between memetics and constructivism according to Heylighen is that constructivism sees knowledge as constructed by individuals or society and memetics sees society and even individuality as byproducts constructed by an ongoing evolution of independent fragments of knowledge competing for domination.[61]

These six theories invite you to recognize that construction of knowledge, of worldviews, must take into consideration which perspective on knowledge acquisition you or others hold. As a leader, you can reflect on your own perspectives on your knowledge by looking at the ways you gather knowledge from one or more of the six differing approaches. What approaches do you value most? Are there some you might disregard and, in the process, potentially devalue the perspectives of others?

Critically important for you as a leader is to be aware that knowledge communities can and do control the flow of knowledge to others, whether through books, movies, music, academic programs or practice. This can result in creating spaces of holders of knowledge (power) and receivers (if lucky) of knowledge. In other words, knowledge has a political aspect and as a leader you must be aware of when you or someone else are bringing this into your work. It becomes possible for the holders of knowledge to exploit those without the same knowledge and this is a barrier to trust.

THE WISDOM IN THE ROOM

A form of knowledge that leaders can draw on is the wisdom in the room. In hosting work and hosting conversations, the underlying assumptions are that the people who are closest to the problems or the issues have the most knowledge of them, people support what they help create and, by providing good processes and methods, the collective knowledge and wisdom can be made visible to be acted upon.

What sources of knowledge you trust, the forms of knowledge acquisition you trust and what you believe to be true all influence and are influenced by your worldview.

REFLECTION QUESTIONS

1. What sources of knowledge do you trust? How do you discern the reliability of your sources of knowledge? How often do you seek out alternate sources of information? What is the nature of your inquiry when you do so?

2. What sources of knowledge does your team trust? What are your go-to references? How does your team react to differing beliefs concerning knowledge? How does your team respond to different approaches or focus of knowledge acquisition by other teams or departments?

3. What sources of knowledge does your organization trust? What sources of knowledge does your organization promote?

CHAPTER 12:
THE STRATEGIC USE OF THE WORLDVIEW INTELLIGENCE SIX DIMENSIONS FRAMEWORK

Several years ago, I was part of a 2-year initiative called the Meadowlark Project. The design of the Project was based on the Change Lab model from Theory U, an approach to change and innovation developed by Otto Scharmer[62]. This approach assembles a team of people representative of the community or business sector that the work is focused on. The Meadowlark Project's purpose was to look at how the region of Minnesota, Iowa, Nebraska and North and South Dakota could begin to address some of its most challenging issues, especially those related to poverty, racial and gender discrimination, youth outmigration and unemployment.

The Lab Team I was a part of was composed of women and men, people of color, all ages, various gender orientations, a range of economic circumstances and conservative to liberal political views. The team essentially represented, in good part, the differing realities, histories, values, ideas about the future, personal and business practices, thoughts regarding the future and ways of gaining knowledge that existed within the Region.

As might be expected, the views on the issues the Project was working were quite varied and the discussions lively. While the Project produced a number of ideas for addressing the issues it set out to explore, the main learning was that we just didn't have the skills to have conversations on difficult topics. We wanted to address issues of racial discrimination, for example, but when conversations focused on racism, while they didn't descend into acrimony, we had a hard time finding ways to common ground that could lead to action.

An aha for me was that while the region had developed the infrastructure to attend to its physical condition through economic development programs, as one example, it had little of the human infrastructure needed to help us address the human relations challenges the Project set out to solve.

Since the end of the Meadowlark Project I, along with thousands of others throughout the Region, have built our dialogic capacity to speak on matters of social and human relations. There is still much to do. It is my hope that Worldview Intelligence contributes to this important societal work.

Jerry Nagel

INDIVIDUAL DIMENSIONS FORM A COHERENT FRAMEWORK

The previous six chapters described each of the six dimensions individually. In this chapter we explore the interrelationship between the dimensions and how this framework can be used strategically to build trust and relationship, develop and implement policy and improve success in change initiatives, including mergers and acquisitions.

As you are now aware, the Worldview Intelligence Six Dimensions Framework provides a structure to understand worldviews by identifying and exploring discrete elements or dimensions that make up a worldview. Looking at the dimensions individually provides a way of organizing our thinking on worldviews that, on the one hand, is pretty straightforward and completely makes sense and, on the other hand, most people have not thought about organizing their thinking or reflections in this way or through this kind of structure. So, not only is it straightforward, it is also innovative and unique. It opens possibilities of new approaches to the leadership skills of self-awareness and self-discovery. Additionally, it is a key to understanding the worldviews of others.

Discussing the six dimensions individually helps us to understand each one in some depth and provides ways to be in productive and strategic conversations, one-on-one or collectively. If an issue centers on one dimension, a deep dive into that dimension can be particularly constructive. For example, if there are unresolved issues in your team or organization due to unaddressed historical influences then a deep dive into history can make hidden patterns visible. If practices are not aligned with stated worldviews, looking at what practices are helpful and which ones are counter-productive is a useful exercise.

In our experience, and you probably already have a sense of this, it is rare that one dimension stands alone at the heart of an issue. Usually a multiple of dimensions are at work when differing worldviews show up. An experience (history) may impact a value someone holds. Or a person's practices may have developed because of the daily reality they experience. In that case, looking at practices could include an historical perspective: what was the origin of the practices? Translated into a current inquiry: do they still serve our purpose? Practices could also be explored from a values perspective: are they still aligned with the organization's values?

When people ask us how to create a new, preferred future or how to align worldviews in an organization or community, the answer resides within the framework – it is in the practices for sure and it might be in valued sources of knowledge or some other dimension. It is certainly in using the framework to create coherence across worldviews that differ in some or all the dimensions. In this way, the framework can be a tool for understanding, for deconstructing worldviews and for aligning worldviews to move forward in a new direction, take action on an issue of relevance or focus on building trust and relationship.

It is rare in our work with clients that we only focus on one dimension throughout the whole engagement. We might use one dimension as a window into specific worldview explorations and the ones we choose to use may vary throughout the engagement as important issues or discussions emerge.

As you will already be aware from prior chapters, we often use the dimension of history to invite people into an exploration of their personal worldview. It quickly becomes clear that history is interdependent with reality. We begin to see how significant influences in our history have brought us to the reality we experience daily, weekly, monthly or annually. And the practices we use to live our daily lives are clearly a component of reality even as it is its own dimension. What we value or our core commitments also influence our reality and arise from our history.

The sources of knowledge we trust can significantly influence or reinforce our belief systems (reality) or our core values or commitments, especially as we continually seek to validate our own experiences and sense of identity. One dimension may provide a window into understanding or awareness and, once in, the interdependence becomes clear. Starting with an exploration of each dimension and then diving into the interrelationship of the various dimensions allows for a more thorough consideration of our worldviews.

When working with the Governing Council of one of our clients, the Council members were first asked to reflect on their worldview as a member of Council through the dimension of reality. Then, through the dimension of history, they were asked to reflect on how their worldview may have shifted since they agreed to step into their governance role. Finally, they were asked to consider the future the organization is working towards and the practices the Council needs to engage to support this future. Working with the interrelationship of these four dimensions helped the Council see how they got where they are, where they want to go and what practices can help them get there.

With another client that provides support to challenged youth in schools and their families, we offered explorations through the history and values dimensions to help them understand their worldviews in relation to the clients they support. They realized that most of their employees are young, white, middle class, educated women with degrees in the field of social work and that they are serving populations that are not. After doing the Worldview exercises they became much more conscious of when they might be imposing their worldviews on their clients and their families and when they needed to listen more and ask different and better questions to understand the worldviews and experiences of those they are intending to help.

WORLDVIEW INTELLIGENCE IS A GAME CHANGER

Worldview Intelligence provides a structured approach, language, skills and strategies to examine the mental models or existing organizational, team and individual worldviews. It also opens the space for the conversations and practices needed to build trust and relationship, to support policy changes and illuminate the blind spots that lead to hidden dynamics and unintended consequences. It enables leaders to ask better, more provocative questions.

The Worldview Intelligence Six Dimensions Framework illuminates where sources of tension, worldview challenges and resistance might reside. It also provides a planning structure with its Theory of Change Planning Model, which we share in Chapter 15, that allows for a thoughtful, strategic, systemic approach to implementing policy, changing organizational culture or aligning worldviews when integrating companies that have been brought together through mergers and acquisitions.

The Worldview Intelligence approach is based in curiosity, empathy and non-judgment. It seeks to get to the root or cause of issues and then work from that foundation up, asking different questions at each stage. These qualities are essential ingredients in building trust and relationship, whether at the speed of change or not, as they are a means to genuinely connect with another person. As we've shared, the shortest distance between two people is a story. When we bring curiosity, we invite story. When we bring empathy, we create a foundation for connection as we offer a space of trust to another person.

Practicing Worldview Intelligence leadership helps you recognize when a conversation is a worldview conversation so you can adapt your stance and your receptivity to open exploratory conversations rather than become defensive.

WHAT IS A WORLDVIEW CONVERSATION?

You may be wondering, what is a worldview conversation? It is one where the participants in the conversation bring different perspectives, often seeing the situation quite differently. If you are not aware that you are in a worldview conversation, you could find yourself being triggered and leaping to persuasion, sometimes bordering on imposition, defensiveness or judgment. Being aware of any of these reactions allows you to press the pause button, step out of your reaction to become curious and more attentive to the conversation and the people with whom you are in conversation. We have written much more on this in Chapter 13: Brain Science and Worldviews: Rationale and Strategies for Working with Fight-Flight-Freeze Responses and Chapter 14: Understanding Worldview and Identity Responses Through Behavioral Science.

Being curious and nonjudgmental enables you to not take offence when your views or perspectives are challenged. This could happen, for example, if you believe initiatives you have implemented in the team or organization are progressive or have moved things forward and are nearing completion, while others may think they are only a starting point. Or, if you believe someone is expressing dissatisfaction with your actions, behaviors or outcomes. Or, if you believe you have been attacked.

Empathy provides you with the capacity to listen beyond the volume or the noise to what is being said or asked. Using the framework helps you discover a path to the future that allows for going back to the organization's collective history as well as forward to the preferred future, recognizing that these points meet right now, in the reality of the present moment. Being Worldview Intelligent enables you to consider different and potentially opposite views at the same time, both individually and collectively. It enables you to acknowledge the existence of differing and possibly clashing views and to create opportunities to build strength from difference, to turn diversity and inclusion into a competitive advantage.

POLICY DEVELOPMENT AND IMPLEMENTATION

Policies don't always work the way they are intended because the heart of this work is not in rigid enforcement as much as it is in the hard work of staying in the challenging conversations that could lead to an alignment of worldviews. For example, there is substantial research that shows that having a Diversity-Equity-Inclusion policy in place does not necessarily mean that an organization is achieving any of its DEI goals, and sometimes the situation gets worse. Why is this? Because having a policy does not automatically equate to actions that lead to increased diversity and, even more important, a workplace that feels welcoming and inclusive. This requires a worldview shift at the bottom of the iceberg first presented in Chapter 4: What It Means to Be Worldview Intelligent. It also requires worldview alignments across the organization and probably the need to put additional supporting structures and practices in place. Most policies stop short of addressing these key foundational requirements.

Getting to policy development is not an easy or quick task, which is why creating a good policy is an achievement. While policy is a structure that influences behavior, in and of itself, it is not enough. It stops short of understanding the mental models that contribute to the current organizational culture and of understanding what it takes to support successful implementation of new policies.

A DEI policy can lead to worldview challenges and clashes. If unresolved this can activate passive and active resistance. There may be no "safe enough" place in the organization to have conversations concerning the challenges that arise in implementation and especially conversations that get to the heart of individual and collective responses to actual and perceived tectonic shifts in "the way things have always been". These elements of organizational culture are implicitly and explicitly understood by the people who work in the organization. Changes can challenge the known "world order", including individual and collective sense of identity.

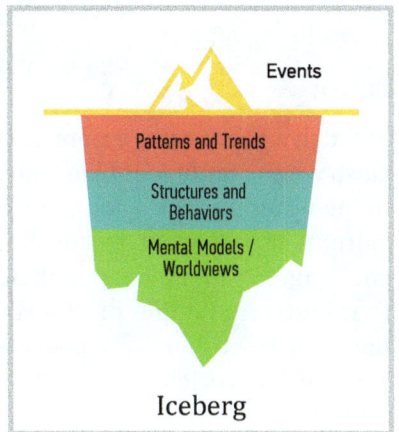

Iceberg

One area where we see this emerge is in how success is measured. If you come from a culture where individual achievement is celebrated, then that drives the structure of the measurement system. However, if you come from a culture where collective success – family, team, community – is valued above individual success, then that

WHAT IS NORMAL – MENTAL MODELS OF DISABILITIES

Western society holds a medical model worldview of people with disabilities. Their condition – the person – needs to be fixed or cured. It is something that people need to overcome. We need to make them normal. But what is normal?

Since the beginning of the Gulf War, soldiers have been coming home with a broad range of injuries that have created physical disabilities for them. Soldiers are often considered heroes by society, even if society still does not offer the best support for them, evidenced by a lack of services particularly related to mental health – a hidden disability.

However viewing soldiers who have become disabled because of wartime injuries as heroes is a different worldview than the medical model society holds for people who are either born with or have acquired a disability that is not wartime related. Perhaps this is a positive new narrative – that people with disabilities, whether soldiers or not, can be seen as strong contributors to our diverse society.

Why do we have different worldviews regarding disabilities? What is your worldview regarding these differing narratives? Would you be interested in helping society move to a more collective worldview where disability is part of the human condition and is as natural as gender, color, sexual orientation – as being human?

will drive the measurement system. These two worldviews can clash when employees from one culture find themselves working in the other one. As a company becomes more global and multicultural it will want to continue to reward achievement. The challenge is to develop policies or reward systems in ways that motivate people of differing cultural lenses and not favor one over the other. This may require a team or organization to explore its worldview on what success means and what that looks like in practice.

There are a whole host of areas where worldview or culture clashes can be found in the policy arena. Jerry recalls listening to a Native American woman, who was an executive in an energy company, describe how she resigned her position in order to grieve the death of her mother in the ways of her culture. The company offered her a few days off for the funeral while her traditional grieving time would be several weeks. The company was not interested in respecting her cultural request.

Because these kinds of conversations are either avoided or undervalued, there may not be enough people in the organization skilled in creating the opportunities or safe enough spaces for them. When making a significant policy change it is important to identify and include other structures or practices that need to shift or be implemented, and any new skills needed to support the success and longevity of the new policy.

WORLDVIEW INTELLIGENCE FRAMEWORK: ILLUMINATE BLIND SPOTS AND IDENTIFY KEY STRATEGIES FOR POLICY IMPLEMENTATION

The six dimensions of the Worldview Intelligence Framework provide a sound structure for illuminating blind spots, patterns and trends with respect to implementation of new policies and strategies in your organization. It can reveal barriers to implementation that can then provide you and your team with information key to developing approaches to successful implementation of new policies.

You might believe that since the policy is in place, your job is done, that everyone in the organization is committed to the new policy. But looking at the situation through the reality dimension you might discover this is not entirely true. If that is the case, then you could develop strategies to address the blind spot. You could look at measurement systems to see if they are measuring relevant information, ask better or different questions, develop the conversational skill sets to address blind spots and the things people don't want to do. This requires the creation of "safe enough" spaces for frank and honest conversations related to differing personal realities within the organization that invite curiosity and learning versus judgment.

Under history, you could explore if policies have been developed based on a particular worldview. You could look at how policy implementation has been dealt with in the past, especially policies that might have challenged worldviews in the organization. How have the questions the policy has been designed to address been addressed in the past? Is there an assumption that while issues from the past may remain, they can just be let go or dismissed – like they are no longer relevant? Looking at history enables you to identify patterns that might be lingering from historical events, decisions or situations. It helps you to recognize if healing may be necessary and to then take appropriate actions.

A look through the dimension of future may prompt questions like: How will policy changes challenge worldviews or identity in or across the organization? Do our employees know where the organization is headed? Do our employees see the new policies as contributing to a stronger and better future for the organization? Through this exploration, worldview and identity challenges can be identified so they can be addressed. Leaders can also ensure the story of the future the organization is moving towards is consistent and clear to those who work in the organization.

Values conflicts might be interfering with the implementation of a new policy or causing overt or covert resistance. Are personal and organizational values in enough alignment to go forward? Are similar or consistent personal beliefs or values held across the organization regarding new policies responding to changes in social attitudes and mores? To address this lack of coherence, values can be made explicit. This would include articulating what they look like in practice, the development of accountability mechanisms to bring values to life and the creation of safe enough spaces for frank, open, honest conversations related to possible conflicts between personal and organizational values or whatever else holds energy for people.

Do the practices of the organization support the new policy or the change effort? What rewards systems are in place and what are they rewarding? Are the practices influenced or shaped by the dominant social system? Are they readily adaptable to any social/cultural system? It might be helpful to check or test the practices (policies and procedures) against a global range of social/cultural systems that could be researched on the subject matter the policy is intended to address to determine the efficacy of the proposed policy. Answers to these and similar questions about practices can help identify any new practices that need to be encouraged (or old practices that need to be let go of) to support implementation of new policies. It will also be important to identify the skills required to develop powerful questions to encourage and support these conversations.

Finally, when it comes to knowledge, what is being measured and does this provide answers that are useful and helpful? Is qualitative evidence or measurement substantive enough? Talking to employees can be a way to measure success if done well and consistently. Identify the key things that will demonstrate the impact of the policies and implement both quantitative and qualitative measurements. Create safe enough spaces for frank, open conversations between executives, HR staff and the whole organization that invite curiosity and learning versus judgment. Then have the conversations needed to continue to advance policy implementation.

WORLDVIEW EXPLORATIONS ARE VIBRANT AND DYNAMIC

The intersection between the worldview dimensions can occur in many ways. The loss of a child can impact someone's daily experience as the memory of the child is ever present and certain events can be a painful reminder. A daily struggle to pay bills can leave a person pessimistic about the future. A desire to continue working in an economic sector that has employed generations of a family or community (mining, agriculture, fishing or forestry as examples) can cause a person to see few other options for future employment and perhaps contribute to resistance to career changes. A person may believe in fairness or equitable treatment for all co-workers regardless of gender, race or sexual orientation and yet the reality is that a glass ceiling exists that works against this goal. There could be a belief that success should be measured by the results of the entire team but the work environment is highly competitive where advancement is based solely on individual achievement and shared success is not rewarded.

As our workplaces, neighborhoods, schools and social lives expand, we encounter more and more diversity in life experiences and outlooks. These life experiences are usually multi-dimensional. Being able to work with the six dimensions interdependently and to explore their inter-relationship can help us discover the full richness of the people we work with, our neighbors and communities. It can take us to new and unexpected explorations and it can help us build trust and relationship as we discover new vibrancy in the people around us.

REFLECTION QUESTIONS

1. How does awareness of the interdependence of the framework dimensions open new possibilities for understanding policy implementation or change management issues you may be dealing with in your organization? What new paths forward might be possible now?

2. How might awareness of the multi-dimensionality of each of us open possibilities for deeper understanding of each other, how we might see a situation differently and how we could have more productive conversations?

SECTION 3
WORLDVIEW INTELLIGENCE, BRAIN AND BEHAVIORAL SCIENCE

CHAPTER 13:
BRAIN SCIENCE AND WORLDVIEWS: RATIONALE AND STRATEGIES FOR WORKING WITH FIGHT-FLIGHT-FREEZE RESPONSE

In 2011, I had the pleasure of being part of a hosting team in Brazil, working with a team of seasoned practitioners and new apprentices. As part of our hosting role in an Art of Hosting Training, we coach teams of participants to "practice" hosting the methods for engaging people and conversations. One of the apprentices was coaching a relatively new method that only that person and I on our team knew or had had any experience with at that time. As the coached team introduced the second stage of the method it was clear to me in the team's instruction to participants that they were not staying true to the guidelines of the method.

When I asked their coach what was going on, the coach realized they had given the wrong instruction and instead of acknowledging that, suggested that learning from mistakes was also good learning for the whole group. While I agree that learning from mistakes is also a rich and honorable learning field, the fact that the team was not, in my view, properly prepared – that they were essentially set up for failure – triggered me and clearly activated an amygdala hijack. I was angry enough to perhaps even be described as enraged, partly because of my sense that people had been set up for failure (contravening values of respect, fairness and responsibility) and partly because it left me with no choice but to step into fierce stewardship, to raise the issue with the whole group. I'm not a fan of confrontation like that and I didn't want to have the team that had stepped into the fire of hosting this process feel that their efforts were being dismissed or that they were wrong.

As participants continued in the method, which required a couple of hours to complete, I tried everything I knew to calm myself down, to regain my center. I took myself outside in nature. I took many deep breaths. I walked. I sat. Nothing brought me back to my center and when I went inside and saw how things were unfolding as my colleague was trying to rectify the situation without much success, it only fueled my anger.

The results of the small group conversations were reported out. The team that hosted the process and participants were asked for their reflections on the method and it was clear that the results were mixed – and more so than I had ever seen before.

With a significant tremble alive in me, I brought my voice and my views in the room of 60 or so people. I explained how the method was designed to work and why it was designed that way. It sparked quite an exchange (whisper translated for me from Portuguese to English) and eventually one of the participants, a mentee of my colleague, accused me of being arrogant, that I could not be sure the outcome would have been different. I responded by saying, "I don't mean to be arrogant, but I am not in my center right now and I know it." Tears streamed down my face as I spoke.

A few more people offered reflections. Some came to my defense, acknowledging that I had spoken in my role as a global steward so this group should pay attention. As the energy began to wind down, I realized the group needed something else. So, I told them, "My colleague and I, we need to have a conversation for sure, but we are okay, and we will be okay." With modest encouragement from the group we hugged each other. There was a collective sigh in the room. The tension and the circle broke. People came over to each of us and there were many more hugs to go around.

In the evening, participants were invited into our hosting team process as was our usual custom. More than half the participants showed up, curious to see how we would handle our relationships given what had transpired. They saw that we hosted each other in this space with empathy and compassion and were able to move on from a stable foundation.

It is rare that I lose my composure like that – particularly in a group I am hosting or facilitating. This is one of the reasons we say never host alone. Some people even think I never get angry which, of course, isn't true. There was a time I would have tried to contain that rush of emotion. However, having had a chance to be in deep learning on what my emotions are trying to tell me, I was learning *that emotions are not necessarily good or bad but we make value judgments concerning them. I knew that if I had tried to hide my responses, people would have sensed the lack of alignment within me; they would have known something was wrong whether I spoke it out loud or not. There would have been hidden dynamics in the team that fueled a tremor in the field.*

The reflections that people shared with me afterwards acknowledging my vulnerability, honesty, lack of defensiveness and allowing the tears and expression of my anger, made it clear that the incident was viewed with respect. It was considered role modeling in powerful and positive ways. It was an experience that will not be forgotten.

Kathy Jourdain

THE POWER IN UNDERSTANDING INVOLUNTARY REACTIONS

This book is obviously not a medical text. We cover the topics in this chapter in a cursory way. We hope to give you just enough information to help you understand your own reactions to stimuli and the reactions of people you relate with, to offer insights and strategies on how to improve communication, relationship and trust.

Understanding your own reactions to situations that impact you – people, art, music, language or even world events – gives you an opportunity to work with your responses in order to find new ways to approach challenging conversations that matter to you. Understanding what might be behind someone else's reactions offers the opportunity to be thoughtful and strategic in how to engage the conversation and the person in ways that advance the issue you are engaged in, your understanding of it or the relationship.

In Chapter 16: Building Trust and Relationship One-on-One, we offer a framework for engaging that challenging conversation. In this chapter we offer the opportunity for personal exploration around your reactions to events, circumstances or situations that trigger or activate your own emotional responses. These are responses you often realize are out of proportion to the situation or, even if they are not out of proportion, they get in the way of your ability to advance progress on the issue. This chapter focuses on brain science research and particularly the impact of the amygdala hijack. Chapter 14: Understanding Worldview and Identity Reactions through Behavioral Science will build on this with a look at some of the behavioral science research.

BRAIN FORMATION

The brain forms from the back to the front, from the most primitive part to the most sophisticated part. This means the action part of the brain forms first at the juncture with the spinal cord. This part of the brain takes care of automatic behaviors like breathing, blood circulation, digestion, elimination systems and growth. It operates in the background most of the time, but it dominates whenever we sense our safety is threatened or our survival is at stake.

An important component of the action part of the brain is the amygdala. It is in the brainstem and it controls automatic responses to situations we encounter. This means the fight, flight or freeze response is activated whenever the action part of our brains registers that we may be in danger. This automatic response is called amygdala hijack and it can be activated in <1/1000th of a second[63]. More on that momentarily.

The emotional part of the brain forms next. This is that part of the brain that allows us to feel and connects us to other people and the world around us. It plays a significant role in transferring information from short term to long-term memory.

Lastly, the thinking or logical part of the brain forms. This part of the brain is responsible for abstract thought. It is involved in our ability to conceptualize, reflect on and learn from our experiences. It is what allows us to create, to innovate and to imagine.

In most of recent society in North America, we have given prominence and preference to the logical brain, believing it to hold the capacity for rational decision making. Rationality and logic have been prized and prioritized over emotion in our

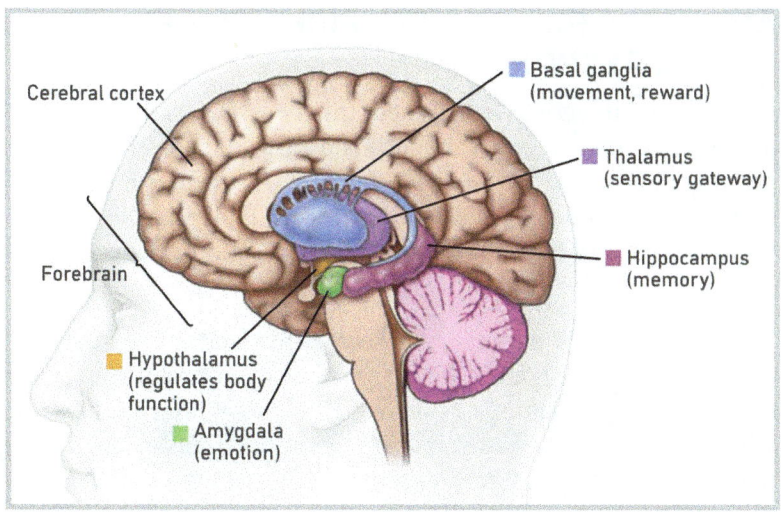

organizations and workplaces. In many organizations, employees have been discouraged from bringing their whole selves to work. Many people, overtly or covertly, are penalized for issues that might affect their work performance. In some workplaces, employees find it necessary to lie if they need a personal day, calling in sick rather than acknowledging the true need for their absence. Issues like burnout or the need to access employee assistance program (EAP) services may go unaddressed or unsupported. This is another aspect of building trust and relationship. What happens when members of your team are under enormous amounts of stress? Is there support or derision within the team? How might they be viewed or judged? Are there support mechanisms in place and, more than that, how are team members or employees treated if they access these services?

Interestingly, Antonio Damasio[64], a Portuguese-American neuroscientist began studying the decision-making capacity of individuals who received damage to the cerebral cortex, or the thinking part of the brain. What he discovered is that it is nearly impossible for these people to make decisions. They encountered too much information or data to sift through. This demonstrated how important the emotional brain is to the decision-making process. Almost all decisions draw on emotion or intuition without us being aware of it. It is not uncommon for decisions to be made based on "gut feelings" and then supported through logic or analysis.

AMYGDALA HIJACK – THE FIGHT-FLIGHT-FREEZE RESPONSE

When the amygdala is hijacked, this is as far away from logic and rationality as you can get. The amygdala (Latin, corpus amygdaloideum) is an almond-shaped set of neurons located deep in the brain's medial temporal lobe. It plays a key role in the processing of emotions, particularly in automatic reaction to stimuli.

The thalamus is a sensory gateway involved in sensory and motor signal relay and the regulation of consciousness and sleep. The hypothalamus regulates the body's internal balance, which is known as homeostasis. The hypothalamus is involved in many functions of the autonomic nervous system, as it receives information from nearly all parts of the nervous system. It is a slower acting system than the amygdala response.

When we encounter sensory data it is sent to the thalamus, the amygdala and the frontal cortex. The amygdala does an instantaneous threat assessment and, if it perceives a threat, it blocks the slower thinking processes. This causes a rapid, automatic, kinesthetic or bodily response that most people recognize in a number of different ways: more rapid breathing, flushed face, faster heart rate, a shock in the system and possible shaking in the body, and the inability to analyze are just some of the possible reactions.

This kind of response was necessary in the early days of human evolution. When life was filled with ever-present dangers, we didn't want to pause to be curious about whether that rustle in the nearby leaves was the breeze or actual danger. The amygdala hijack was central to survival. For most people today, even though there is no actual physical danger, this same response can kick in and it is less helpful and more problematic. This is why awareness of it and what happens when it happens to you is a useful Worldview Intelligence skill. This awareness can give you a strategic advantage in situations where emotions or passions are running high.

TYPES OF AMYGDALA HIJACK TRIGGERS

Also of note, amygdala responses can be as easily activated by small, almost trivial things as much as by the big ones. When was the last time you put your hand in your pocket to retrieve your phone or your keys and they weren't there? Was there a little adrenalin rush? This is a common experience. The quick fright response before the rational brain kicks in to tell you where else to look or give you the clue to where you last had your phone or your keys, plus the distraction until you find them, takes you out of being present.

Once we were in a meeting prior to Kathy catching a flight out of Fargo, North Dakota, to head home to Halifax, Nova Scotia. Her cell phone pinged and the visible part of the message was: "Your flight is now departing…" The amygdala hijack kicked in with a full body response including visibly shaking hands. The full message was: "Your flight is now departing from Gate 1 at 1:05 pm." That time was a few hours from this moment, a time we had scheduled our meeting around. Even after this message was absorbed, it took a while for the shaking to subside and her breathing to go back to normal, and this was a long way from a dangerous threat.

Another variation of a hijack response is the slow burn. This could be a small incident that happens, someone said something to you and it didn't register in the moment but as you reflect on it you begin to put new interpretations and nuances on it until you reach a boiling point. If you act on this delayed reaction it can completely catch the other person off guard. We often speak of the "itty-bitty-shitty committee" that sits on your shoulder and tells you how bad something was or what an awful mistake you made, playing the same message over and over again. This is another version of that kind of dialogue and you have an opportunity to turn it off sooner with awareness.

In Chapter 4: What It Means to Be Worldview Intelligent, we mentioned the Worldview Intelligence skills of curiosity and compassion. This is a good place to put them into practice on yourself and your thoughts. Why am I thinking this way? What is going on? Might there be another interpretation of the person's actions or words? Were they intentionally meaning to offend? If they were, what might be behind that? No matter what, unchecked thoughts that fuel emotions that cloud your ability to respond will not help you sort out useful solutions to the issues in front of you; so learning to change your thinking can be a valuable practice.

We have had the privilege of working with Native American youth in a Youth Build program in Leech Lake Nation, Minnesota. The youth in this program have already lived many challenging experiences and for many this program is a last lifeline. Life experiences for these young men and women include violence in the home, alcoholism, being in and out of detention facilities, living on the streets, sleeping in cars or couch surfing and teenage parenthood. In this program they prepare for their high school equivalency certification or GED, learn a skill like carpentry and are exposed to additional life skills. The first year we worked with the youth, there was a young man in his early twenties who was working hard to turn his life around. He had isolated himself from many of his friends and other influences on his life he wanted to shift away from. When we shared information on the amygdala hijack and the triggers exercise he commented on how profound this information was for him. He said, "My emotions spoke louder to me than I could speak to myself." Realizing this also helped him shift from harsh self-judgment to an awareness that he could develop the ability to manage his emotions.

GAS AND BRAKE PEDALS

If the amygdala is like the gas pedal, the hypothalamus is like the brake pedal. When the amygdala hijack happens, it is like pressing the gas pedal all the way to the floor, going from 0 to 100 in no time. There is growing evidence that this is what happens to some people suffering from PTSD. Their amygdala is easily and quickly hijacked. They can go from calm to angry in a fraction of a second. By the time the hypothalamus catches up, the fight-flight-freeze response is already in full motion action and it takes longer for the brake to be applied and for the thinking brain to catch up. People suffering from PTSD have an especially difficult time applying the brakes once hijacked.

NEURAL PATHWAYS

Information travels through the neurons or nerve cells of the brain, creating what are called neural pathways. A lot of the programming in the body is "hard wired" into us before we are even born. Each time we travel down a neural pathway through a pattern or habit, specific neural pathways are strengthened. Each time a belief or strongly held opinion is reinforced, a neural pathway is strengthened and deepened. It becomes like a rut in well-travelled roads where the tires of the car follow the rut in the road. Moving to a different part of the road can feel risky in addition to requiring intentional decision and focused movement. The flip side or opportunity is that every time we experience something new and different we also begin to create new neural pathways. Even if this initially happens by happenstance, we can also be intentional in reinforcing these new neural pathways. While it is often said to take 21 consecutive days of consistent effort to change a habit or develop new ones, thanks to the work of Maxwell Maltz and his 1960 book, Psycho-Cybernetics, newer research from a 2009 study suggests it is more like two months[65]. If the new neural pathway is to deepen, it needs to be reinforced so patience may be required.

If your tendency is to defend your worldview, and it is the human tendency, then every time you argue in support of the way you already think, you impact your brain by deepening these specific neural pathways. The more you do this, the harder it is to change your thinking.

When a circuit is activated, the synapses get stronger. If that circuit inhibits another circuit, like a competing belief or habit, that circuit gets weaker. Repetition strengthens synapses. It doesn't matter if what is repeated is true or not, a threat or opportunity or not. The brain doesn't know the difference between what is real and what is imagined. This is why visualization of goals works so well for many people. Remember the athlete before they begin their run or their routine. They go internal to visualize what they are going to do. The difference between gold, silver and bronze in many elite competitive sports is often miniscule in terms of time or score. What makes the difference is not necessarily the physical training, it is the visualization.

When someone experiences constant or continuous amygdala hijacks due to actual or perceived threats in their environment, the amygdala gets bigger. When this happens, the hypothalamus becomes smaller. This means the amygdala can go into overdrive with little counteracting balance from the hypothalamus. This is a dynamic present in early childhood trauma and other forms of trauma like PTSD, both of which are beyond the scope of this book and the work of Worldview Intelligence. If you are interested, there are dedicated bodies of knowledge and resources like the work done in the Adverse Childhood Experiences Study (ACES) on childhood trauma.[66]

For the purposes of Worldview Intelligence, for those who have what might be considered "normal" exposures to amygdala hijack, there is an opportunity to become aware of these responses and develop strategies to deal with them. This awareness does two things. One is, it helps you understand what events, situations, people or behaviors activate your own fight-flight-freeze responses. As you grow your awareness of this you are better prepared to observe rather than fully engage in your own response. Second, if you can step out of your responses to be more present to the situations that typically activate you, you can then respond in a manner more consistent with how you prefer to respond rather than this automatically activated response. You can train yourself to reduce the amygdala reaction and tune into the wisdom available when the hypothalamus kicks in.

TRIGGERS OR ACTIVATION POINTS

The amygdala response can be activated when you are triggered by an event, situation or other person. Triggers can be certain people or situations that cause you to react quickly, without thinking, and in ways you may regret later. There are people you know who can activate the amygdala response simply when their name appears on your phone or email. The response is visceral and can be in full swing before you even answer the call or look at the message. This provides an excellent practice ground for deciding how you prefer to respond and to develop a trigger response plan you can put into action every time it happens. It is easy for us to write about this, it is a lot harder to do, which is why it is a practice. The good news is, as you do this for any one person or situation, you grow your capacity to apply it in a variety of situations.

Kathy often speaks of a challenging person in her life who has been known to trigger a response the second their name appeared on her phone or in email. The responses ranged from mild to dramatic which could include uncontrollable physical shaking. This is due to a traumatic history. In the past this was someone she needed to stay in some form of relationship with over a period of years for a variety of reasons, otherwise she would have stepped away completely. Over time, she trained herself in her response. When the email came in she would wait a bit to open it. Once opened, she would read it and then put it away. She would decide if it required a response. If it did, she waited at least a day and maybe more. There is nothing that says we need to respond immediately to a situation that triggers us.

She would re-read the email more clearly a second time, realizing where she may have read things the first time around that weren't there or weren't as bad as her initial response. Then she would respond only to any essential part that needed a response and leave the rest go, no matter how challenging that was. Over a period of time, she learned to manage even her initial reactions, but it took intentional practice and a strong desire to shift that particular amygdala response. Despite this practice, it doesn't mean it always works.

In Chapter 2: Worldviews, How They are Formed and Why it Matters we described how when your worldview is challenged you may react as if your mortality is threatened.[67] When you are in this response, in addition to the amygdala hijack, chemical and hormonal responses are also activated. The thirty or forty hormonal and hundreds of chemical changes include a reduction in IgA (immune system hormone) and DHEA (anti-aging hormone) and an increase in Cortisol (nicknamed the stress hormone). Research at the Heartmath Institute based in Boulder Creek, Colorado, has shown that these physical impacts can linger for as long as twelve hours.[68] Even more distressing, they can be reactivated and reinforced just by remembering the situation that caused the triggered reaction, if you step fully back into the emotional reactions. The good news is, that in learning to mitigate your amygdala response, you can also neutralize and reverse these chemical and hormonal changes. So, if learning to be your best and most Worldview Intelligent self was not incentive enough to change your own behaviors, maybe understanding that you improve your health and decrease the aging process as well as improve your ability to think might be added incentive.

TRIGGERS – AND EMOTIONS – AS A GUIDANCE SYSTEM

Triggers can be a guidance system that you can learn to work with. This does not mean being emotionless or hiding your emotional responses. We all have emotional reactions. Pretending you don't gets in the way of building trust, because people see or sense that something is up. This creates distrust. Emotional maturity means you are able to access your own emotions and, for ones that might be volatile like anger or rage, frustration or feeling like you've been betrayed, learning first to acknowledge them and then express them in healthy ways will role model for your team helpful ways to express experiences and reactions. Naming your response rather than lashing out at someone or something that provoked your response is a useful strategy. As we mentioned in Chapter 5: Introducing the Worldview Intelligence Six Dimensions Framework, when your actions are out of alignment with your worldview and your experiences, it is communicated in so many ways in addition to the words you use.

REFLECTION QUESTIONS

1. Think of a time you were triggered and reflect on what happened. What was the situation? How did you react? What happened in your body or what was your physical reaction when this happened? What thoughts went through

your mind during this time? Were you in a fight, flight or freeze response? How did this reaction influence your communication or relationship?

2. What practices do you have, or could you develop, that would bring your physical responses back to a "normal for you" baseline, like conscious breathing, tapping your body with your hands, closing your eyes? What are thoughts you could deliberately choose to bring your mind back into presence?

CHAPTER 14:
UNDERSTANDING WORLDVIEW AND IDENTITY REACTIONS THROUGH BEHAVIORAL SCIENCE

For 500 years or so, the fishing industry had largely shaped the lives and communities of Canada's Atlantic coast. Much of the economy of the four Atlantic Provinces (Newfoundland, Prince Edward Island, New Brunswick and Nova Scotia), especially in small towns and villages, depended on the fishery. Not only did it shape the identity of individuals and families for generations but fishing, fishing boats, fish factories were the fabric of these communities. They celebrated good catches together and mourned tragedies together, such as loss of boats and their crews in fishing accidents and lost to the sea in storms that ravage the ocean from time to time.

In 1992 the Canadian Government declared a moratorium on the Northern Cod fishery due to a dramatic decline in cod stocks. This had an immediate and devastating impact on the communities in Atlantic Canada and on the lives of individuals and families that depended on this way of life. When the federal government announced retraining initiatives for fishermen and their families, the fishermen said, "I don't want retraining. I want to fish." On the surface, this seems ungrateful, irresponsible and unrealistic given there was no indication of when or whether the fishing stocks would rebound. Understanding it now from a Worldview Intelligence perspective, if I've been a fisherman all my life, my father and his brothers were fishermen, my grandfather was a fisherman, the fishing boats and fishing licenses were passed from one generation to the next; my grandmother, my mother, my aunt all worked in the fish processing factory, then my whole identity and that of my family and my community is intertwined with fishing. My history, reality and anticipations concerning the future are significantly defined by fishing. Knowing that, might we find a different way into that conversation? Might we have more compassion for people we label as resistant to change? Might we find another way to engage that relationship and even build trust?

Not every coastal town has survived or is surviving. Those that are, have expanded their worldview about who they are and what opportunities exist. Some are thriving tourist towns now. There continues to be a dynamic tension in these communities on whether the future can be an extension of the past or if it needs to be dramatically different. People long for a quality and way of life they feel is threatened.

Substitute farmer and farming family and community or miner and mining family or community for fisherman, fishing family and community, and you can see how this dynamic plays itself out all over the world. This is identity rooted in history, a way of life or reality, anticipation of the future and values and practices passed from one generation to the next.

Kathy Jourdain

IDENTITY AND WORLDVIEWS

As we described in Chapter 2: Worldviews, How They are Formed and Why it Matters, worldviews are closely linked to identity. Psychological research tells us that when our personal identity is threatened, we respond as if our life has been threatened.[69] This is why sometimes a person's reaction to something you said seems out of proportion to what was said, or maybe it was a reaction you had that logically you knew was out of proportion to the situation, but you couldn't prevent the response.

The more we work with worldviews, the more we see how the behavioral and brain science research (referenced in the previous chapter) provides explanations for why we are so attached to our worldviews. When we know this, we can offer Worldview Intelligence strategies and skills for addressing situations where worldviews, or how attached we are to them, contribute to the challenges at hand or stuck issues. We can then find ways to create exploratory space to make progress on these issues. As a leader, you can examine your own attempts to build trust and relationship and evaluate your strategies for success, failure and new opportunities. The information on cognitive and behavioral science research may provide you with new insights to employ in your Building Trust and Relationship at the Speed of Change strategies.

This research also helps us understand why certain conversations are becoming more fragmented and more polarized to the point that we are often asked some version of this question: How do I have a conversation with my neighbor or family member or coworker who has a different worldview than I do? Most commonly the focus is on social or political views on topics like same sex marriage, gender identity, abortion, euthanasia, immigration, race or a specific political candidate.

COGNITIVE AND BEHAVIORAL SCIENCE RESEARCH

Cognitive and behavioral science research tells us that reason is not rational without emotion. For many people this will seem counterintuitive, especially in a society and workplaces that have emphasized the value of logic and rationality. As human beings our relationship to facts is interesting. According to one definition, facts are specific, observable and verifiable. Any two or more people looking at the same thing should be able to name the same set of facts. This is where it becomes challenging as we shared in Chapter 2, because our worldviews influence what we see and interpret as fact. Interpretation of facts can become even more varied and challenging to discuss when we bring our values into play and frame facts from that interpretive lens.

How often in your conversations, do you say something like, "The fact is...." But is it really a fact or is it more likely an opinion, a belief or your experience? When you refer to something as a fact or as fact, do you mean that you think or believe it is true or correct? It may not be. It may be an interpretation of an experience. It may be a belief or a firmly held conviction on something – so firmly held, you believe it to be true. Most arguments are not won or lost based on facts. Persuasion is more likely based on passion or conviction, substantiated or not.

It can be a frustrating experience when you attempt to convince someone of your point of view with the facts you have at your disposal, only to have the other person dismiss your facts or counter with their own, often different and sometimes opposite, facts. Reflect on a time you changed your mind about something that was important to you. Did you change your mind based on facts first or based on something else, like the opinion or view of someone you respect? How long did it take? How quickly are you expecting or hoping someone else will change their mind regarding a position they hold? Our expectations of how quickly someone else could or should shift their opinion, view or belief may be completely unreasonable.

FACT AND TRUTH(S)

We often equivocate between fact and truth. There are very few, if any, truths that are universally held (outside of a few scientific truths like gravity) as we explored in Chapter 6: Reality. What is true for you may not be true for someone else. Facts are knowledge or information based on actual occurrences that can be verified. However, the interpretation of facts can vary significantly. Jerry has a graduate degree in economics. Setting aside economist jokes, it is a common occurrence in the profession for economists to have the same set of facts or data and interpret them differently. A good example is rate increases for consumers of electricity. One economist may argue that the data indicates a need for an increase of some amount and another may argue that the data does not support an increase or a much lower increase is warranted.

Facts also get confused with opinions. Opinions are a view or judgment formed on something that is not necessarily based on fact or knowledge but is a personal view, attitude or appraisal. Opinions, like beliefs strongly held, can feel like facts to us. We hold opinions so strongly that we are often unwilling to shift from them. Your opinions, like your worldview, begin to form before you are even aware of it. You may or may not question some opinions you hear or absorb early on. Your experiences inform your opinions, again like your worldviews. Once you state your opinions, you may be asked to explain them. As you explain them you can discern how attached you are to them, unless you are engaged in a debate, in which case you may find yourself looking for reasons or explanations to support your opinions and thus become more attached to them. As we shared in the previous chapter on brain science, every time you argue a specific point, you change and deepen those neural pathways in your brain, creating super highways along which the information travels faster and faster.

Your opinions are often reinforced by people around you who think like you, who view the world like you; essentially your reference group or groups. It is these reinforced opinions that are likely to get you into those deeply polarizing conversations.

When you consider your team, while there may be many shared views or opinions, how often are there discussions of facts that create debates when the facts in question may more likely be interpretations of facts or experiences?

HUMAN BEHAVIOR/DYNAMICS

Behavioral science research goes a long way toward explaining the human behaviors and dynamics we regularly see and experience, many of which are also typical worldview responses or reactions when worldviews are challenged. Understanding this can be quite influential in developing a strategic advantage when it comes to planning communication and in building trust and relationship.

As human beings we are constantly making decisions at lightning fast speeds, mostly without conscious awareness that this is even happening.

As we offered in Chapter 2, where we first shared the Ladder of Inference, from the time you see something, interpret it, make conclusions about it, and decide which action to take, less than 13 milliseconds, or .013 seconds, will have passed. That is faster than you can blink your eyes. It is less time than it takes you to read this paragraph. This also supports why and how the amygdala hijack response, described in the last chapter, happens with such speed.

Your eyes are finding concepts and your brain is trying to understand them all day long. Even after the image has disappeared, the concepts may linger for processing in your brain, adding

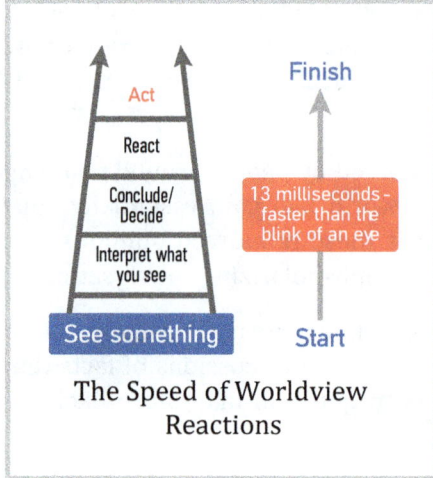

The Speed of Worldview Reactions

more interpretation, reinforcing your belief systems about people, ideas and situations.

This rapid processing helps keep you safe, much like the amygdala hijack is intended to do. In this case, it enables you to recognize complex patterns so you know instantly who familiar people, places and/or situations are and it enables you to develop habits to move through your days quicker. It also gets you in trouble when your interpretation, conclusions and reactions are wrong.

While this particular information came from a study done at MIT,[70] much of the research on how fast your brain processes information is funded by marketing companies and political parties that want to ensure their messages influence you, your thoughts, beliefs and actions in a particular direction, before you have a chance to think. They don't have enough time to intervene in your reaction so, if they have a good idea of your worldview or starting point, they can present you with information that fits within your worldview, knowing how quickly you will pay attention and react to it.

CAMBRIDGE ANALYTICA

Understanding how we process information was the opportunity that Cambridge Analytica capitalized on before, during and after the 2016 US election and in the lead up to and post the Brexit vote, also in 2016. Targeting people through their social media habits by segmenting specific messages to individuals, Cambridge Analytica used its knowledge of how messaging to the brain works and how behavioral science shows how we seek to confirm our views. They manipulated massive amounts of information using algorithms they created to see what links people clicked on. Then they showed people similar articles and posts to keep reinforcing their views. In this process, Cambridge Analytica became more and more targeted in their approach. Much like niche marketing, select groups of people received specific, targeted social media feeds, almost to the exclusion of anything else. There was no balanced perspective on any issue, only the perspective that grew people's attachments to the way they were already thinking.

In this way, groups of people would have no crossover in news feeds or articles with other groups of people. If I am only seeing one stream of thinking and you are only seeing another stream of thinking, there is no middle ground, no infusion of competing ideas that might link us together or catalyze creative thinking. Then we wonder how people have such dramatically different views. "How could they possibly think the way they do?", we wonder. It doesn't make sense to us because it doesn't link to any of the information we have been receiving or any of the views we have formed.

Worldview Intelligence provides the opportunity to short-circuit this kind of unconscious messaging. Suggestions on how to do this are offered in this chapter and the next. Worldview Intelligence gives you the awareness, knowledge and skills to press the pause button, to be curious about your interpretations so you can act more mindfully, intentionally, skillfully and strategically. It provides ideas on how to do this with your team so you can build an environment of curiosity that invites questions and explorations, regularly seeking to broaden sources of information and access the most diverse views available within your team and beyond.

BEHAVIORAL SCIENCE – HOW BEHAVIORS AND ACTIONS ARE INFLUENCED

There are a host of behaviors that science has identified and described. We focus on a few that have been most helpful in the

Worldview Intelligence work in understanding typical human behaviors and providing strategies and tactics to broaden perspectives.

NAÏVE REALISM

This starts with the idea that we are not aware of, do not understand or accept our own biases. As human beings we tend to have a built-in bias that we are not biased – naïve realism. This makes us believe our own view is reasonable, even if it isn't, while it causes us to be more likely to dismiss other people's views as we name other people as having biases. We might miss the opportunity to be curious about our own biases. Knowing this, however, means you can continually ask yourself what implicit biases you may be bringing to your understanding of any situation. This may invite you to ask yourself the question from the Worldview Intelligence dimension of Knowledge: how do I know what I know and how do I know if this is true or false?

CONFIRMATION BIAS

When you scroll through your social media feed, what stories or links do you click on and what ones do you move past? We have a voracious need to continually confirm our own point of view by looking at and for information, data and facts, perspectives, opinions and beliefs that support our worldviews, otherwise known as confirmation bias. Your worldview will deliberately and unconsciously filter out information that does not support your view and allow in information that does support your views. The more you see, experience and hear something, the more you believe it, even if it is not true. If you only click on the things that support your worldview, as we discussed in Chapter 11: Knowledge, you may not be able to discover how or why someone with completely different views sees the world the way they do.

A quick antidote to this is to develop a practice of deliberately seeking out views that are different from your own, stopping yourself from sliding on by that disconfirming headline and take a few minutes a day to read something that offers you the opportunity to expand your awareness of other's worldviews. When you don't stop to try to understand how another person may have come to see and experience the world the way they have, it is not just easy to dismiss their views, but it becomes easier to dismiss the person as an illogical, irrational human being.

MOTIVATED REASONING

If confirmation bias is consciously or unconsciously confirming and reconfirming your current views, motivated reasoning goes to a much more active level of commitment and recommitment. Once you have decided something, anything, you have an unconscious tendency to process information in a way that supports and validates that decision. Your unconscious motivations, desires and fears shape the way you interpret information. Decisions, whether they concern where you live, something you purchased, who you are in relationship with, or where you work become associated with your sense of identity. One of the reasons political parties want you to give them money, even small amounts, is because that donation represents a commitment. The more you confirm and reconfirm your sense of identity or commitment, the more attached you become to your decision or your point of view and the more important it becomes to resist information that threatens your sense of identity. You become even more motivated to support your decisions.

An excellent example of motivated reasoning is a story from 19th Century France. Officers in the French military discovered that someone was selling military secrets to the Germans. They quickly decided, after a cursory investigation, that the culprit was Capt. Alfred Dreyfus. They made this decision despite the fact he had a sterling record and no history of wrongdoing, no motive as far as they could see. He was the only Jewish officer at that rank in the army and, at that time, the French army was highly anti-Semitic. Although they continued to look for evidence to support their suspicions, when they didn't find any evidence, they did not conclude his innocence. Because they had already determined his guilt, they were motivated to support that decision. So much so that they determined he was that good a spy that he left no evidence and they convicted him anyway. How do you counter an argument like this? This is what motivated reasoning looks like: conviction in the rightness of your belief or view even when it is not supported by the information or data, even when there is evidence to the contrary.

Eventually Dreyfus' case was taken on by Colonel Picquart who, unwillingly at first, began to see that the facts did not add up, including the fact that the Germans still seemed to be receiving sensitive information concerning the French military. Fascinatingly, when he took on Dreyfus' case, he became the target of derision among his fellow officers who were still highly motivated to continue to support the decision that had been made and their investment in it. Yet, Picquart stuck to his mission, despite serving time in jail for disloyalty to the army over this cause and was eventually able to get Dreyfus exonerated, more than a decade later. This is what attachment to worldviews looks like.

This may seem like an extreme example, yet we can't help but wonder how many innocent people are sitting in jails because someone had decided they were guilty and was unwilling to stay in curiosity and exploration until the conclusion matched the facts.

Here, the antidote is to continue to pay attention and be willing to question your own assumptions and biases, to entertain the disconfirming facts that come to your attention rather than dismiss them out of hand.

COGNITIVE DISSONANCE

One reason disconfirming facts are dismissed out of hand has to do with cognitive dissonance. When you hold a core belief that is strong, when you are presented with evidence that works against that belief, the new evidence cannot be accepted. It creates a feeling that is extremely uncomfortable, and this is called cognitive dissonance. Because, as human beings, it is important to protect our core beliefs, which contribute to our sense of identity, we will rationalize, ignore and deny that which does not fit with the core belief.

This dissonance is especially painful when conflict arises between your view of yourself and information that disputes that view. By dismissing the new or contradictory information, this response to cognitive dissonance enables you to stay committed to your sense of self, beliefs and to your worldview. But that can be a disservice to yourself if a different or expanded belief system or worldview would offer you better ways to navigate the world around you.

Another way this does a disservice is when it comes to the multiplicity of worldviews. When we are challenged by a worldview that is different than our own, the preference is to dismiss the other worldview to calm the dissonance it creates. One unintentional impact of that is that it also dismisses and invalidates the experience or identity of the person who holds or conveys that worldview. The ability to hold opposing views at the same time is a Worldview Intelligence skill. To be able to ask questions that look for connecting points or alignment of those views is also a skill. To create the opportunity for those opposing views to meet each other in an exploratory space could take everyone to unexpected places that may offer a richness of learning and insight that grows everyone involved in the encounter.

In your own personal development, having an awareness of when you are in cognitive dissonance and learning to intentionally hold open that space is a solid Worldview Intelligence leadership practice. It is a practice you can bring as an invitation to your team. This invitation can appear as a diversity of ideas and, almost more importantly, it creates the space for your team members to bring the fullness of their own worldviews, with their unique realities, histories, futures, values, practices and knowledge to your team discussions. Imagine how much richer your conversations can be when infused with the wisdom and experience of each person on the team.

In a client meeting with United Way Halifax, as the organization was digesting a report on Poverty Solutions created as a result of deliberate and authentic community engagement, the organization was now trying to discover how best to incorporate the findings into the fabric of the organization. A young woman who had only been employed at United Way for a month was staying quiet. Her background was with a grass roots organization that received funding from United Way. When the team lead asked her opinion or view, she was hesitant in her response, but finally she said, "If it was me, I would do something radical."

Now, radical for the organization she was with previously and radical for United Way does not necessarily look the same. However, that word energized the room and changed the nature of the conversation. If she hadn't been invited to speak up, this opportunity would not have existed.

LOSS AVERSION

When we describe the term, Loss Aversion, there is always an immediate resonance with our clients. It comes from Ron Heifetz, author of *Leadership Without Easy Answers*,[71] who notes that change is mainly about the management of loss. When change is happening so quickly in our organizations or the larger environment, we get a sense of the magnitude of this. If you, as team leader, are focused on continually moving into a new and exciting or anxiety inducing future, what does this mean for your team's emotional response or for the organization as a whole? Maintaining trust in fast moving circumstances is a skill and strategy unto itself.

Loss aversion says we are usually more fearful of losing something than we are excited to gain something that may be better or greater. Your promises about a future I don't know don't hold as much persuasion as the reality I do know where there is a predictability that gives me stability, even when that predictability or known reality is uncomfortable. Some people call it the comfort zone, but we call it the familiar zone since it is not always comfortable. Think about people you know, maybe even yourself, who stay in jobs or relationships long past their "best before" dates, because the familiar is known and the future cannot be predicted, or at least it feels that way. Since reality is one dimension of worldview, the way you currently live your day-today experience has a strong hold. Considering a different future evokes lots of questions that you may not want to entertain: Will I fit there? Will I know how to act? Will I have the skills needed to fulfill the responsibilities required of me? Will I be alone for the rest of my life?

As a leader operating in environments or circumstances of rapid or ongoing change, you are likely out ahead of what we call the change curve. What are your strategies to make sure your team feels supported? This is a good time to understand what the risks and rewards of both success and failure are to ensure the supports in place don't work against the culture and environment you are trying to create, remembering the iceberg in Chapter 4: What It Means to be Worldview Intelligent.

Providing team members with opportunities to express what they are experiencing and feeling or are concerned about goes a long way to building trust. It can sometimes be difficult for people to express themselves because their concerns feel silly, illogical or inconsequential. This includes things like office changes, title changes and different roles or responsibilities. Creating safe enough spaces for the expression of these concerns is key. If they go unexpressed, they don't go away. They become buried and reappear as hidden dynamics. Leaders can be reluctant to create these opportunities because they just want to get on with the change or they fear that allowing the expression of these kinds of concerns will sink or slow down the change effort. However, what you resist, persists.

SUNK COSTS

Have you ever approached the check-out counters in a store, looked them over to decide which was moving the quickest and then went to that line only to see the one next to you moves more quickly? Did you change lines? Most people don't. Once we analyse a situation and make a decision with respect to it, we tend to stick with that decision. The analysis becomes a sunk cost or investment, and we stick with our investment. Other examples include a relationship you have invested a lot of time in that is no longer healthy; a job that no longer brings satisfaction; a project that continues despite becoming clear it might not offer the solution that was anticipated.

The Canadian Federal Government's implementation of the Phoenix Pay System is a good example of sunk costs. The new system was launched in 2016 and immediately resulted in issues. Federal government employees were either not paid, over paid or not paid the proper amount. They tried to fix the system which, according to news reports, was under resourced during implementation but the issues continued for years. The Government had sunk a lot of investment into this failed system and was trying to fix it, requiring more investment rather than admitting the failure and moving on quickly.

The idea of sunk costs also holds true for worldviews. Once we make a decision based on conscious or unconscious analysis, it becomes part of our identity and we stick with it, even if contradictory information shows up.

THE LAW OF GROUP POLARIZATION

Periodically, throughout this book, we mention reference groups. This is an important concept because we each have reference groups and our reference groups tend to contain people with similar social or economic status, age, color, spiritual beliefs, culture and similar or aligned worldviews. Our reference groups support our experiences and our points of view, validating us and the way we think or act. They confirm our hopes and our fears.

When you are constantly around people like you, who have the same or similar worldview as you, you can become more extreme in your views. Consider an animated discussion you've had with a group of people who think like you on a given topic, whether religion, politics, human rights, or sports teams. The conversation often becomes more animated and vibrant as people agree with each other and views expressed may become more extreme than you might normally consider in mixed groups. If you do have a different view, it may become harder to bring your voice in and if you do, you can be drowned out by the increasing voracity of the discussion. When this happens, when our views become more extreme thanks to the groups we associate with and the neural pathways mentioned in the previous chapter are reinforced, we become less empathetic or understanding of people who see things differently. This can happen in mild to extreme forms.

A milder version might be a generational clash as we often see between Baby Boomers and younger generations. Each categorizes the other generation in particular ways and then becomes dismissive of what they deem to be certain characteristics of that generation. The use of technology and assumptions regarding what that means or doesn't mean, often related to beliefs on the implications for personal connection is one example. There is a widely held perception that the use of social media and smart phones by younger generations means they do not have true relationships with people or don't know how to communicate face-to-face. At a restaurant it can be common for some generations to look at younger generations on their phones while sitting at a table together and make a judgment about the behavior. However, reading the newspaper or a printed book, which could essentially be the same kind of behavior using a different medium, gets a pass. This kind of assumption or judgment rarely leads to violent clashes, but it does create challenges in communications and, even more so, in the workforce where values, practices and ideas on how to get work done or in considering the future can be different.

More extreme versions of group polarization include trends toward Nativism* or White Supremacy on one end and groups like Antifa♦ at the other extreme. Members of these reference groups, in communication with each other, embolden their ideas and receive encouragement from some visible political leaders in many different countries. They are dehumanizing the subjects of their vitriol whether people of color, immigrants, refugees

---

* Nativism is the protection of the interests of native-born or established inhabitants against those of immigrants.

♦ Antifa is a political protest movement of autonomous groups affiliated by their militant opposition to fascism and other forms of extreme right-wing ideology

or business owners. Their ideas become more fully entrenched and it is harder and harder, though not impossible, to open exploratory space with them. It may be somewhat easier on a one to one basis than group to group.

We have certainly seen examples of where individuals or groups have opened exploratory space. One of the most well-known examples is the discussions in Boston hosted by the Public Conversations Project between Pro-choice and Pro-life groups that happened several years ago. Personal views weren't changed but understanding and relationship were built.

A key first step is to build relationship with another person with differing views. It is much easier to be in dialogue on difficult issues when the starting point is relationship. It takes focused, intentional skill, curiosity, compassion and humility to do this. You have to care enough, and it has to be important enough to you, for you to try. In the next chapter we offer strategies for doing this. As noted before, one of Jerry's close friends is someone with different political views. Over the years they have built relationship and trust, which allows them to work, travel and speak of their different political and social views.

Back to the more mundane or milder forms of group polarization. With your team, one thing to watch for is the nature of the dialogues concerning other people, other parts of the organization, other organizations or community. If the conversation is only negative with respect to another group, if it is dismissive in any way, this may point to blind spots within your team. It is hard to be in healthy relationship when this happens and almost impossible to have productive collaborations or partnerships. It is your responsibility as a leader to monitor any predilection you may have towards this. As pointed out in Chapter 5: Introducing the Worldview Intelligence Framework, your actions will convey more to your team about what is and is not acceptable practice than anything you say to them. You may also want to have a collective practice with your team of shining the light on any of the team's tendencies so you can continue to engage in conversations and practices that change outcomes and advance goals and objectives.

ILLUSORY CORRELATION

There are many misperceptions that abound and illusory correlation helps to remind us to distinguish between fact, opinion and perception. Many people think there is a disproportionately high percentage of black-on-black crime, compared to say, white-on-white crime. However, white-on-white crime is almost never talked about as a thing, while black-on-black crime is discussed or referenced often, particularly when there has been an act of violence against black or brown people. A look at crime statistics shows there is virtually no percentage difference between black-on-black and white-on-white crime. So, within a small group and a larger group, if negative behavior is the same percentage in the two groups, the larger group tends to believe the smaller group has more of the negative behavior and this is illusory correlation.

Another example is alcohol consumption and alcoholism among Native populations. It is widely believed that Native Americans and First Nations people have serious alcohol issues, much more so than the white populations they are compared with. However, this is also an illusory correlation. In 2016, researchers from the University of Arizona used nationwide survey data to compare the drinking habits of more than 4,000 Native Americans to 170,000 white people. They found that around 60 percent of Native Americans do not drink at all, compared to 43 percent of whites. Native Americans were also more likely than whites to be "light/moderately-only" drinkers. Both groups showed similar binge drinking habits, with around 17 percent of each population reporting to have consumed five or more drinks one-to-four times over the previous month. The study helps to shatter the notion that Native Americans are genetically more susceptible to alcoholism than other groups.[72]

TEAM PRACTICES

Looking to cognitive and behavioral science research on typical human patterns and dynamics is revealing. You can likely see now how it is connected to worldviews. Simply having an awareness of these typical responses can be enough to allow you and your team to question some of your own automatic responses. As a leader and with your team, you may want to incorporate some simple practices of inquiry, especially when any of you notices any of these behaviors or dynamics clicking in, individually or collectively.

REFLECTION QUESTIONS

1. Consider a time you changed your mind about something. What was it that changed your mind? An opinion, fact or belief? How long did it take?

2. Of the different concepts offered in this chapter, which ones have you and your team experienced? In what ways?

3. What practices can you and your team adopt to stay mindful concerning the impact of human behavior on your discussions, beliefs and actions?

SECTION 4
BUILDING TRUST AND RELATIONSHIP: APPLICATION ONE-ON-ONE AND IN TEAMS

CHAPTER 15:
WORLDVIEW INTELLIGENCE THEORY OF CHANGE PLANNING MODEL

After delivering the first one-day Worldview Intelligence Program in Halifax, we realized that one day was not enough. A few months later, we held the second program in Minneapolis, and we offered it over two days. The mix of participants was quite diverse. During the morning of the second day Kathy inadvertently said something that upset a number of the participants who were women of color.

We recognized this as a critical moment for us and for how Worldview Intelligence would develop going forward. Together with our colleague Dave Ellis, we met over lunch to determine the best way forward. Since Kathy was linked to the clash of worldviews, it was determined that someone other than her should begin the afternoon – which is one of the reasons we advise against hosting alone.

It was agreed that Jerry would open the afternoon by acknowledging the clash that emerged in the morning and suggesting we approach discussing what happened through a worldview lens. This moved the conversation from one that could have become quite personal to one of exploring how we each see and experience the world and how that might influence ways we speak and interpret what is said. The conversation moved from possible recrimination to learning and personal growth for those who do not experience the discrimination and racism that the women of color do. For many participants, this was a worldview expansion moment.

When we did a check-out at the closing of that day, one participant remarked that they had arrived the day before with a boulder on their shoulder and now they were leaving with just a small rock on their shoulder and a deeper self-confidence regarding their interactions with others.

Jerry Nagel and Kathy Jourdain

A COMPREHENSIVE PLANNING APPROACH

We first started bringing the idea of worldviews into our work in 2011. We introduced it as part of other training programs and consulting work. As we paid attention to the conversations that the worldview language and a simple, earlier version of what is now the Worldview Intelligence Six Dimensions Framework were generating, we realized there was more potential for progress using a Worldview Intelligence approach. Our journey working specifically with Worldview Intelligence began in August 2014 with the creation of a one-day program that we offered in Halifax, NS. Participants were roughly half white, half African Nova Scotian thanks to local collaborators. This program and the nature of the conversations between participants served to confirm our early realizations and inspired us to go deeper.

Over the next few years, we brought Worldview Intelligence into consulting work with many of our clients, using this approach for a variety of applications. We were delighted with the flexibility and adaptability of the Worldview Intelligence Six Dimensions Framework whether through personal, professional, organizational, cultural, community or social systems explorations. Other people could see it as well.

In speaking with our clients, we discovered they described their experience with us and Worldview Intelligence as having new language and a new structure to work with that made them feel like they had a secret weapon. The approach and the framework stayed with them and worked in them over time. As one client said, it is not a one and done deal; it has a quality of "stickiness" to it. People felt like it gave them strategic and tactical advantages.

Soon, people were asking for more. While we were applying the framework within the context of the planning frameworks and models, we have used in our consulting practice all along, it was an implicit extension of our planning, preparation and design approach. It was just what we did, how we had our conversations, how we developed our understanding of the issues, how we wrote our proposals and created process designs. When we finally recognized that people were asking us to make explicit what we did unconsciously, it took very little time to draw out our thinking on our own processes, methods of application and practices. We also realized that our clients were interested in a comprehensive approach and body of knowledge, essentially a one-stop shopping experience. This brought us to articulating our Theory of Change Planning Model (CIDA-W) complete with:

- A set of principles which guide the Worldview Intelligence Approach
- Identification of starting points, skills and outcomes within the planning model
- What is in each stage of the Worldview Intelligence Theory of Change planning model and some of the hows of each stage
- The SHEER framework for planning challenging conversations and a template for this purpose (found in Chapter 16: Building Trust and Relationship One-on-One).

These have become powerful additions and strategies to our work, and they make this approach more robust. Like the Worldview Intelligence Six Dimensions Framework itself, the Theory of Change Planning Model is adaptive to a wide variety of applications including mergers and acquisitions, strategic planning, leading change, challenging conversations, diversity-equity-inclusion and community engagement.

FIVE PRINCIPLES OF WORLDVIEW INTELLIGENCE

We identified five principles that guide the Worldview Intelligence Approach, some of which are based on the social constructionist origins of the worldview work. They are:

1. Each of us has a unique worldview (as does each family, team, organization, community, system, culture).
2. Worldview Intelligence is a relational approach recognizing that individual and collective experiences are locally and socially constructed.

3. The ability to hold and invite multiple perspectives (or worldviews) allows us to build strength from differences, to make better decisions and to make progress on issues that matter.

4. It is in the intersection between worldviews where the greatest opportunities and innovations lie.

5. Worldviews do shift and change, and we can be intentional in how this is invited personally, professionally, individually and collectively.

WORLDVIEW INTELLIGENCE IS A RELATIONAL APPROACH

The clients we work with who have the best results are those who choose to be collaborative and are open to fine tuning as we go, based on the experiences and feedback available – essentially a relational approach. On occasion we have run into a worldview clash with a client or potential client who is looking to "buy" something from us to fix a problem or are looking for a quick fix, wanting only that sprint referenced in our introduction. Not that there isn't value to be gained or added when a client is only interested in what we can do for them now as a transactional exchange, but there is little fertile ground for Worldview Intelligence to take root to change outcomes or to offer the truly transformative impact of changing mental models or worldviews.

Worldview Intelligence is a relational approach to connecting, entering challenging conversations, developing strategy, engaging stakeholders, working with teams and systems change. This is how we work with and for our clients. Part of the strategic advantage offered by Worldview Intelligence is that it considers longer-term relationships, growing connections that support the building of trust, being collaborative and co-creative with value added exchanges. We bring a solid body of Worldview Intelligence theory, knowledge and academic research along with years of practical experience in applying it and decades of expertise in facilitation and hosting methods and techniques. The client brings their own industry or sector specific knowledge as well as intimate knowledge of their own organization and its inner workings, its people and existing challenges and opportunities. This is valuable when it comes to identifying patterns, hidden dynamics and blind spots, a key element in the ability to develop strategic approaches to changing outcomes. We are vested in each other's success.

THEORY OF CHANGE – WORLDVIEW INTELLIGENCE CIDA-W PLANNING MODEL

The Worldview Intelligence CIDA-W Theory of Change Planning Model outlines a four step iterative process to apply Worldview Intelligence approaches to project planning and implementation, human resources, working with complexity, merging departments or organizations, public engagement and more. The facets of the Worldview Intelligence Theory of Change Planning Model are independent and interdependent as well as iterative.

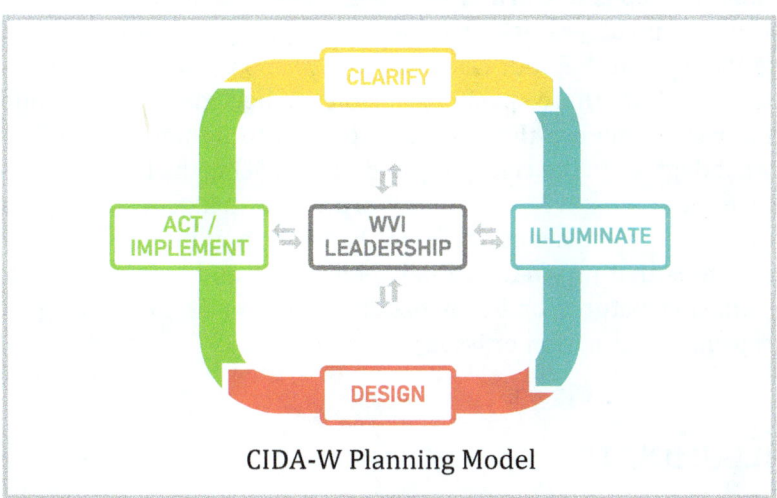

CIDA-W Planning Model

WORLDVIEW INTELLIGENCE LEADERSHIP

At the heart of the model is Worldview Intelligence Leadership. This is the ability to work effectively with many worldviews, beginning with self knowledge of your own worldview and activation or trigger points and then applying Worldview Intelligence leadership strategies to work with team members, internal groups and departments or external partners and stakeholders. The Six Dimensions of the Worldview Intelligence Framework – history, reality, future, values, practices and knowledge – provide a coherent way of organizing thinking, seeking points of connection and difference, offering insight into patterns and dynamics as well as a path to solutions for many pressing issues. It provides insight and strategies for building trust and relationship. Worldview Intelligence Leadership informs and is informed by each step in the CIDA-W planning model and, as you have seen, this book highlights these skills throughout.

CLARIFY

When applying the Worldview Intelligence Theory of Change, the first step is to clarify the issues, challenges or opportunities and the outcomes desired for your work, project or future. What is the need to be addressed and the purpose that will address the need? Are there specific principles to be articulated to guide the work, who are the people who need to be involved and to what degree? In the clarifying stage, referencing the Iceberg from Chapter 4: What It Means to be Worldview Intelligent, we inquire into the specific event, issue or challenge, any interventions or solutions that may have already been tried, and any patterns or trends, structures or behaviors that seem to be influencing or causing the situation or issue.

ILLUMINATE

The Worldview Intelligence Six Dimensions Framework is a key structure for illuminating dynamics that often are hidden. It can be used to make the multitude of worldviews, or specific dimensions that are inherent in any situation, visible to work intentionally with them, to find connections and alignments or disconnections and misalignments, and turn them into strategic advantages.

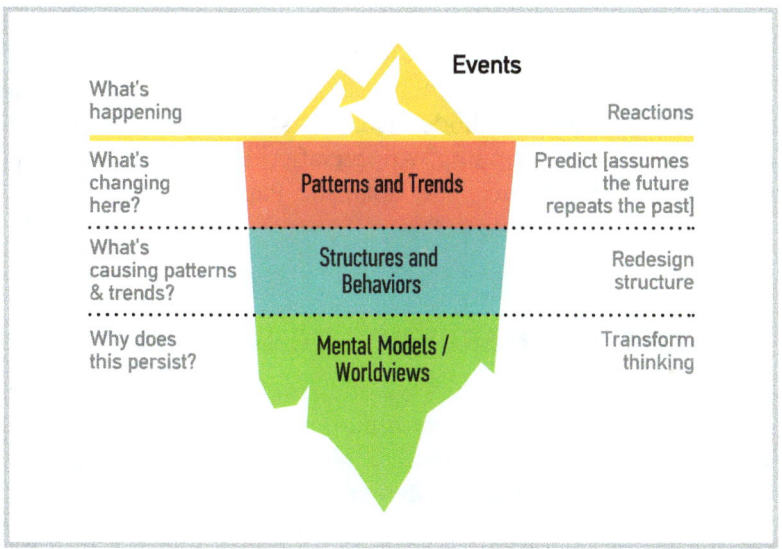

In the illuminating stage, more information may come to light that further clarifies the need, purpose and scope of the work to be done. Sometimes illumination can be done with a small planning team and other times it becomes a key part of the structure and design of the project or initiative or both.

One key aspect of illuminate is, together with the client, to be in inquiry to go further down the iceberg. What structures are in place that inhibit different results from being achieved? How do behaviors illuminate helpful and hindering structures? What clues do they give us to the worldviews that are predominant in the reality of the organization or community we are working with? What is the worldview shift in thinking, practices and action that would enable an intervention to be designed that would successfully achieve the outcomes identified?

DESIGN

A more comprehensive understanding of the issues at hand and probable causes of the problem or concern coming out of the first two steps allows for appropriate process designs to be created to address the need, purpose and outcomes of the project or initiative. Processes, systems and structures are then designed or developed in consultation with the client and modified based on experience to support these outcomes, drawing on a wide variety of tools and methods including systems thinking, social system and asset mapping, Appreciative Inquiry, Divergence-Emergence-Convergence, the Chaordic Path and the Chaordic Stepping Stones to name a few.

DIVERGENCE-EMERGENCE-CONVERGENCE

When working with clients we often explain how Sam Kaner's description of Divergence-Emergence-Convergence offers a powerful pattern to use as a planning framework and in understanding human group dynamics.[73]

Typically, in a planning process or in a team conversation the pattern will look like this: methods or practices to make the available information visible to all, seeing what new information emerges as a result and then converging on a few ideas or a few actions required to continue to move plans forward. Sometimes the team hits a groan zone where conversation seems to get bogged down and people get tired or frustrated with the process. Making it through groan zones consistently is a skill that is learned and welcomed as teams see the productive results that emerge.

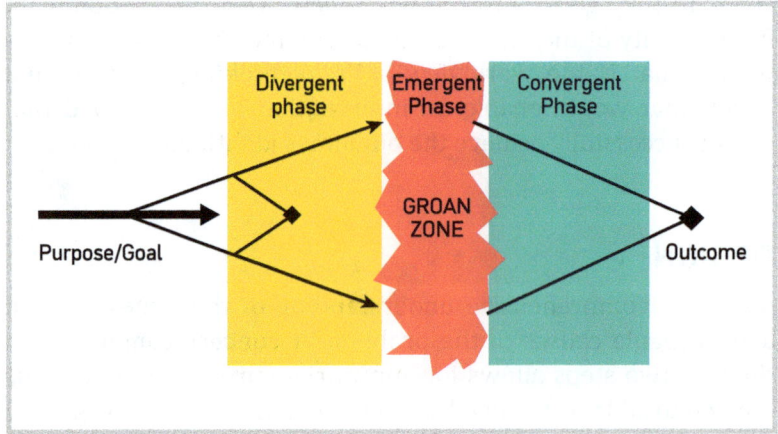

The diamond in the divergent phase in the following diagram illustrates early convergence or an early decision. The team has not yet explored all the possibilities. They have converged early because of the illusion that they need to save time and just get on with actions. They may have wanted to try to avoid the groan zone. Or, some of the more vocal or persuasive people may have dominated the discussion and advocated for a certain decision. However it occurs, you know decisions have been made too early when they are revisited in a future meeting or when resistance to next steps shows up. This is an indication there is valuable information and discussion still to be had.

This pattern is described in more detail in Chapter 17: Building Trust and Relationship in Your Team.

APPRECIATIVE APPROACH

We bring an appreciative approach to our work often drawing on Appreciative Inquiry. AI was pioneered in the 1980s by David Cooperrider and Suresh Srivastva, two professors at the Weatherhead School of Management at Case Western Reserve University. It is based on social constructionism and is both a worldview and a process for facilitating positive change in human systems. Its assumption is simple: every human system has something that works right–things that give it life when it is vital, effective, and successful. AI begins by identifying this positive core and connecting to it in ways that heighten energy, sharpen vision, and inspire action for change.[74] We reference the application of Appreciative Inquiry in Chapter 18: When the Team is Dysfunctional – Is It Possible to Build Trust and Relationship?

The Chaordic Stepping Stones is another powerful, iterative planning framework that is embedded in our design work. The Stepping Stones are Need, Purpose, Principles, People, Concept, Limiting Beliefs, Structure, Act and Harvest. These stepping stones can be used by a planning team to clarify and illuminate why a planning process is being undertaken, what it hopes to achieve, what the principles are that will guide the work and who needs to be involved. Before articulating structure, there is an exploration of possible design concepts as well as an illumination of the limiting beliefs that can get in the way of moving forward. It can be a challenging framework to learn; it takes practice and experience to embody each stepping stone and the questions and conversations that evoke the power of this framework.

ACT

Nothing gets done without action. This involves the strategic use of conversational or engagement methods and practices to get work done, to address issues or challenges and solve problems and provide continual illumination and alignment of worldviews. It also includes the alignment of worldviews that gets people and the organization on the same page for moving forward. This is the stage where project plans or operational plans with accountabilities and timelines are developed and implemented, action items are completed and progress takes off.

As we have offered often in this book, the personal and leadership alignment between worldviews and action is essential. The outcomes of actions feed back into the planning model, assessing whether the outcomes have been achieved or, as the environment, conditions or understanding of the issues changes or evolves, how responsive the team or organization needs to be to the changing conditions. It may inform next steps or new initiatives to be undertaken.

Throughout this, as a leader of your team, you will want to ensure your practices continue to maintain and grow trust and build relationship.

WORLDVIEW INTELLIGENCE CIDA-W THEORY OF CHANGE PLANNING MODEL APPLICATIONS

As mentioned previously, the Worldview Intelligence CIDA-W Theory of Change planning model is as adaptive and responsive as the Worldview Intelligence Six Dimensions Framework. It can be used for a number of organizational planning needs or interventions including:

- Leading change
- Strategic planning
- Strengthening high performance teams and team cohesiveness
- Challenging conversations
- Mergers and acquisitions
- Diversity-Equity-Inclusion
- Community engagement

\multicolumn{3}{c}{**Worldview Intelligence CIDA-W Theory of Change: Examples of What and How**}
WVI Model Stage	**What (examples)**	**How (examples)**
Clarify	• Understand the nature of the issue, question or system to be addressed • Identify and articulate need, purpose, outcomes/wobjectives	• Inquiry • Research • Check assumptions
Illuminate	• Worldviews at work • Hidden dynamics or patterns • The complexity of the system of interest	• Worldview Intelligence Six Dimensions Framework for explorations: personal, organizational, systems etc. • Complexity theories • Systems thinking
Design	Create the conditions for: • Connections • Challenging conversations • Explorations • Culture shift	• Worldview Intelligence Six Dimensions • Framework • Influence of behavioural and brain science • Apply systems thinking • Strategy development • Change management • Prototyping

Act/ Implement	<ul><li>Plan of action/ implementation</li><li>Align worldviews across the organization</li><li>Create the structures for the work to be done</li><li>Experiment with prototypes</li></ul>	Templates and practices for:<ul><li>Strategic conversations</li><li>Change management</li><li>Stakeholder engagement</li><li>Addressing the influence of behavioural and brain science</li><li>Learning/feedback loops</li></ul>
Worldview Intelligence Leadership	<ul><li>Prepare to engage</li><li>Self awareness – personal Worldview Intelligence explorations</li><li>Understand your role as a leader in the inquiry / initiative identified</li><li>Understand worldviews at work and how to assess them and their impact</li></ul>	<ul><li>The Worldview Intelligence Six Dimensions Framework</li><li>Work with triggers or activation points – personally and with others</li><li>Understand and utilize the power of story</li><li>Break out of hardwired programming to develop adaptive responses (response mechanisms)</li><li>Worldview Intelligence leadership development plans</li></ul>

STARTING POINTS, SKILLS AND OUTCOMES OF WORLDVIEW INTELLIGENCE

It became clear in the early stages of the development of Worldview Intelligence that it offered a set of skills that lead to a wide variety of potential outcomes. As we worked with colleagues, trusted advisors and clients, it also became clear that individually and collectively there are what we have come to call "starting points" that contribute to the successful application of this approach. These starting points are qualities of being that can be developed for greater effectiveness and even mastery. They are essential leadership qualities and speak to a basic inner orientation or stance.

STARTING POINTS OR STANCE

It is next to impossible to open exploratory conversations from a place of judgment, needing to be right or from a starting place of superiority, arrogance or ego. In our experience of applying Worldview Intelligence in a variety of contexts we have learned that foundational to powerful, and sometimes profound, application are the qualities of curiosity, compassion, empathy and humility. These are qualities or neural pathways that can be developed and deepened over time with practice and experience. They are also qualities essential to building trust and relationship.

CURIOSITY

We always say, and people now quote us, that curiosity and judgment cannot exist in the same space. When you find yourself feeling judgmental, which could also mean being defensive of your own ideas or dismissive of someone else's, turning to curiosity is a powerful game changer. Curiosity can be applied in a range of ways:

- To yourself and your own reactions,
- To the other person and why they may be acting the way they are or saying what they are saying,

- To begin to imagine how they have come to see the issue the way they have, and
- About the situation in general.

Not only is it a learning stance, the quality of curiosity changes the quality of the exchange.

COMPASSION

Compassion is the ability to understand the emotional state of another person or oneself. Being compassionate invites you to bear suffering with another and to feel for and seek to understand the misery and suffering of others. This can be a challenge. It involves learning how to hold totally different perspectives when it comes to how you perceive others and their actions. Combined with curiosity it indicates a willingness to understand another person or group and where they are coming from rather than judging them for behavior that might be different than your own behavior or your expectations of appropriate behavior.

EMPATHY

Empathy is a worldview starting point. Empathy and sympathy are often used interchangeably, so it is important to distinguish between the two as we referenced in Chapter 7: History. In general, sympathy is when you share the feelings of another person or agree with them or their point of view. Empathy is when you understand their perspective and how they came to it or understand why they feel the way they do concerning something, but you do not necessarily share the same sentiments. In understanding them, you can bring compassion to the situation or exchange. There are many worldviews out there you might not agree with or sympathize with, but if you can find a way to empathy or even curiosity, you can open an exploratory space for conversation and understanding that cannot exist otherwise. You do not open a conversation by condemning another person's views, even if you strongly disagree with them. If you do wish to influence or try to change another person's perspectives then you need to find an entryway or invitation that, at a minimum, opens a conversation.

Kathy and a colleague were recently in a conversation with a new friend originally from Kenya, currently living in Bermuda. He talked about his grandfather and his grandfather's five wives. In western societies, the concept of polygamy can spark disbelief and outrage. He was amused by the differences in worldviews and the worldview reactions to his and his family's history and practices. Bringing curiosity to that conversation invited an exploration of what it was like for him growing up with five grandmothers who each had their own domain and how this socially acceptable practice in that country has been changing through the generations.

HUMILITY

Humility is a quality of remembering you don't have all the answers and you can always be learning. It is being able to listen well and appreciate the contribution of others. This is particularly valuable when encountering worldview clashes. The need to be humble and open to other perspectives can show up in many ways and especially when power dynamics are part of the situation. Both Jerry and Kathy have been through the teenage years with their children. And both have experienced the worldview clashes that can emerge between parent and emerging young adult. These clashes are natural and can lead to real conflict. They have both learned that this is a time when the person (the parent) with perceived or real power does well to step back, be more humble and listen fully or be present to what is being said and what is true for the one without power. Jerry often says that his learning as a parent to be humbler and more present to his children's experience has helped him in his professional work.

PERSONAL WORLDVIEW AWARENESS IS A KEY STARTING POINT

Knowing in general what your personal worldview is becomes

an important starting point to any conversation. Taking time to reflect on your view on a specific situation, person or upcoming conversation can help the conversation be more productive and help you better manage your emotions or reactions to differing views or challenges to your perspectives that may be part of the conversation.

WORLDVIEW INTELLIGENCE SKILLS

There are several skills that Worldview Intelligent leaders cultivate in themselves and in their teams. They are interconnected and include presence, deep listening, and inquiry.

Presence is the ability to bring yourself fully into the present moment, to tune out distractions and to become an open slate for listening or being in conversation.

Presence is a prerequisite for deep listening where you give your full attention to another person, listening not just for the words, but for the pauses in between the words, for what is not being said, for the body language and energy vibrations coming from the other person. It is applying the stance of Worldview Intelligence: curiosity, compassion, empathy and humility. We will sometimes say, "Listen for the song in the words".

All these skills can be applied to inquiry which involves being genuinely curious about another person's stance, asking questions to learn more and inviting yourself and the person you are in inquiry with to a deeper exploration.

These are also essential skills to Building Trust and Relationship at the Speed of Change. As a leader in your team or organization, it is a mistake to think you don't have time for this, when things are changing so fast. There are some basic structures, patterns and practices you can put in place with your team that will help you operate in healthy and strong relationship. We explore them more directly in the Chapter 17. When these structures, patterns and practices are not in place, relationship and trust can waver. Sometimes, trust wavers so much that relationship devolves into dysfunctional teams – or you may have inherited a dysfunctional team in which case building trust and relationship is that much more difficult, sometimes not even possible, as we explore in Chapter 18.

These are skills that can be honed with practice and none of them needs to take a lot of time. Although we cover this in more detail in Chapters 16 and 17, here are a few quick hits. Focus your attention. Put your phone down. Pay attention to the nature of the questions you are asking. Be genuinely, authentically curious regarding the person, team or work right in front of you. When do you deliver your best work? When you are passionate and you know you and your contributions are valued. It is as simple as that. Do you show up fully to the other people on your team, in your organization or in your family?

When these skills are well honed, a Worldview Intelligent leader, with their team, or with the help of a consultant, can illuminate hidden patterns and dynamics that may be present in a relationship, team or organization. Identifying hidden patterns means different and more comprehensive strategic approaches or interventions become possible.

With these skills, a Worldview Intelligent leader grows the capacity to change the nature of conversations, as we illustrated in Chapter 9: Values. This is not to be manipulative or to ignore issues at hand, but to move a conversation from stuck debate to generative conversations, from a narrow perspective to a broader view or from a clash to an exploration.

A Worldview Intelligent leader has the ability to build connections between themselves and another person, among members of a team, across an organization, with collaborators or partners or between worldviews. In the increasing complexity of today's world and the issues in front of us, the skill and ability to find and build connections is essential to advancing issues and agendas.

WORLDVIEW INTELLIGENCE OUTCOMES

What differences does Worldview Intelligence make? A few

that we see repeatedly in the work with our clients are:

- Increased productivity
- Fewer conflicts
- Better results on divisive or polarizing topics
- More creativity and innovation
- Stronger connections
- More inclusive, diverse, welcoming work environments
- More cohesive teams
- Better relationships with customers, partners and stakeholders
- Faster decisions by management and/or teams
- Greater alignment in mergers and acquisitions
- Improved governance

REFLECTION QUESTIONS

1. What opportunities for addressing your organization's issues do you see in the Worldview Intelligence CIDA-W Theory of Change Planning Model?

2. Which of the Worldview Intelligence starting points or skills resonate with you and why? Of these, which are you skilled at and which would you like to develop more? How might you act on that?

CHAPTER 16:
BUILDING TRUST AND RELATIONSHIP ONE-ON-ONE

Many of us have at least that one person who is always challenging to talk to. It could be a family member, a partner of a family member, neighbor or co-worker. It seems that the conversation always gets stuck in some way so we go out of our way to avoid conversations with them, even when we are in the same physical space. This was the situation for me with one of my brothers. When we were younger, we often had opposing views or differing enough perspectives that created tensions that carried into adulthood. We pretty much avoided each other and only had contact at family events when it couldn't be avoided. Yet, I have always held my brother in high respect as he has done many good things for people living in difficult circumstances, like bringing medical care to rural areas of Central America. And we pretty much share the same political views (whew!).

At a family event a few years ago, something happened that caused emotional hurt for my brother. I became aware of this because of his abrupt departure from the event. After some reflection, I decided to initiate a conversation with him, albeit first through email. I asked what had happened and if I was responsible for the hurt. If so, I expressed a sincere apology. I then offered that I hoped our respective children, the cousins, would continue to be friends. Finally, I suggested that while we may never be best friends, I hoped we could be closer.

It turns out, I was not responsible for what happened. However, I gained some insights into the history of the situation, how my brother's reality was not respected and how some values were discounted. The outcome is that we are now on good terms, have spent some social time together and no longer avoid each other at family events. And when I moved recently, my brother came and helped.

From a Worldview Intelligence approach to conversations, I sought to define or clarify the situation, acknowledge my role, if any, in it in order to illuminate any blindspots I might have. I identified the outcomes I was hoping for prior to engaging the exchange and allowed my own vulnerability to surface. I prepared for the possibility that I might be in the wrong. This is an example of how working with the Worldview Intelligence Six Dimensions Framework has become engrained in my way of thinking and approach.

Jerry Nagel

SHEER CONVERSATION PLANNING FRAMEWORK

A question we are frequently asked is how to have that conversation with someone you have a different worldview from, where opinions can range from somewhat different to polarized. It is important to note that, while we are obviously huge advocates of worldview shifts and exploratory conversations, there may be some conversations you are better off not having. One of them includes when you know for certain that there will be no opportunity to expand the conversation, or you know you will be attacked in ways that are not helpful and you know this from experience not from supposition. We are not suggesting you put yourself in a position to be abused and we are also not suggesting you be the attacker or abuser in a conversation.

Having said that, it is not enough to simply believe that there is no room for exploration. You need to determine this from your experience. If your experience tells you that the conversation always gets stuck, always circles around the same exchange or doesn't move beyond a certain point, there may be an opportunity to shift it using SHEER and the conversation planning template offered in this chapter. If the conversation is one you haven't had yet but are anticipating will be challenging, the opportunity to think through how to approach it may offer you strategies and questions you would not have thought of without this structure.

If you've been frustrated by previous attempts at this conversation or find yourself annoyed with the other person, this book has already offered a wealth of ways for you to enquire into why. They include:

- Examine your own worldview
- Know what triggers you
- Be conversant with some of the brain and behavioral science as it may offer you clues into your own reactions and behaviors as well as the person you want to engage in the conversation

If you can get to the heart of what's frustrating you (beyond it is the other person), then you have the potential to change the way you enter the conversation and that just might change everything.

In addition to the behavioral science, you can use the knowledge of amygdala hijacks to consider how the person you want to engage in conversation might respond, why that would be so and what your own response to that might be. As you're in the conversation, be attuned to clues, both within yourself and from the other person. Being present in the conversation, fully listening, being in inquiry and not interrogation are Worldview Intelligence skills you can cultivate. They will be your most valuable allies for this work.

It is also incumbent on you, as the person initiating the conversation, to create the exploratory space. This is one reason there is so much emphasis in this book on knowing your own worldview. This is the first of the five steps in the SHEER Conversation framework: Starting point or stance. The other steps are: Hoped for Outcomes, Empathy, Engage and Results. The following chart outlines guidelines for initiating worldview explorations with people or groups that may have a differing worldview or a different understanding of the situation. Following this is a template you can use to plan your conversation.

S	*Starting point or stance:* know yourself and your own worldview (apply Worldview Intelligence Leadership and the six dimensions of the framework to your situation and analysis), be clear about your own starting point on this topic, understand where and how you get triggered on the issues or in conversations to be able to mitigate your own response
H	*Hopes, hoped for outcomes* of the conversation: identify your intention and motivation in engaging the conversation and what you hope to have achieved by the end of it
E	*Empathy:* put yourself in the shoes of the other person by thoughtfully considering what their worldview might be, how they may have come to see and experience the issue, topic or situation the way they have – recognizing you may have to check your assumptions once you engage the conversation. When you consider what the other person's perspective might be, how might this change how you engage the person and the conversation?
E	*Engage* the person and the conversation: Consider how you make the conversation space invitational and exploratory, be aware of your own presence in the conversation and how it makes the other person feel by observing their reactions and adjusting your stance
R	*Results, Resolution, Reflection:* identify any openings or movement in the explorations, acknowledge points of agreement or connection, name any resolution that arises (if any) and later reflect on the experience for learning, what worked, what didn't, what surprised you, what affirmed the experience

A LIVED EXAMPLE OF SHEER

In 2008, when she was in her mid-forties, as mentioned in a previous chapter, Kathy found out she was adopted when her two biological sisters reached out to contact her. On the one hand, it was a disorienting shock. On the other hand, a few "facts" of her life clicked into place in interesting ways and, within a short period of time, she came to believe this information was true. Her mother's mental, cognitive and physical functions had declined due to dementia and she would soon be admitted into long-term care. When considering engaging her mother in that conversation it was unclear whether she could contribute anything and there was a possibility it could spark some kind of crisis for her. This meant she needed to have a conversation with her father, who was then 75 years old.

KATHY'S STARTING POINT

At this point in her life, Kathy had already worked with life coaches a few times to work through or understand her own life journey or path as well as stuck points and she was, at this very moment, working with a life coach. She had gained good insight into her actions, reactions and choices. But she had been feeling like there was a block to further personal and professional development so when this new information on a significant unknown thread of her life came to light, it was a possible answer to that question. Despite the shock, curiosity was the main inquiry she was holding.

From the Worldview Intelligence Six Dimensions Framework, her reality was both dramatically different and completely the same. She was still a mother of three children, still married (at the time), still a consultant living in Nova Scotia, still had two parents living an hour's drive away. However, her reality now included a whole other network of biological family members and their extended relationships.

Some of her history was in question. Things she thought to be part of her history may not have been and a series of unknown events that led to and included her adoption were now revealed to her as part of her history.

The future held some questions – particularly concerning relationships. Her values remained the same and the practices she had been developing over the course of decades held her in good stead. However, how she knew and trusted what she knew was in flux.

HOPED FOR OUTCOME

Kathy had no doubt of the strength of her relationship with her father and knew it would hold steady through this revelation. The most significant outcome she sought was to know, or in this case confirm, the truth while maintaining the good relationship.

EMPATHY

When a good friend heard of this new development in her life, Kathy was asked, "Aren't you angry?" The question surprised her and she responded, "If I thought about this from the perspective that people have been lying to me the whole of my life, maybe I would be angry." Instead, she put herself in her parents' shoes. She knew how much her parents loved her, how much they had supported her over the years through many different and difficult life events and she realized there is never a good time to reveal family secrets, especially the longer they go on. She gave her parents the benefit of the doubt and, instead of accusing her father, she was able to bring inquiry.

ENGAGE THE CONVERSATION

The hardest part of engaging the conversation was waiting for her mother to go to bed. Normally, she went to bed quite early because of her dementia, but not this night. Something was in the air, and it was also the day of her parents' 50th wedding anniversary. As part of engaging the conversation, she had determined having her mother present would bring no benefit and only distraction.

When her mother finally went to bed, Kathy turned toward her father and began. "Dad, something happened this week and I just need to know the truth." She had his attention. "Two women have contacted me and they seem to think I might be their sister." There was a dramatic pause and finally he replied, "Well, that is another long story."

They talked for half an hour. He shared her parents' fears about her possible reactions to learning she was adopted – rejection of them being primary among them. He gave her background to the story, fearful of what would happen to their relationship now. She told him they were good and acknowledged their 46 years of history together. He wondered if her brother, who was their biological child who had been born soon after Kathy's adoption, knew and what his reaction would be. She was able to say her brother knew and he was accepting of the information, once he got over his own shock. Her dad offered for her to change her name back to her birth family name, which she had no interest in, Jourdain being part of her identity for a lifetime.

RESULT AND REFLECTIONS

After this first conversation, it was some weeks before her father raised the topic again, out of his own curiosity. He was supportive of her meeting each of her birth family members, including her birth father who was still alive at the time and lived a three hour drive away. Over time, there were more conversations with respect to meeting biological family members. When Kathy's older birth sister arrived for a visit, a relationship from her childhood was renewed.* A decade later, they continue to have a close relationship despite living on opposite sides of Canada.

---

* Kathy shares this story in detail in her memoir: Embracing the Stranger Within: A Journey to Openheartedness

PREPARING FOR A CHALLENGING WORLDVIEW CONVERSATION

Exploring and understanding the perspectives of others is important to knowing how to open conversations with them and how to act in thoughtful, generative ways. While you cannot know for sure another person's worldview before having a conversation with them, you can give some preliminary thought to what it might be by putting yourself in their shoes. Using the following worksheet you can identify the person you are reflecting on, define the outcomes you want to achieve, identify what your own blindspots might be, what judgments you might be bringing, what curiosities you could genuinely bring. Then reflect on the other person and what their worldview might be by reflecting on the six dimensions. After that, consider how to begin the inquiry and any other approaches you might take to the conversation and the person you are engaging.

In addition to the worldview considerations, identifying the hoped-for outcomes can be a game changer for these conversations. Most people haven't considered outcomes beyond the need to have the conversation or resolve a stuck issue. Thinking about the outcome often offers insight into different ways into the conversation. You can choose to name it at the beginning of the conversation if you wish or use it as your own internal guide. Some examples of outcomes include:

- I want to hear what the other person thinks
- I would like my perspective to be heard
- I would love for us to come to an agreement
- I want to begin a conversation I want this conversation to continue one or more times
- This relationship is important to me and I want it to be intact at the end of the conversation
- We seem to be unable to make progress on this issue. I am curious to hear their perspective and how they have come to see this issue the way they have.

Occasionally, someone will realize they don't want a conversation; they just want to download their own position and sometimes that makes them think better of having the conversation in the first place.

Strategizing a Worldview Conversation		
The person or situation I am reflecting on is:		
The need for this conversation is:		
Clarify (Starting point and hoped for outcomes)	Outcomes I want to achieve	
	My/our possible blind spots	
	Judgments I might have about this situation/person that might influence my communication	
	Genuine curiosities I could bring to the person or situation	
Illuminate (Empathy)	Worldview Intelligence Six Dimensions Exploration	
	Dimensions	What their worldview might be
	Reality	
	History	
	Future	
	Values	
	Practices	
	Knowledge	

Design (for engagement)	Where could I begin this inquiry?	
	What approaches might I take to achieve the outcomes identified?	
	What are some good questions I could use?	
	How can I create an invitational and exploratory space?	
Act (Engage and Reflect)	When will I have this conversation and why is this a good time to have it?	
	Where will I have this conversation and why is this a good place to have it?	
	What will I do to prepare myself for this conversation (emotionally, energetically)?	
	What actions did I take?	
	What was the result?	
	What am I relieved about? Excited about? Disappointed about?	
	What could I do differently next time?	
	What is a good next step in this conversation or process?	

Worldwide Intelligence Leadership Skill	What was my stance? (Curiosity, compassion, empathy, humility)	
	Which skills did I use? (Presence, deep listening, inquiry, illumination of hidden patterns and dynamics, the ability to change the nature of conversations, building on connections)	
	Which skills can I improve on?	

Some additional considerations before entering the conversation include:

- Are there power dynamics that are impacting this conversation/relationship? If so, what is the nature of the power dynamics and who has power?

- Are there cultural, social or faith contexts to be taken into consideration? If so, what are the contexts and what needs to be considered?

- Might the effects of trauma be a part of this situation for either me or the other person? If so, how does this inform how to approach this person or conversation?

In the Worldview Intelligence programs, this conversation planning worksheet is often praised as valuable for planning challenging conversations, for the insights it offers, even before engaging the conversation. Routinely people say to us, I have never considered the perspective of the person I need to have this conversation with, or it never occurred to me to identify the outcomes I want from the conversation. Some also realize the conversation they need to have is different from the one they thought they wanted to have.

CREATING INVITATION AND TRUST

Part of *Building Trust and Relationship at the Speed of Change* on a one-to-one basis is how you create the environment or invitation into the conversation. If you begin with strongly held pre-conceived notions about the other person or by projecting your anger, frustration, disappointment or other strong emotion onto the person you need to be in the conversation with, you immediately put them on the defensive which creates the opportunity for each of you to dig in your heels. Does this mean you need to be emotionless or emotionally neutral? No, of course not. The question is more, how do you express those emotions and how do you do it in such a way that you can also hold the space for the conversation? To be able to name your emotions or your experience, "I'm angry....", "I'm frustrated....", "I'm disappointed...", "I'm struggling....", when done well, opens the space for honesty, vulnerability and authenticity for you both.

Checking your motivations and becoming fully present in the space changes the quality of the interaction. Focusing on what the other person is saying – truly listening to them – means you are not allowing your assumptions to fill the space or your mind, and you are not simply waiting for the opportunity to have your say. When you change the quality of your listening, you change the quality of the conversation.

A key question for you personally and as a leader is, "Do I give other people someone they can trust?" These one-on-one relationships, whether around challenging conversations or in general, provide the opportunity to build trust and relationship in your team and across your organization. They offer you the opportunity to be as honest and authentic as you are capable of in those moments.

A good place to begin practicing challenging conversations is in your personal relationships. This may be the most challenging and rewarding place to practice. We (Jerry and Kathy) try to live what we preach in both our shared personal and professional lives. We have found that this dual practice has enriched both parts.

REFLECTION QUESTIONS

1. What is a challenging conversation you are anticipating and who is it with? What is the nature of the conversation and why do you believe it will be or is challenging?

2. Use the worksheet in this chapter to plan your conversation. Let us know what you discover.

CHAPTER 17:
BUILDING TRUST AND RELATIONSHIP IN YOUR TEAM

A long-time client of Kathy's was bringing a significant culture change to their membership-based organization with a staff complement of thirty people. Because of their ongoing relationship, a key contact had been hearing about Worldview Intelligence and could see the possibility of this approach in supporting their culture change initiative.

The staff explored their personal worldviews and then their teams' worldviews, looking for the points of connection and differences so they could find the alignment of worldviews across the whole organization. In the discussions, they had a flash of insight, one that once illuminated was obvious but until then was subtly influencing their interpersonal dynamics. And the insight was frustrating for them. It was that internal communication was an ongoing challenge. People did not know what other people did. Information was not traveling between departments. This is the same work the organization had focused on periodically over the years.

It hit home that building trust and relationship is not a one-time deal. It requires dedicated attention to relationship and communication on an ongoing basis. For this organization, Worldview Intelligence grew their skills and ability in communicating and collaborating across departments, reduced conflict and enabled departments to have more animated conversations amongst staff.

Kathy Jourdain and Jerry Nagel

CHALLENGES TO BUILDING TRUST AND RELATIONSHIP

Many things can interfere with maintaining strong positive, productive team dynamics. Some key challenges that interfere with Building Trust and Relationship at the Speed of Change are poorly addressed interpersonal communications or relationships, lack of transparency, information not shared across teams, departments or organizational silos, lack of role clarity and poor or poorly articulated decision-making processes. Whether an organization has 30 or 30,000 employees, it is typical to see communication challenges, silos where departments operate independently and sometimes at cross-purposes with other departments and people not knowing what each other does. These have been identified as problems that get in the way of efficiently addressing work issues and goals or outcomes in organizations. They are age old, reoccurring problems and the solution requires enduring attention to structures, processes and practices that support building trust and relationship.

Stability in a team can come through predictable, consistent structures, as processes and practices even as the team, the organization or the very nature of the work is subjected to the fast pace of change. Additionally, there is a "sweet spot" that can be attained in teams that enable them to become and maintain high performance. The sweet spot is the interdependence between learning, work and relationship. In this chapter, the sweet spot is explored, followed by looking at how stability is created through consistent structures, processes and practices.

THE SWEET SPOT BETWEEN LEARNING, WORK AND RELATIONSHIP FOR HIGH-PERFORMANCE TEAMS

High performance teams are highly valued and often difficult to cultivate in the world of teams and team development. To be clear, not every team needs to be a high-performance team to deliver results. However, leading edge, innovative or fast changing organizations interested in attracting and retaining highly motivated employees want to encourage high-performance teams, and the leadership that grows and sustains them, as a competitive advantage.

In that Google study of high-performance teams mentioned earlier,[75] Google discovered that the most successful teams provided the opportunity for all members to have equal voice or contribution and team members had higher levels of social

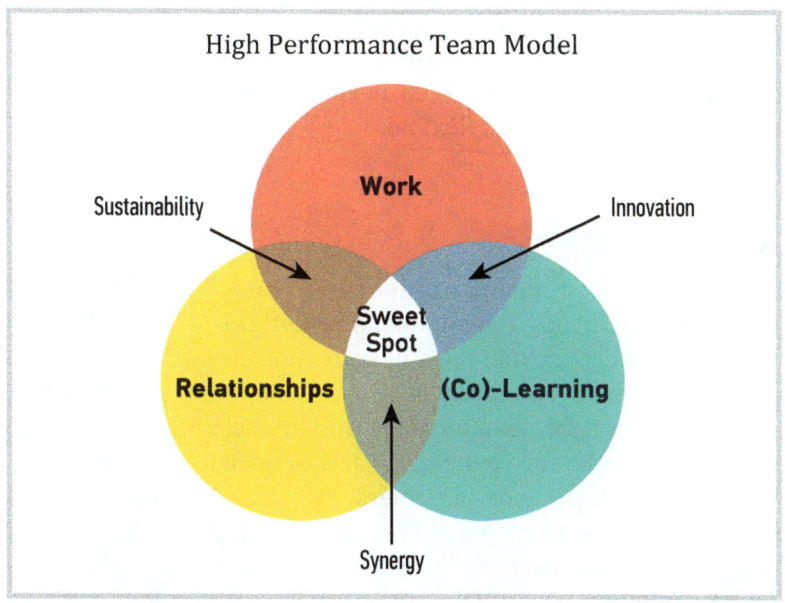

sensitivity. Worldview Intelligence offers insights into both aspects. It explicitly invites multiple worldviews by looking to the intersectionality of views rather than the dominance of one or a few. The frameworks, templates, practices and processes of Worldview Intelligence provide a means to increase social sensitivity by offering each or all the Six Dimensions as lenses into understanding more about another person, team or organization and their views. This enables both increased connectivity and the opportunity to align views to powerfully move forward on issues that matter.

In our work with teams, we present a model for cultivating high-performance in teams that has three components: learning, relationship and work. At the intersection of these three components is the sweet spot of high-performance teams. High-performance teams have mastered the ability to take *learning* concepts into practical application at *work* and sustain the results or impact over time thanks to healthy, constructive *relationships*. Success comes from an appropriate emphasis on each of these aspects of team development and performance. In high-performance teams, members seamlessly adjust the emphasis on each of these aspects based on changing circumstances, and without ignoring any one of them for any length of time. Tuning into what is needed most at any given time and stepping outside of the pressures of time when needed means these teams are dynamic, responsive and flexible.

RELATIONSHIP

Sustainability of high performance to reach desired outcomes is supported through relationship. Relationship, or relational leadership skills, include the ability to build connections through a genuine interest in others, to cultivate long term relationships, to be collaborative, engage value-added exchanges and create environments that are generative and responsive to emergence. High-performance team members are vested in each other's success and have a high degree of trust. This supports innovation, creativity and connectivity, which are solid outcomes of healthy relationship practices.

The Worldview Intelligence Six Dimensions Framework has proven versatile and adaptable in illuminating the influence of worldviews on relationships in workplaces and in communities, particularly in uncovering sources of tension, conflict and hidden dynamics. It is a powerful resource in identifying blind spots that can negatively impact relationships, torpedo change initiatives or affect policy implementation.

Once discovered, blindspots, sources of tension, conflict or hidden dynamics can be directly and specifically addressed using Worldview Intelligence frameworks, processes and strategies.

High-performance team members learn how to be in lively, animated conversations, discussions and debates in honest, open, healthy and productive ways. These kinds of generative conversations create a synergy that elevates a team beyond even the individual capacity of each team member. The whole is greater than the sum of its parts. This gives an organization or team a strategic advantage in achieving results, leading to greater motivation and higher performance. Understanding how to use Worldview Intelligence frameworks, processes and strategies effectively provides ways and means of inviting the available worldviews into team discussions so that the team sparks and enhances its creativity and innovation. In high- performance teams, leadership and responsibility are shared and rotate, based on what each member brings to the team and the knowledge, skills or abilities needed in the moment.

LEARNING AND CO-LEARNING

Learning in a team often means that some or all of the team members learn new skills, attend conferences or educational seminars or have common reading lists. What is learned is then put into practice in the work environment. This could include a teaching component for individuals to share new knowledge with the rest of the team. Worldview Intelligence learning also applies to the learning of a team over time. Many teams do not take the time to make visible or share what they are learning about the work they are tasked to do, how they are working together and what past learnings might impact the current work tasks.

Teams commonly assume that members share similar knowledge. Our work with worldviews has shown that these assumptions are often wrong. People bring into any work situation their own worldviews on the tasks at hand and how they can be accomplished. Taking time to understand each team member's perspective on the work and process and continually checking in on what is being learned can keep a team focused, innovative and productive, with greater connectivity and limited diversions.

Two of the Worldview Intelligence Six Dimensions are applicable here – practices and knowledge. High-performance teams use practices of open communication and personal awareness, which helps them stay innovative and productive. They also regularly check-in on their practices to make sure they don't get stuck in a rut of continually doing things the same way and to ensure that their team practices continue to do what they were intended to do. High-performance teams question their sources of knowledge to be sure the information they are working with is accurate and complete. They recognize that knowledge can be emergent and so hold open the space for new information, ideas and possibilities to emerge.

WORK

Ultimately, high-performance teams are tasked with getting things done. Knowing that the team's interpersonal relationships have been attended to, trust is in place, and recognizing the importance of keeping what is being learned on the table, members of the team and the team as a whole can focus on the tasks they have been charged with. The attention, creativity and energy of the team can be focused directly on the work.

Here several of the dimensions can be used to advance the work. In considering reality, what is the context for the application of the work of the team? Be sure not to work in a bubble of your own personal or team perspectives or reality. Consider any historical factors that might impact implementation of policies or strategies, including cultural, gender or societal factors that may impact how people might respond, whether customers, clients, social groups or other stakeholders.

How the team individually and collectively anticipates the future is another area to be given consideration within the scope of the work. People consider what the future offers in varying ways, as discussed in Chapter 8: Future. It is important for the team to reflect on how the people impacted by the work might view it from their perspective on the future. Will they welcome what is offered or might they see it as a threat to their well-being. A few years back we were working with a group of union organizers who were quite resistant to discussions of a different way to work in the future as they thought it was a ruse to get rid of them. Because of this, a contentious discussion emerged between the organizers and union leadership. After several minutes of heated exchange, one of the longer-term members of the union walked through the past 30 years of the union's history reminding people how they had changed their organizing practices and perspectives at different times in response to the changing situations. This historical overview helped alleviate some of the suspicion and shift the thinking on the change that was ahead and on how to approach the future.

Other key considerations affecting work tasks include checking to be sure that the approach to the work fits within the company's or organization's values and that the outcome of the proposed action will also fit within the company's values. Related is that the practices used to accomplish the work align with company values, are attentive to learning and are relational.

High-performance teams are created and developed through attentiveness to cultivating the right conditions for the team and its members to flourish. Attending to relationships, learning and work is a game changer in sustaining high-performance teams over time.

SITUATIONAL HIGH-PERFORMANCE TEAMS

During the time Kathy was the Executive Director of an Atlantic Canada-based charitable organization, the organization decided to take on a special event fundraiser for the first time. It was a big labor-intensive event, an experience they had not previously had. The planning horizon was short and it required all hands on deck for an intense couple of months. The event, a long-distance bicycle ride, required organizing of, and then working with, volunteers in several communities along the route, sponsorship and communication with sponsors, RCMP and liaison with the ham radio operators association.

Every staff person, no matter their role, became part of the team and pitched in for the organizing. The office boardroom became the Project Management Office. Because of the urgency of the situation, people would come in and out of meetings as they responded to phone calls on logistics or other questions. No one questioned roles and decision-making was either shared or localized to the person who had taken over responsibility for particular aspects of the organizing efforts. Trust was high and so was the energy – especially as registrations came in and as the amount of money raised neared the fundraising goal.

Patterns of communication and relationship were established that served the purpose of successfully completing the event. Then, staff went back to their "regular" roles in the organization. One interesting unintended consequence was that the patterns of communication and work that were established during the event planning process carried over into the re-establishment of routine. For instance, the coming and going in staff meetings continued, leading to some discussion about this. The leadership now required was noticing the new patterns and a deliberate re-introduction of norms that served the regular workflow. This meant reestablishing attendance and participation in staff meetings and breaking the pattern of urgency that had consumed the team for months that was no longer valid.

BUILDING TRUST AND RELATIONSHIP AT THE SPEED OF CHANGE

In these days where there is increasing diversity in the workplace and in community, where change seems to move faster every day, where conflicts seem more persistent and it is harder to have constructive conversations, Worldview Intelligence provides a strategic advantage in building trust and relationship, even at the speed of change.

QUALITY OF RELATIONSHIP

Relationship tending is often taken for granted. After all, how difficult can relationship building be? Most of us know or have a sense of how challenging it can be and would prefer to pretend it's easier than it is. Or we get lulled into a false sense of security when things are going well. We know, though, when there are budget issues or competing demands on time, the activities, processes and practices that build relationship are often the first line items sacrificed. This is especially likely when things are changing rapidly and there is so much that demands attention.

However, it is the quality of relationship that supports or gets in the way of accomplishing the task, the goals or outcomes. People who like each other enjoy working together. They are more inspired, motivated and get far more done. They are more likely to have animated conversations that lead to new discoveries and creative solution finding, less likely to take offence and are more likely to look forward to going to work. Isn't this the kind of team you want to be working with or for? As a leader of a team that has good relationships, your role is to continue to provide the leadership that allows those relationships to flourish. What structures, processes and practices will support trust and relationship in your team or organization? And what is the difference between them?

STRUCTURE

Structure is how something is put together. It is a construction or framework of identifiable elements that defines their relationships and, in this case, relationships between parts of an organization. Structure brings or imposes order, connecting parts together in an organized way. Physical structures in organizations include everything from the building or office the organization is in, to the office layout, rooms available for meetings and the set up of those rooms. Other non-building structures include organizational charts, roles and responsibilities, job descriptions, procedures and policies, performance management systems, formal reporting structures and more. Structures support or hinder the team in doing its work.

Think for a moment. What are the structures that are in place to support your team? What structures might get in the way? In what ways does your team work around the structures in place? Are there other structures that could provide additional support, especially as it relates to trust and relationship building? We will often ask, what is the minimum elegant structure that needs to be in place to do the work you need to do, to accomplish the results you need to accomplish? Too much structure, too many policies or procedures are just as likely to get in the way. Some of the best creativity arises as people find ways to work around structures that are not helpful.

It is common for individuals and teams to experience the impact of silos, even in small organizations. People tend to share information with the people closest in physical proximity to them, especially when working on the same project or initiative. They forget that it might be valuable to include people in other parts of the organization and, for that matter, other partners or collaborators in their conversations. This can sometimes be intentional if people think knowledge is power. More often it is a function of structure and "out of sight, out of mind".

There is also the possibility of worldview clashes showing up. If one department basically has the role and responsibility of community organizing, another department is responsible for revenue generation and another is responsible for distributing funds, they sometimes forget that sharing of information could be beneficial to all. The same can happen in healthcare amongst care providers and revenue generation and administration. Or in business between marketing, research and development and finance. People with differing departmental worldviews may see competitive agendas more so than aligned purpose and outcomes that can be collectively worked towards. It requires persistent effort to work across silos or organizational structure to capitalize on the best thinking or worldview perspectives of the people involved.

Another point of contention within teams often comes with lack of role clarity and clarity of accountability and responsibility of team members. When members of the team are not clear about the scope of their responsibility, things can fall through the cracks and impact trust and relationship. The same is true when there are several team members vying for certain areas of responsibility. Too much overlap can happen, efforts are redundant or create confusion and no one is happy. Making sure roles are clear and being in the practice of conversation around them when they are not clear makes a significant contribution towards making or breaking trust and relationship. If your team members are feeling competitive with each other or protective of what they believe is their area of responsibility, you have work to do.

PROCESS

Process refers to a series of actions or steps taken in order to achieve a particular end; it could be a set of activities or tasks resulting in the delivery of a service or product or the accomplishment of an organizational goal. If structure is the what, process (and practices too) are the how. Policies and procedures may lay out hiring processes but hiring people is enacting the process. In addition to processes that come out of structural elements, there may be certain meeting processes that are followed, methods of engagement, meeting notification, communication processes and more.

When the people in an organization follow and are held accountable for the processes it has articulated, trust is built. When its own processes are not followed, people lose trust, not just in the process and people but in the organization. Important questions to ask include: Are all the processes needed? Are they in their simplest form possible? Are they inclusive? Do they do what they are intended to do? If not, are there ways to address the matter within the organization or team?

DECISION-MAKING PROCESSES

Decision-making is a process, although not always thought of in that way and not always well thought out. Lack of clarity regarding when and how decisions are made and by whom is a key area of challenge in many teams and organizations. This could include whether decisions will be made authoritatively by an individual or collectively by a team. It also includes clarity around when a decision has actually been made. It is a common occurrence that some people on a team think a decision has been made and they attempt to move it forward while other people are still questioning whether this is the case.

DIVERGENCE-EMERGENCE-CONVERGENCE

The divergent phase, represents an opening and an invitation to exploration, focused on the purpose or goal that has been identified. It is an opportunity to surface the ideas people have brought into the room, to identify and build on possibilities. Divergent thinking typically generates alternatives, has free-for-all open discussion, gathers diverse points of view and unpacks the problem. The divergent phase is non-linear and often needs "chaos time." This is the phase where we get out everything we currently know so we can all see it together.

If the divergent phase closes too soon, the level of newness or innovation will be less. Ideally a group will stay in inquiry in the divergent phase until new shared ideas emerge or when new paths forward are seen collectively. This phase may close early if there are dominant, persistent people in the room, if not all the views or perspectives are invited or considered, if people feel constrained by time or they want to avoid the "groan zone". A sign that this phase closed too soon is when decisions are revisited, the next steps lack clarity or they lack the energy to enact them.

The emergent phase, between divergence and convergence, is also fondly known as the "groan zone". It is the phase where different ideas and needs are integrated and where truly emergent ideas and solutions evolve. It may require stretching our own understanding to hold and include other points of view, perspectives or worldviews. It is often called the groan zone because it can feel messy, where people are frustrated, energy is low, and solutions sometimes feel unreachable – just before they emerge.

When teams learn they can successfully navigate the groan zone, they grow. High Performance Teams have confidence in their ability to be successful in these conversations and communication in this phase. They trust that shared solutions will emerge that have benefited from the collective thinking. When these solutions appear, there is often a collective shift in the team as everyone recognizes the power and potential of the ideas or solutions at the same time. Energy and focus pick up again.

The convergent phase is goal oriented and focused. It is more linear, structured and could be subject to time constraints. The intent is to get results and it may require quick decisions.

Convergent thinking means evaluating alternatives, summarizing key points, sorting ideas into categories and arriving at general conclusions.

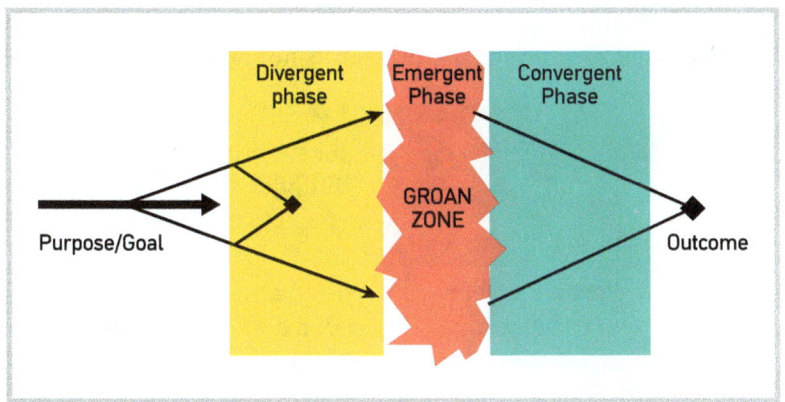

POLARITY MANAGEMENT

In his book *Polarity Management*,[76] Barry Johnson distinguishes between making decisions and managing polarities. Not all dilemmas call for a final or clear decision, some are essential polarities to a process and being aware of that means you can work with it explicitly. Polarities are related on a continuum and remind us that each pole has value and has a positive and a negative aspect. Remembering this, you can better understand what is needed in any given moment. Decision-making is one area where polarity management can be quite useful, especially for an organization that values employee engagement and collaboration.

There are times when collaborative decision-making is extraordinarily helpful and strategic. This could be when there is a need to have the input or voice of as many people as possible in the process, or when a team is establishing principles of communication or an organization is establishing the values or the mission and vision that will guide the organization. It is also important when an organization or community wants to have widespread support for an idea, strategy or new way of doing things. It can be essential when the issues are complex and the solutions require collective thinking or collective implementation to understand the complexity to find ways forward that no one individual is able to do on their own. The downside to collaborative decision-making is that it takes time, planning and authentic strategy to do well. Some people get frustrated with the pace of this kind of decision-making and just want to get on with it, if they lack patience or the process is not held well.

	Collaborative Decision Making	Leader or Individual Decision Making	
+	Positive aspects of collaborative decision making	Positive aspect of leader decision making	+
-	Negative aspects of collaborative decision making	Negative aspects of leader decision making	-

There are other times when leader or individual decision-making makes more sense, is more strategic or is a function of certain organizational imperatives requiring more directive decision-making by a leader or other individual. This could be when decisions need to be made quickly, when there are non-negotiables in a new strategy or a change initiative or when a new leader has an inspired vision to communicate to the entire organization or community. The downside is that, when it is not done well or not clearly communicated, people feel like they are not a part of the decision or the decision-making structure in the organization and they can become disaffected. Sometimes the decisions do not consider all possible available information held by others in the organization and can have unintended consequences.

It is not a matter of right or wrong. It is a matter of the best use of time, resources and knowledge at the time and with respect to the decisions to be made. And it is a question of clear communication of what is happening. When it becomes problematic is when people expect to be part of a decision-making process and they're not included and don't know why, or when they are expecting decisions to be made by the leadership in the organization and that's not happening. This can be further befuddled by a lack of transparency.

Remember a time when you have been part of a discussion where decisions have been re-opened because some people thought a decision had been made and some people didn't. A team Kathy worked with on re-building trust and relationship with each other recognized during the course of this process that they didn't pause to explicitly finalize a decision before moving on to the next topic of discussion. This created uncertainty about what decisions had been finalized and should be acted on and what decisions were still being worked through. They learned to stop themselves and take themselves back to the discussion to be clear amongst everybody on the team whether they had made a decision and what it meant practically for the team or other people impacted by the decision. It was a game changer for them, and it might be for you.

Clear decision-making processes and practices that are consistently followed can go a long way to alleviating issues related to decision-making responsibility and accountability.

PRACTICES

All of Chapter 10 is dedicated to practices. For our purposes in this chapter, practices refer to the application or use of an idea, belief or method – the how of how we hold our meetings, invite a diversity of worldviews, invite all the voices to contribute or engage others in our process. Practices define how we treat each other, interact with each other, how we enter conversation and how we give life to or follow process. If practices do not support processes, one of two things needs to happen: practices need to be created and followed that do support processes or processes need to be reviewed and evaluated for their usefulness and practical application. And not just reviewed, but decisions concerning the alignment of processes and practices need to be made.

What are the practices that need to be present in your team in order for your team to feel supported in its work, for people who don't look or think like the rest of the team to feel like valued members of the team, and for you to draw out the diversity of views and opinions that will strengthen your team and your work? What practices can build relationship and trust within the team? Are the team's practices congruent with its history or values or how knowledge is accessed and used? In many ways, the practices used within a team tell the story of the team.

Some form of invitation to hear every voice is a valuable practice. This might mean using some form of circle practice or process, with agreements that are acknowledged and supported by the people in the room. Agreements (part of process) from Peer Spirit Circle Practice[77] might be useful, including listening with attention, speaking with intention, everyone is responsible for the well-being of the group and silence can be part of the conversation. Agreements could acknowledge decision-making processes or any other principle that is important to the team. We have some clients who want to make sure they remember the voices of people not explicitly in the room. It could mean creating a talking piece practice which assists with moderating the tempo of a discussion – slowing it down when needed and inviting participants to bring their perspective on a lively topic. You might have agreements on how to talk about the hard stuff that comes up. This is, of course, where Worldview Intelligence and its language, skills and frameworks can also be useful.

ADDRESSING CHALLENGES AT THE POINT OF ACTIVATION

In the end, you can have as much structure and as many processes as you can think of, but it still comes down to relationships and developing the skills to have the needed conversations at the point and in the relationship where they are needed. Some teams and organizations try to address issues of trust through rules and policies, but rules and policies and the enforcement of them do not create or build trust when trust in a team has become an issue. Nothing builds unhelpful policy and procedures like creating one to deal with the one or two people who bring negative influences to the team or organization or who abuse the policies.

Building more or more detailed policies to address each new problematic situation that requires attention puts the locus of responsibility somewhere external to the relationships. This makes policies or procedures more complex than they need to be in the pursuit of trying to close loopholes. We hope to stop the people least likely to follow existing procedure and not penalize the people most likely to follow them. The right conversation and the right consequences in the right moment goes a long way towards alleviating behavior that does not fit with the team culture or in reinforcing behavior that does. This is, again, where Worldview Intelligence skills and the SHEER framework for conversations can be of value.

It comes back to your role as a leader, in bringing as much transparency and authenticity as possible given the circumstances and the environment in which you work. This is why the personal and professional worldview explorations matter and why understanding your reactions to challenges to your worldview can be a game saver. In addition to building processes that can be and are followed consistently, honoring practices that may have been collectively created and agreed to take you to the heart of what it means to Build Trust and Relationship at the Speed of Change.

REFLECTION QUESTIONS

1. What structures are in place that support – or hinder – the ability of your team to do its work? Are there structures that might be missing that would be helpful? Are there structures that should be revisited or reviewed to assess their impact?

2. What processes are in place that guide the functioning of your team? Are they consistently used by your team and by your organization – essentially, are they trustworthy? Are there other processes that would be helpful?

3. What practices are used regularly in your team to bring in all the voices, allow for animated discussion of ideas

CHAPTER 18:
WHEN THE TEAM IS DYSFUNCTIONAL – IS IT POSSIBLE TO BUILD TRUST AND RELATIONSHIP?

I once facilitated a conversation between two groups that had been collaborating on an important and costly initiative for several years. Significant distrust had developed between the two groups. I began the process by interviewing many of their staff and Board members to get the lay of the land. It became clear that much of the distrust was personal and related to differing views concerning power and control over finances.

Then I hosted an all-day meeting of the two groups that included a representation of staff, from the CEOs to the janitors, and Board members. We began in circle. I first outlined process agreements that had been distributed earlier and made sure they were collectively confirmed. We began with a check-in and a review of what I had learned from the interviews before moving into the heart of the work.

Three questions had been developed around the current reality from my interviews that were less oriented towards airing personal grievances and more towards making the differing worldviews more explicit. There was a focus on how to move forward to resolve the issue of mistrust and to explore how they might re-establish relationship.

We used a watch as a talking piece. Each person was invited to speak to the first question for three minutes, timed by the previous person who spoke. The intent was to equalize power in the room. As the watch moved around the room and came to one of the CEOs, he began talking with an assumption he had all the time he wanted. But when his three minutes were up and the watch landed in his lap, he had to stop talking as this was the process we had agreed upon. When the watch came to him the next time during the second question, he was much more precise in offering his reflections. This equalization of power through time management gave everyone's voice equal status with others.

During the reflections on the three questions, I harvested key points for potential action. In the afternoon, small groups were formed to develop a priority for action steps to be taken and more specific actions within each of them. Over time the groups came to realize that they were not compatible collaborative partners, but this conclusion came from thoughtful analysis and conversation instead of a break-up based on mistrust and animosity. They were then able to develop a clear contractual relationship regarding financial responsibilities instead of one dependent upon personalities and based on assumptions that they shared worldviews.

Jerry Nagel

THE DEVASTATING IMPACT OF DYSFUNCTIONAL TEAMS

When things go wrong, trust is compromised and when trust is compromised it is hard to regain. Some teams never recover. Thankfully, not every team experiences this level of dysfunction. When a team does, there are remedies; however they are often resource and time investment heavy in the recovery process, so the risk and opportunity must be assessed and believed to be worth the investment.

Beyond the sheer frustration and challenge of the inability to accomplish tasks and outcomes effectively and with efficiency, falling into this level of dysfunction can have devastating impacts personally and professionally for the team and for each member of the team. In our experience working with challenged teams, the professional reputations of everyone on the team are often at stake because the issues have become widely observed or evident in the organization and team members are being made aware of what is being said on the rumor mills.

When there is a lot of dysfunction, team members either barely speak to each other or speak sharply when they do, likely due to the impact of heightened and persistent amygdala hijacks. Tensions run high, trust is low or non-existent, blame is rampant and team members undermine each other in any number of ways, intentionally and unintentionally.

For teams in conflict, accomplishing work tasks is at risk. For teams that want to address the conflict, it requires a significant investment of resources and time. These are the very things that seemed in short supply. It also asks the leader and team to focus on relationship, the very thing that seemed self-evident as not needing tending before chaos ensued. Once these patterns are established and become entrenched, it is incredibly difficult for the team collectively, and members individually, to change the dynamics without external support.

Addressing the human dynamics of teams in deep conflict is a several stage process that takes thoughtfulness, care and intentionality. It is necessary to institute practices that make it safe enough to proceed with the needed challenging conversations. One of the biggest mysteries for team members who find themselves in this situation or dynamic is the disbelief that this is happening. Most people are reasonable. They've demonstrated competence in their careers, they're intelligent and now, suddenly, they find themselves in circumstances that challenge their self-perception, self-confidence and self-esteem – their identity – to their core.

People become trapped in patterns they no longer know how to disrupt and their usual strategies for coping no longer work. When you are buried in it, it is hard to know where or how to come up for air. This is where Worldview Intelligence brings a strategic advantage in working with dysfunctional teams. The structure of the Worldview Intelligence Six Dimensions Framework brings new perspectives and insights. It allows people to step out of personal attacks and defensiveness and invites them to work first with their own responses and then collectively with the patterns of the team, bringing newfound curiosity to all these explorations. This uses a combination of personal, professional, team and possibly social systems worldview explorations to advance the conversations.

For the above reasons, the support of a consultant can be valuable to the team over a period of a few months. It also allows the leader to participate fully in the process which is usually needed by both the leader and the team.

WHEN IT DOESN'T WORK

There are several reasons why an intervention might not work or why dysfunction might not be able to be resolved. Here are a few of the possibilities.

People can be reluctant to deal with relationship issues and challenges, which are often labeled as soft skills or denigrated as warm and fuzzy work. They may expect an intervention to be successful in a day or two, which is an unrealistic expectation when teams have been operating in dysfunctional patterns. The result is they stop an intervention before new patterns and practices have an opportunity to take root. If a team is experiencing a lot of challenging relationship dynamics, one or two meetings will not resolve a stuck issue. 'Soft skills' is a misnomer as this is some of the hardest work a team will ever do. These are essential skills.

If a team leader is complicit in the dysfunction and is either unwilling or unable to acknowledge their complicity, they may run a hidden agenda underneath the overt agenda. When they are skilled at this, it can be hard to spot at first. If they aren't interested in solving the issue, they can sabotage the process. Yes, this happens and we have, on occasion, experienced it.

Sometimes, people just want to check the box. Yes, we did that team thing, but without a real interest in resolving the issues. Sometimes this is because they don't want to invest the time, other times because there are power dynamics in the dysfunction that suit them and they prefer to play there. It could also be because of the fear of the unknown or loss aversion that we covered in Chapter 14: Understanding Worldview and Identity Reactions Through Behavioral Science.

Another reason issues aren't dealt with is related to power dynamics. This happens if the team leader looks at all matters through a power dynamic lens, is attached to or identifies with the power they wield and sees change as a potential threat.

If there is no clear direction or leadership, either from the team lead or the person higher in the organization they report to, then the lack of role clarity and responsibility allows people to manipulate the process. We have experienced people saying all the right things but continuing to rule their fiefdoms in the way they want because accountability and consequences are lacking. Obviously, the potential risks to reputation either are not a factor or are not yet evident, so no progress is made.

FOCUS ON RELATIONSHIP AND CO-LEARNING

Because the work of rebuilding trust and relationship initially requires a lot of focus on relationship, it can be frustrating to team members who just want to get on with achieving goals. This is, of course, why it is better to maintain trust and relationship in the normal course of team functioning. However, as the work of building relationship and trust tentatively moves forward, the team conversations can begin to shift to include more and more tasks until the balance between relationship and task is back to a productive level and the checks and balances or structures, processes and practices are in place, as described in the previous chapter. Trust is renewed while making progress on the work at hand.

When we are invited to facilitate a team intervention, we use Worldview Intelligence as a way of helping people remember who they are, remember who their team members are and offering new language and different structures and methods to support the conversations the team needs to have. They are in co-learning together about new concepts that help them learn to be in relationship differently.

An intervention could include any or all the following steps, remembering that a foundation for team trust and relationship needs to be created or recreated, learned or relearned to support the rest of the work and the hard conversations.

CLARIFY AND ILLUMINATE: INDIVIDUAL TEAM MEMBER INTERVIEWS

The purpose of individual interviews is four-fold. First, it is to give everyone an opportunity to individually tell the story of their experience, not to be confused with the facts of the situation. Each person is invited to tell the story from their perspective or worldview and can express any frustrations they have, speaking openly and honestly.

A second purpose is to provide an opportunity for each individual to reflect on the situation, how they may be contributing to it and what happens if the situation is not resolved. Essentially this is the cost to them personally and collectively of not being able to move forward or change the outcome.

A third purpose is for the consultant(s) to build connection with each person individually prior to having the team meet to address the issues. It is common for people on a team to point to an individual as being the primary cause of the problem when it is actually the structure or the system. These interviews help uncover the system or patterns that have evolved and the hidden dynamics.

A fourth purpose is to discover the themes and patterns across the individual stories to create a more holistic and dynamic view of the situation at hand. This picture is then presented back to the full team.

The same interview guide is used with each member of the team. Team members are assured that the conversation will be confidential. Usually an hour is allotted for each interview and it may seem like a lot, but you may be surprised to know that most people we work with regardless of their position or role in the organization are more than willing to block that time in their calendar. While the interviews can be done in person, most times this is done on the phone. It is a deep sensing interview, designed to invite the interviewee back into their humanity and to go deeper than simply asking them what is wrong or what needs to be fixed now. It is important in conducting the interview to ask each question, even if you or the interviewee believe they may have already answered it in a previous response. We might say, "You may have already answered this, but I will ask it anyway." It is surprising what additional information can be surfaced by not making an assumption.

Questions in this type of interview will include learning a bit about the career path of the individual, why this job now, what they hoped to accomplish when they took it on, what issues need to be addressed, what has been done in the past to try to address the issues, what is everyone pretending not to know and what is the one conversation that is not being held that if it could would change everything. It is amazing what comes to light with these kinds of questions.

Following the interviews, the information is compiled into themes and patterns as an offering back to the team in the first face-to-face meeting. This might be compiled in some form of mind map or some other mechanism to make the themes visible to the people in the room at the same time. We assure team members that nothing will be mentioned in the themes and patterns unless it has been heard from at least three people.

CIDA-W APPLICATION

We use the Worldview Intelligence Theory of Change Planning Model we presented in Chapter 15 to address the issues of team challenges.

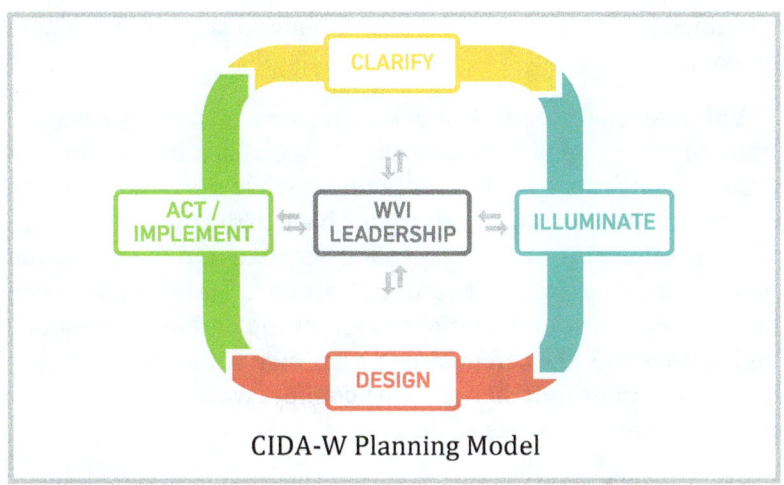

CIDA-W Planning Model

COLLECTIVE CLARITY AND ILLUMINATION: A FIRST MEETING

The first meeting with the team following the interviews is always interesting. Team members do not know what to expect. They are often nervous. They don't know what will be revealed and they are anxious in anticipation of conflict, particularly related to any conflict that might be directed towards them. Individual team members know their own perception of the conflict and often think they will have fingers pointed at them by others. They feel isolated.

REMOVING BARRIERS

We use a circle practice – with or without a table in the middle. We prefer to use circle without a table, without the protective barrier of something in front of people or something to partly hide behind. Team members are invited to bring all of themselves fully into the room.

When people arrive and the form is unexpected or unfamiliar, as in how the room is set up, it is often immediately disruptive and uncomfortable. As consultants facilitating this work, we have developed skill in being at ease with others' discomfort and create an environment that helps them breathe through it. Being proficient in the Worldview Intelligence starting points and skills identified in Chapter 15 gives us a strategic advantage in this kind of work.

With one team we worked with, when the team leader walked into the room she was immediately taken aback by the circle of chairs. There was a projection table on wheels by one wall. She sat in her chair, also on wheels, rolled back to the projection table, put her coffee on it, awkwardly rolled her chair and the projection table back to the circle as a source of support. The group watched her with curiosity and a bit of humor. At the end of our first day and half session, she commented on her own behavior, noting her initial discomfort and her growing comfort with the form of our meeting as progress was achieved.

PRACTICES AND METHODS

We start sessions with a check in, often using a talking piece to slow down the process. This allows people to be thoughtful and intentional in what they share and to invite attentive listening into the space. The check-in could focus on each person's hopes for this process, naming any concerns related to the day, or tensions they might be carrying, or any other check-in question or reflection that is relevant to the outcomes of the day. The check-in brings each person's voice into the process early and quickly. There are no wrong answers and showing an acceptance of everyone's contribution begins to set the stage for the conversations to come.

One client Kathy worked with had experienced a significant downsizing that included going from three floors of offices to one. Internal communication and relationship had become exceedingly difficult. The check-in question asked what gave them hope during this time. Nine of the eleven people offered a response to the question, the tenth person said nothing gave them hope and the final person was even more despondent than that. They both broke down in tears, apologizing for not answering the question properly. Assurances were quickly given that their responses were true for them and their experience, therefore fine, and tears, in this case (not every case), were part of the process. Instead of moving directly to the next part of the pre-established design for the meeting, with the permission of the group, a detour was taken to share and discuss the change curve, including grief and survivor's guilt. After making room for this, we were able to return to the process designed for the work.

After the beginning of the session either as part of the framing of the work to be done or just post the check-in, we review the themes and patterns that emerged from the interviews. This may be physically placed in the center of the circle as we begin or prominently displayed on the wall.

With one team we worked with, it took until the end of the first day of working together for someone to become brave enough to say, as they looked carefully at the mind maps that had been created to collate the interview themes, "That could have been my interview." You could hear the collective sigh of relief as everyone else acknowledged the same thing. It was a shock and a relief to them to discover that what they had each been carrying individually they were also holding collectively – similar experiences, similar fears, similar hopes. It was common ground they had not witnessed in a long time.

Occasionally a team has so much pent up frustration that it needs to be released before progress can be made. If this frustration isn't released it can continue to sit beneath the surface and impact everyone. The key is to recognize that moment when the tension can be attended to or released and hold the space for this to happen in healthy ways. When this moment of increased tension or conflict shows up, usually when people start raising their voices and interrupting each other, we will pause the conversation and remind people of any agreements we have been working with. We bring the talking piece in, ask people to be intentional in what they share and to not make personal attacks. We ask them to offer what they are hearing, feeling or perceiving. We will take as much time as necessary to be sure everyone has offered fully what they need to. Once the tensions and frustrations are released there is often a palpable shift in energy in the room and the conversations move forward in a different, more collegial and productive way.

APPRECIATIVE INQUIRY

We might use an Appreciative Inquiry (AI) based approach since even in the most distressed teams there is always something that has worked or is working now. Reminding people of this by asking them what their best experience of collaboration has been, their best experience of resilience, their best experience of team, their best experience of the organization or other relevant topic, reorients them to what has and does work. It helps them understand they can make it work again while also surfacing what it is each person values about the organization, the team, each other, or themselves. We might also use Appreciative Inquiry to collectively generate the principles by which the team wants to engage this work of building or rebuilding their relational field by drawing on their experiences of when things worked well.

By investing time in this, the foundation for the team to enter the difficult conversations is created in a healthier space of curiosity, generosity and possibilities rather than defensiveness, debate and blame, where they can hear each other instead of only wanting to be heard. Where the conversation goes from there depends on what is most alive for the team, what has surfaced in the themes and patterns and what the team needs in order to engage in good work together.

When a team is in this level of disarray, these initial meetings focus almost exclusively on tending to relationship until the relationship is strong enough, even tentatively, to deal with the tasks and goals, supported by new structures, processes and practices that allow for the acknowledgement of progress they make, no matter how small or large. Part of the meeting practice is to explicitly identify new achievements and accomplishments, reinforcing that the new practices they are adopting are producing outcomes and delivering results. The team must slow down to go fast later.

DESIGN AND ACT: ONGOING MEETINGS

Issues and patterns that have become entrenched in a team are not easily shifted. Neutral, external support can bring voice to things the team itself cannot name. They can bring new strategies and patterns into an existing situation and can challenge the team in gentle or fierce ways regarding its patterns and interactions with each other.

There are many reasons for ongoing meetings. One is simply that entrenched patterns cannot be shifted in a day. It takes reminding, accountability, learning and progress made explicit to trust that new patterns produce different results, like experiencing how using a check-in and check-out process for each meeting changes the quality of the meeting and the quality of relationship. The consultant provides accountability and role models the practices with the team, as well as helps the team illuminate success.

A check-in practice brings people into the room mentally and emotionally even after they have arrived physically and sets the tone for the conversations that are needed. Check-out seals the day, allowing people to express what is most present for them, like gratitude, reflections, questions. Sometimes what arises in the check-out provides purpose and intention for the next meeting.

A consultant can explicitly bring in patterns of human dynamics that help people name and understand the dynamics they are experiencing, like the divergence-emergence-convergence framework, or surface hidden dynamics through systems mapping, or provide strategies for thinking or planning differently.

Sometimes it is as simple (and difficult) as holding space for the team to be in its own discomfort. For one team we worked with, the first meeting was held in a hotel meeting space. Everyone went completely silent whenever the wait staff came into the room. Not a peep out of anyone. No one wanted to speak when there were people in the room who were not part of the team. The wait staff were asked to come and serve the break or the meals and leave directly afterward, leaving clearing the room for later. It was remarkable to witness the transformation of this team over the course of the first three meetings. The tension in the room dissolved from one meeting to the next as issues were resolved, conversation became more positively animated and continued no matter who was in the room.

In addition to the one-on-one interviews and the presentation of the themes and patterns, we used a "parking lot" for the topics that began to spin around without resolution or which no one seemed prepared to address in the moment. Once an issue was 'parked', we moved to the next topic of discussion. The team developed experience in addressing issues and conflicting ideas. When we later came back to the topics listed on the parking lot, it was gratifying to see how easily most of those issues could now be resolved, if they hadn't been addressed in the course of the other conversations. More foundation and less edge. More experience with conversations that advanced with success. More trust and relationship within the team. More willingness to be in exploration.

HONORING PROGRESS

Another benefit of meeting with teams on a regular basis is that the team gets to surface and review its progress, to be in learning about their relationship and team dynamics – something not always tended to in the regular course of meetings and interactions but a key part of building high-performance teams as we shared in Chapter 17: Building Trust and Relationship in a Team. We can identify dynamics that get in the way of team effectiveness – like lack of clarity of role or no discernable, reliable decision-making processes. Once the team addresses these issues there is more ease in relationship and a greater possibility of having a conversation rather than operating from assumptions. The team develops its own common language and short cuts into conversations or dynamics identification.

Initially the consultant might have to offer the purpose or intention for each meeting, to attune people to where they are in the process and keep things on track. Before too long, the team can collectively elicit the purpose and intention on its own by tuning into what's been going on since the last meeting and identifying anything they feel needs their collective attention.

As soon as it is reasonably possible, the focus of the meeting needs to tune into the work of the team and a reasonable balance between task and relationship tending must be established. As people see the impact of relationship tending on moving the task along or easing work flow, they are more willing to invest the necessary time.

CONCLUDING THE PROCESS

At some point, the consultant is no longer needed on a regular basis. The goal is for the team to become self-accountable with shared leadership and shared responsibility. With one team, our last meeting was in a boardroom at a hotel. The leader, the one who had the initial adverse reaction to the first circle, mentioned prior to the meeting that there was a big board table in the middle of the room and was feeling regret that it would impact the circle. She arrived to find out the board table had been pushed back against the wall, leaving room for our circle.

Another team we worked with began using their resources more effectively following the intervention. When trust was low, three or four members of the team would attend a meeting when realistically one or two would do. As they addressed their issues and grew trust, they were able to trust that the perspective of the team could be conveyed by one individual. Instead of undermining each other in meetings with others, behavior that contributed to the whole organization seeing their dysfunction, they began to support each other, even when they did not fully know what their team member had in mind. Instead of challenging their ideas in their absence or in front of others, they now would offer something like, "I'm sure if my teammate has suggested this as a possibility, it has merit and we should all be seriously considering it."

The whole organization began to see and sense the difference before they could articulate what they were seeing. Like magic. Only it wasn't magic. It was hard work that paid off.

SKILLS LEARNED WORKING WITH TEAM DYSFUNCTIONS ARE TRANSFERABLE

We are bound to work with or on challenged or even dysfunctional teams at some point in our careers although not all teams need the degree of intervention described in this chapter. Some teams disband because team members take on new challenges. Sometimes a re-organization in the company breaks the team up. The experience in challenged teams can be difficult but the skills learned during this kind of experience addressing team dynamics are transferable to many different situations. Individuals see, and others witness, that they have grown their leadership capacity.

Worldview Intelligence offers leaders a rich array of frameworks, planning models, worksheets and templates for supporting success, even with the most challenged teams. The skills and characteristics of Worldview Intelligent leaders and organizations is a game changer that changes outcomes and enables the building of trust and relationship, even at the speed of change.

REFLECTION QUESTIONS

1. Have you been part of a team where relationships were extraordinarily challenged? What seemed to the nature of the challenge or dysfunction? What was your level of trust in this team? What was your level of trust in yourself while working with this team? What level of responsibility did you have for this team? What actions or practices might have been helpful to restore trust in this team?

2. What leadership skills have you learned from working in dysfunctional situations?

CONCLUSION:
A WORLDVIEW INTELLIGENCE APPROACH TO BUILDING TRUST AND RELATIONSHIP AT THE SPEED OF CHANGE

Wow! This book has been a journey – at least for us. We hope it has been for you as well. We started out by asking if you were familiar with the word "worldview". If you have made it this far, you not only understand what we mean when we use the word worldview, but you have had the opportunity to reflect on worldviews generally, your own worldview, that of people close to and around you or your team, your organization, even your family and family members, and maybe even a few situations we haven't thought of yet.

We also hope that you will benefit from being able to put Worldview Intelligence into action in your environment and that it brings value to you as you Build Trust and Relationship at the Speed of Change within your teams and organization. Worldview Intelligence provides a means to sprint or begin fast when contemplating your work and environment while it prepares you for the marathon or the ability to stay with your strategies over time. By applying the Worldview Intelligence Six Dimensions Framework, the CIDA-W Planning Model and the SHEER framework to the various issues and challenges you are confronted with on a regular basis, you are equipped to build and maintain trust in times that are changing quickly, growing in complexity and diversity.

It can be as simple as holding onto the notion that everybody has a worldview that influences how they see and experience the world. Bringing curiosity to that idea as you encounter people you are just meeting and people you know well is the beginning point for shifting the nature of conversations from potentially oppositional to exploratory. It can be as complex as finding the way to the bottom of the Iceberg to dig into the underlying causes and formative influences of events we can see and track.

Being in it for the long haul means you and your team will hone the Worldview Intelligence skills that allow you to change the nature of conversations, be in inquiry around the sources of issues facing you so you can build from the foundation up as you implement change, create new structures, processes and practices or develop policy. Worldview Intelligence skills enable you to create lasting opportunities for inclusion, to invite all views, perspectives and voices into addressing the issues that arise in these times of complexity and change.

When we are delivering Worldview Intelligence programming for a client or in open enrolment groups, we do not have the time to go in-depth on each of the Worldview Intelligence dimensions. We give a quick overview with stories to illustrate them. We know through our own research and experience there is so much more to each of them. This book gave us the opportunity to provide the background and depth that some people have been seeking. Before this book, there was no other book that addressed this topic in the way we have been developing and presenting it. Now, this is that resource. It fills in the gaps of the questions people have been asking. We were delighted to write about the framework and its origins as well as explore each of the six dimensions – reality, history, future, values, practices, knowledge – in more detail, and to wrap up that section by giving examples of the coherence and interrelatedness of the dimensions in application.

Colleagues who had an early introduction to Worldview Intelligence kept asking us how we do what we do. In one way it was intuitive, but intuition that built on decades of experience. The examples that we share in Chapter 12: The Strategic Use of the Worldview Intelligence Six Dimensions Framework demonstrate the interrelatedness of the dimensions and illustrates some of the thinking that goes into the design of processes or interventions for our clients. We always ask how the Worldview Intelligence Six Dimensions Framework and overall approach can be skillfully used in addressing issues that matter.

Attending to amygdala hijacks, trigger points and the wealth of information available through brain and behavioral science research provides you with many opportunities to both self-reflect and to strategize how to influence your communication and relationships in helpful, healthy ways.

We shared lots of examples in the final section of this book on application. We hope it inspires you to put ideas and possibilities into action. We encourage you to be creative and adaptive in applying the concepts in this book. After all, that is how the body of knowledge we present grew in its depth and breadth of application. We think of it as a living body of knowledge grounded in core concepts, strong academic foundation, systems thinking and a decade of practical application on the issues our clients have brought to us for strategy and implementation.

We welcome a growing Worldview Intelligence community and invite you to join us by searching for our website www.worldviewintelligence.com, joining our mailing list or through our Facebook group. These forums will alert you to any new community platforms we might engage. We also welcome conversation and interaction with anyone who wants to go deeper or wants to share their experiences with anything they have tried from this book. Please reach out to us.

Finally, when we look out over the state of affairs in the world, it can be easy to become discouraged, to still see in existence the fragmentation and polarization that sparked Leo Apostel to begin a worldviews exploration and conversation and to feel that this is increasing in strength and voracity. However, we continue to draw hope from the people we encounter and those who we know are out there doing good work in the world, building bridges across divides, educating on differences, calling us to attention to what needs to be done and what is being done in the world. We draw hope from people like you because you are drawn to books like this to continue your own personal development and the development of your leadership skills and ability to do good work in the world – even when that means "just" in yourself, your team, your organization, your family or your community, because really, there is no "just" – it is all important work. The world needs each one of us to shine our light as a beacon for others to find the roads of hope we carve out as we act with intentionality in this world. Thank you for all you do and all that you will do.

ACKNOWLEDGEMENTS

It has been quite the journey. This work has been an unfolding gift that on one level has felt like divine guidance and on another level would not have been possible without the support and trust of so many people. We have had many influencers and people who have inspired our thinking along the way from individuals to organizations.

Since the beginning our local and international colleagues have challenged our thinking about Worldview Intelligence. We saw so much potential in the Six Dimensions Framework, adapting it to a variety of applications, proving its flexibility and applicability. Our colleagues liked the framework but they wanted more; they wanted "inside our heads" and the planning models we use intuitively in our work. Formalizing the models was an important breakthrough in the evolution of the work.

There are many people from around the world to acknowledge for challenging our thinking and supporting our efforts. They are influencers, inspirers and co-conspirators. They promoted open enrolment programs, were or became clients, read our book and looked for openings and opportunities.

From Canada: Carolann Wright and Tracey Jones-Grant were part of the first open enrolment program in Halifax and have been frequent advisors, particularly on questions of diversity and inclusion. Jaime Smith, Geoff Wilson and Max Chauvin are other Nova Scotian friends who have offered helpful input into our work and created opportunities for us to apply it in a variety of ways.

From the US: LeMoine LaPointe, Mai Thor, Myrna Peterson, Greg Trahan, Dave Ellis and Loretta Ellis, each of whom reminds us of different ways of seeing and engaging with the world, expanding our own worldviews in the process. Maggie Shelton has helped us see the power of language when inviting people into deeply personal reflection. Tanis Henderson and Mary Hess have helped bring the work into the fields of education.

From Europe: Nancy Bragard was inspired by the Worldview

Intelligence approach from the first moment she heard about it. She was instrumental in organizing open enrolment programs and a few follow up Community of Practice gatherings in Germany and France. Rolf Schneidereit, a colleague from Germany, joined us in many conversations and also in organizing open enrolment programs. It was often in the lead up to these programs and in the ongoing conversations that clarity in describing the structural aspects of our work emerged. We met Stephan Krajcik, Vanessa Mannavarayan, Fabien Vial, Isabelle Rambaud Carassus, Sabine Schott, Marie-Helene Elleboudt, Audrey James, Alexa Lorenz, Helga Schenzer, Waultraud Heller at the first European Open Enrolment program. Their questions and insights sparked the articulation of planning models, inviting us to become clear and visible about our process. Stephan helped organize an open enrolment program in Geneva after experimenting with the Worldview Intelligence approach on both a family level and with the Geneva Model United Nations. Michaela Sieh jumped in to create a way for us to present to members of the European Participatory Leadership Community of Practice, an opportunity that provided valuable feedback and encouragement.

From Bermuda: We first met Kerry Judd, Pamela Barit Nolan and Gil Nolan at an Art of Hosting training in New Hampshire in 2015. Each has seen the value in the work and have created opportunities to bring Worldview Intelligence into client and open enrolment offerings in Bermuda.

In Australia, long time friend and colleague, Stephen Duns invited us to bring early versions of the Worldview Intelligence approach into a local client and worked with us on an open enrolment offering. Dee Brooks is a nomadic Australian, steeped in a cross section of dialogic methodologies who continues to see the connections among the various approaches she uses.

James Gimian, co-author of The Rules of Victory and Executive Director of the Foundation for a Mindful Society, was an early reader of the book and offered his reflections. He graciously agreed to write the Foreword. Robert Slob is Kathy's book accountability partner since both joined the Self Publishing School in 2018. They have been encouraging each other along the self-publishing path and have become good friends in the process. He was an early reader and he has a keen interest in the Worldview Intelligence work. Alain Wouters is a friend who not only inspired some of Jerry's early thinking about his own worldview shifts, but has seen the potential of Worldview Intelligence and attended an Open Enrolment program in Geneva. Rowan Simonsen, a Dane living in Columbia, has been an early advocate and continues to look for ways to partner.

The Meadowlark Institute, led by Jerry, is a non-profit organization and as such has a board of directors. The members of this board have been incredibly supportive of the unfolding work of Worldview Intelligence and the partnership between Jerry and Kathy that evolved over the years. They have provided guidance, oversight, provocative questions and their blessings. Some have opened doors, some have been clients and some have provided feedback on the book. All have been appreciated for what they bring and offer. The Meadowlark Board includes Don Bottemiller, Diana Vanderwoude, Rod Holth, Ron Vantine, Christine Hamilton and Lorin Brass.

The Meadowlark Institute has a long-standing relationship with the Blandin Foundation which supported community engagement through both Art of Hosting and Worldview Intelligence. Key champions and friends there include Bernadine Joselyn, Kathy Annette, Sonja Merrild, and Becky LaPlante. It was through this relationship that we had the opportunity to work with Julie Gordon who coordinates the Leech Lake Youth Build Program. Martin Jennings, who is on the Board at Blandin, also supported the Worldview Intelligence programs through his program work at the Northwest Area Foundation.

There are a few organizations in particular from which we have drawn inspiration. They include the Institute of Noetic Sciences (IONS) whose early work on understanding worldviews and the impacts they have inspired Jerry to pursue the topic in his PhD; the Centre Leo Apostel (CLEA) in Brussels who early on encouraged us to make Apostel's work more accessible and practical; the Taos Institute and its program that makes it possible for working adults like Jerry to complete their PhD; and the Self-Publishing School.

Kathy joined the Self Publishing School in January of 2018 to access a process and information to help her write her second book. The process can be daunting but the resources available through a supportive group like SPS takes the guess work out of next steps and allows you to draw on the experience and expertise of an amazing group of authors, editors and more.

Many of our clients have also been significant influences and inspirers in this work, the full extent of which is still unfolding. Clients who signed on early to experience Worldview Intelligence allowed us to bring our new, innovative approach to the work they were doing. We have built enduring relationships with clients who have stayed with us as Worldview Intelligence has grown into a thing of substance. Our clients keep pointing us in the direction of what is possible with the Worldview Intelligence Six Dimensions Framework and what happens when the nature of conversations changes.

We would especially like to acknowledge our wonderful colleagues at Sanford Health where there were early indications of how impactful Worldview Intelligence was in making visible the inter-relationship of geographic worldviews with departmental or office location, the power of making worldview assumptions clear with social systems mapping exercises and the gift of creating exploratory space for people who have been brought together in growth through mergers and acquisitions. Acknowledgements include Diana Vanderwoude, Kelly Soyland, Deb Letcher, Julie Berndt, Angela Heibult, and Linda Heerde as part of their leader development work, including online learning, and Amy McCloud for development of many of our graphics.

We met Rich Wilson and Mike Ritzius when they came to an Art of Hosting training in Minnesota in 2015. Thus began a journey with The New Jersey Education Association (NJEA) that included the support of Michael Cohan, Steve Svetzky and Amanda Adams among so many others. This relationship brought us to the Massachusetts Teachers Association (MTA), supported by Courtney Derwinksi and Dan Callahan. Victoria Rees and Darrel Pink at the Nova Scotia Barristers' Society rose to the challenge of bringing Worldview Intelligence in to support their innovative work in changing the nature of how law society's are regulated.

And then, there is this book. It started to take shape in August 2018 and was edited several times in exchanges between the two of us. However, the writing was brought to a whole new level thanks to the readers who took the time to read part or all of the book and brought us thoughtful questions, suggestions and insights that only expanded the quality of the book. It wouldn't be what it is without you. Thanks to James Gimian, Eliot Glassheim who edited the book, Darlene Rabello Coehlo, Dee Brooks , Tenneson Wolf, Edie Farwell, Ted Trahan, Jude Rathbun, Don Bottemiller and Rod Holth.

There are several people who have made us and our work look more professional. They include Mark Lewis from 3 O'Clock marketing who developed our website and collaborated with us on the book launch. Claire Fraser who was fresh out of school when we came across her and her videography skills. Michelle and John Coleman, dear friends who we have worked with, took the great pictures of us which adorn the website, the book and other places where pictures are helpful.

It has been said to us that this work is noble work. It has also been said to us, it would never have come about without our partnership. This feels true as we have been curious about what was emerging around our teachings, the framework and so much more. It was our thinking together as we listened to what people were telling us, as we saw a vision for what was possible emerging through each conversation we had with clients, potential clients and colleagues that kept the energy and momentum building. Our own conversations have often been incredibly generative – whether planning for client engagements, open enrolment programs or planning for and writing this book. You can't do this work without living it and we have been living it in our relationship over the years.

We each have children and grandchildren. While the grandchildren are too young yet to know what it is we do, and our children might not always know exactly what it is we do, the support, enthusiasm and appreciation for us, our relationship and the work we do in the world is a constant reminder of how important it is to be relational in a world that often wants to be transactional, polarized and fragmented. We live in two places – Minnesota and Nova Scotia and it is our families that keep us grounded in both places.

ABOUT THE AUTHORS

Jerry Nagel and Kathy Jourdain are transnational partners and the co-founders of Worldview Intelligence. The innovative, thoughtful approach they have created to understanding the impact of worldviews on how we each see and interact with the world around us has been well received in a variety of business and community environments, as a general practice and to advance specific issues. Jerry received his PhD from Tilburg University in the Netherlands in 2015. His research and dissertation on worldviews form a strong foundation for the Worldview Intelligence work. Recognizing the profound impact of worldview explorations on the quality of conversations on issues that matter the two of them began the work that eventually led to the writing of this book.

They have brought the Worldview Intelligence approach to dozens of clients in the US, Canada, Bermuda and Australia. They have offered open enrolment programs in each of these countries and in Europe. Clients include health care companies and provincial health authorities, education unions, foundations, member associations and not-for-profit organizations, private businesses and different levels of government in the US and Canada. They work in the private, public and not-for-profit sectors, across systems in rural, urban and suburban settings and across generations.

They are both global stewards and practitioners of the Art of Hosting Conversations That Matter. They have partnered on consulting and training work since 2011. Kathy and Jerry have extensive experience in planning, hosting and facilitating community and stakeholder engagement. They have trained people to lead community engagement. Between the two of them they have trained well over 3,000 people in Art of Hosting skills and practices in the United States, Canada, Brazil and Australia. They have also brought Art of Hosting practices to clients applied to strategic direction, leading change, innovation, high performance teams and understanding systems.

Kathy and Jerry are currently working with a multi-state,

multi-national health care organization to integrate Worldview Intelligence into their organization-wide, in-house leader development program.

KATHY JOURDAIN, MBA

Kathy and her company, Shape Shift Strategies Inc, are based in Bedford, Nova Scotia, Canada. Prior to embarking on her two-decades long consulting career, she was the Executive Director of an Atlantic Canada health charity. She was the youngest leader in that role across the country and also made significant contributions to the national organization, on committees and issues.

During that time, she chaired HealthPartners, a regional coalition of heath charities. She was a well-known local and national leader of the Canadian Society of Association Executives, where she completed the two-year Certified Association Executive program in one year, acquiring her CAE designation. During her tenure on the CSAE National Board, she contributed to a significant transformation of the governance structure. Under her local leadership, the Nova Scotia Chapter won the award for best performance in the Country. Kathy's leadership has been recognized with awards locally and nationally.

She is known for her expertise in customized leadership development, building team capacity and working with large scale, long-term strategic and systemic change. Kathy was a driving force behind Envision Halifax (now Engage Nova Scotia), a voluntary organization whose mission is to ignite a culture of civic engagement where she co-designed and co-facilitated the leadership development program over a five-year period and where her leadership was recognized in 2009.

Kathy has taught various programs in the Executive Development Programs at Saint Mary's University in Halifax, Memorial University in Newfoundland, Carleton University in Ottawa, Schulich University in Toronto, the University of Winnipeg and Texas A&M University in Houston. Program offerings include Worldview Intelligence to the SMU MBA students, Communications in the Project Management Masters

Certificate Program, Leadership Development and Innovation.

Her memoir, Embracing the Stranger in Me: A Journey to Openheartedness, has been hailed as a deeply authentic sharing of the journey that has shaped who she is today. That book details her experience discovering as an adult, that she had been adopted, her mother's journey with dementia and death and her deepening spiritual journey over a decade or more. Her second book is ready to be published: Accessing Your Healing Power Within and she is a contributing author to Gift of the Hit.

Kathy is certified in Strategic Planning and Strategic Change Management through the International Center for Strategic Management headquartered in San Diego, CA. She holds an MBA from Saint Mary's University in Halifax, Nova Scotia and she is a graduate of the Banff Centre for Management's Executive Leadership Program.

JERRY NAGEL, MA, PHD

Jerry is President of the Meadowlark Institute, based in Minnesota. Meadowlark is committed to developing individual and collective capacity to be responsive during times of rapid change, to be comfortable with uncertainty, to hold multiple points of view simultaneously, and engage in meaningful conversations with those who hold different traditions, values and goals.

He was Executive Director of the Northern Great Plains Rural Development Commission, a Federal Commission established by Congress to look at the future of the 5-state region of Minnesota, Iowa, North Dakota, South Dakota and Nebraska. He co-led the international Trade and Transport project initiated by Congress to specifically look at the relationship between the region's transportation infrastructure and international trade development.

Jerry organized and co-led the Meadowlark Project. The Project was funded by the Bush, Blandin, Bremer and Kellogg Foundations and the US Department of Agriculture. Its purpose was to bring a project team representative of all walks of life using the Change Lab (Theory U) approach to explore how the region could address some of its most intractable problems, such as high unemployment within Tribal Nations while nearby hundreds of jobs went unfilled. A key outcome was the recognition that while the region had built a strong economic development infrastructure at the local and State levels, it did not have the human infrastructure to host difficult conversations. This led to formation of the Meadowlark Institute and support by the Bush and Blandin Foundations to bring Art of Hosting trainings to Minnesota.

He co-authored Talking Wires, a history of North Dakota's rural telephone cooperatives for the North Dakota Rural Telephone Cooperative Association. The hardcover book was distributed to coop members. He authored "Aid to the Poor: Am I My Brothers Keeper?", a study guide used in a series of community humanities seminars. Jerry is co-author of several NGP publications including "The New Marketplace in European Agriculture: Environmental and Social Values within the Food Chain," "Private Sector Protocols: Threats and Opportunities for American Farmers," and Towards New Horizons: Trends in Transportation and Trade – Moving the Northern Great Plains Region to a Stronger Economic Future, which was written under contract for the Minnesota Department of Transportation. He was an editor of Renewing the Countryside-North Dakota, which was written under contract for Renewing the Countryside (RTC), a Minnesota non-profit. The hardcover book was both given to various organizations and sold in bookstores by RTC.

Jerry received an MA in economics from the University of North Dakota in 1984. He has taught economics classes at the University of North Dakota and University of Minnesota-Crookston. He received his PhD in Social and Behavioral Sciences from Tilburg University, the Netherlands in May 2015. Jerry has attended the Senior Executives in State and Local Government program at Harvard University as a Fannie Mae Foundation Fellow and is a Donella Meadows Sustainability Leadership Fellow. He has served on numerous Boards of Directors over the years, including Dakota Sun, Greater Minnesota Housing Fund, the Consensus Council, and Great Plains Sustainable Development. A lifelong fan of public radio, he is the past Chair of the Board for Prairie Public Broadcasting.

ENDNOTES

1 Hosking, D.M. (2010) "Moving Relationally: Meditations on a Relational Approach to Leadership" in A. Bryman, Collinson, D., Grint, K., Jackson, B., & Uhl-Bien, M. (eds) *Sage Handbook of Leadership*. Thousand Oaks, CA: Sage Publications.

2 ibid

3 Hosking, D.M. (2011) *Telling Tales of Relations: Appreciating Relational Constructionism*. Organization Studies, 32 (1), pp. 47-65.

4 Hosking, D.M. (2010)

5 Hosking, D.M. (2007) *Sound Constructs: a Constructionist Discourse of Sound Processes and Listening*. Revue Sciences de Gestion. 55, 55-75.

6 Brene Brown quote

7 https://www.washingtonpost.com/posteverything/wp/2014/07/06/how-diversity-actually-makes-us-smarter/?utm_term=.1acb85f3b98a

8 https://www.fastcompany.com/3046358/millennials-have-a-different-definition-of-diversity-and-inclusion

9 https://insight.kellogg.northwestern.edu/article/better_decisions_through_diversity

10 https://innovationmanagement.se/imtool-articles/why-diversity-is-the-mother-of-creativity/

11 https://hbr.org/2013/12/how-diversity-can-drive-innovation

12 Sire, J. (2004) *Naming the Elephant: Worldview as a Concept*. Downers Grove, IL: InterVarsity Press.

13 Schlitz, M., Vieten, C., Miller, E., Homer, K., Peterson, K., & Erickson-Freeman, K. (2011) *The Worldview Literacy Project: Exploring New capacities for the 21st Century Student*. Petaluma, CA: Institute of Noetic Sciences.

14 Koltko-Rivera, M. (2004) *The Psychology of Worldviews*. Review of General Psychology. 8 (1), 3058.

15 MIT News, http://news.mit.edu/2014/in-the-blink-of-an-eye-0116

16 Schlitz, M., Vieten, C., & Amorok, T. (2007) *Living Deeply: The Art & Science of Transformation in Everyday Life*. Oakland, CA: New Harbinger Publications.

17 The Famous People, Sun Tzu Biography, https://www.thefamouspeople.com/profiles/sun-tzu-261.php

18 Gimian, J. & Boyce, B. (2008) *The Rules of Victory: How to Transform Chaos and Conflict: Strategies from the Art of War*. Boston, MA: Shambhala Publications, Inc.

19 Come From Away Musical Production, https://comefromaway.com/

20 LeBaron, M. (2003) "Cultural and Worldview Frames" in *Beyond Intractability*, eds. Burgess, G. & Burgess, H.

21 "What Google Learned From Its Quest to Build the Perfect Team", New York Times, Feb 2016

22 Gimian & Boyce. 2008

23 Aerts, Diederik, Hubert Van Belle, and Jan Van der Veken (1999) "Worldviews and the Problem of Synthesis" in D. Aerts, H. Van belle & j. Van der Veken (eds.) Einstein Meets Magritte. Brussels, BE: Kluwer Academic Publishers.

24 Aerts, Van Belle & Van Der Veken, 1999

25 Aerts, Diederik, Leo Apostel, Bart De Moor, Staf Hellemans, Edel Maex, Hubert Van Belle, and Jan Van der Veken (2007) *World Views. From Fragmentation to Integration*. Brussels: VUB Press. http://www.vub.ac.be/CLEA/pub/books/worldviews.pdf

26 Heylighen, F. (2000) *Foundations and methodology for an Evolutionary World View: a review of the Principia Cybernetica Project.* Foundations of Science. 4.

27 Aerts et al. 2007

28 Aerts, Van Belle & Van Der Veken, 1999: xix

29 Aerts et al. 2007

30 Aerts et al. 2007: 8

31 Aerts, Van Belle & Van Der Veken, 1999: xv

32 Aerts et al. 2007: 24

33 Aerts et al. 2007: 9

34 Aerts et al. 2007:7

35 Aerts et al. 2007:8

36 Vidal, Clément. "An Enduring Philosophical Agenda. Worldview Construction as a Philosophical Method." Submitted for publication (2007) http://cogprints.org/6048/.

37 Heylighen, 2000

38 Aerts et al. 2007: 8

39 Vidal, Clément (2008) "What is a worldview?", in Van Belle, H. & Van der Veken, J., Editors, Nieuwheid denken. De wetenschappen en het creatieve aspect van de werkelijkheid, in press. Acco, Leuven.

40 Vidal, Clément (2012). "Metaphilosophical Criteria for Worldview Comparison." *Metaphilosophy* 43 (3): 306–347. doi:10.1111/j.1467-9973.2012.01749.x. http://homepages.vub.ac.be/~clvidal/writings/Vidal-Metaphilosophical-Criteria.pdf.

41 Vidal, 2012

42 Vidal, 2012

43 Alan Page Wikipedia page: https://en.wikipedia.org/wiki/Alan_Page

44 Aerts et al. 2007

45 Hosking, D.M. (2010) "Moving Relationally: Meditations on a Relational Approach to Leadership" in A. Bryman, Collinson, D., Grint, K., Jackson, B., & Uhl-Bien, M. (eds) *Sage Handbook of Leadership*. Thousand Oaks, CA: Sage Publications.

46 Vidal, 2008

47 Johnson, B (1992) *Polarity Management*. Amherst, MA. HRD Press

48 Aerts et al. 2007: 17

49 Aerts et al. 2007: 17

50 Vidal, 2008

51 Funk, K. (2001) *What is a Worldview?* http://web.engr.oregonstate.edu/~funkk/Personal/worldview.html

52 Gimian & Boyce, 2001

53 Aerts et al. 2007

54 Heylighen, 2000

55 Funk, 2001

56 Debold, E. (2002) *Epistemology, Fourth Order Consciousness, and the Subject-Object Relationship or...How the Self Evolves with Robert Kegan.* Enlightenment? 22/Fall-Winter.

57 Heylighen, F. (1993) *Epistemology, Principia Cybernetica;* http://pespmc1.vub.ac.be/EPISTEMI.html

58 Heylighen, 1993

59 Heylighen, 1993

60 Heylighen, 1993

61 Heylighen, 1993

62 Scharmer, O. (2009) Theory Y. San Francisco, CA. Barrett-Koehler.

63 Daniel Goleman coined the term Amygdala Hijack in his 1996 book *Emotional Intelligence: Why It Can Matter More Than IQ.* Drawing on the work of Joseph E. LeDoux, Goleman uses the term to describe emotional responses from people which are immediate and overwhelming, and out of measure with the actual stimulus because it has triggered a much more significant emotional threat. He notes the speed of an amygdala hijack at 1 millisecond.

64 Antonio Damasio's research in neuroscience has shown that emotions play a central role in social cognition and decision-making. His work has had a major influence on current understanding of the neural systems, which underlie memory, language, consciousness.
https://www.ted.com/speakers/antonio_damasio

65 Here's How Long It Really Takes to Break a Habit, According to Science, Signe Dean,
9 JUN 2018, https://www.sciencealert.com/how-long-it-takes-to-break-a-habit-according-to-science

66 Centers for Disease Control and Prevention, https://www.cdc.gov/violenceprevention/childabuseandneglect/acestudy/index.html

67 Koltko-Rivera, M. (2004)

68 https://www.heartmath.org/

69 Koltko-Rivera, M. (2004)

70 MIT News: In The Blink of an Eye: http://news.mit.edu/2014/in-the-blink-of-an-eye-0116

71 Heifitz, R. (1994) *Leadership Without Easy Answers*. Cambridge, MA: Harvard University Press.

72 https://www.rawstory.com/2016/02/the-stereotype-is-dead-researchers-show-that-native-americans-drink-less-than-whites/

73 Kaner, S. (2014) *The Facilitator's Guide to Participatory Decision-Making*. San Francisco, CS: Jossey-Bass

74 Center for Appreciative Inquiry, https://www.centerforappreciativeinquiry.net/more-on-ai/what-is-appreciative-inquiry-ai/

75 Work Issue, NY Times 2016 What Google Learned From Its Quest to Build the Perfect Team https://www.nytimes.com/2016/02/28/magazine/what-google-learned-from-its-quest-to-build-the-perfect-team.html

76 Polarity Management, Johnson, B. 1992

77 Baldwin, C. & Linnea, A. (2010) *The Circle Way: A Leader in Every Chair*. San Francisco, CA: Berrett-Koehler Publishers, Inc.

A REQUEST FROM THE AUTHORS, JERRY AND KATHY

If you enjoyed *Building Trust and Relationship at the Speed of Change* or gained benefit from reading it, please consider posting a great review on Amazon.com so other readers will learn about it.

We also invite you to become part of the Worldview Intelligence Community by signing up to our list at

http://worldviewintelligence.com/a-request-from-the-authors/

or by joining us in the Worldview Intelligence Facebook Group:
https://www.facebook.com/groups/worldviewintelligence/

or the LinkedIn Group:
https://www.linkedin.com/groups/8154323/

You could join our secret book group at
https://www.facebook.com/groups/BuildingTrustandRelationshipattheSpeedofChange
where you will have interactions with the authors and other readers as well as access to short videos related to book content.

By joining the Worldview Intelligence community you will be informed of new developments in our work, opportunities to engage in learning and you will be notified when the next book is ready.

And, you can reach us directly at
Authors@WorldviewIntelligence.com.

Thank you,

Kathy and Jerry

www.ingramcontent.com/pod-product-compliance
Lightning Source LLC
Chambersburg PA
CBHW070913030426
42336CB00014BA/2395